D1081977

Can a Good Christian Be a Good Lawyer?

Notre Dame Studies
in Law and Contemporary Issues

Volume Five

The University of Notre Dame Press gratefully acknowledges the
generous support of The Honorable James J. Clynes, Jr., of Ithaca,
New York, in the publication of titles in this series.

Can a Good Christian Be a Good Lawyer?
Homilies, Witnesses, and Reflections

Edited by
Thomas E. Baker
and
Timothy W. Floyd

University of Notre Dame Press
1998

Copyright © 1998 by
University of Notre Dame Press
Notre Dame, IN 46556
All rights reserved.

Manufactured in the United States of America

Library of Congress Cataloging-in-Publication Data

Can a good Christian be a good lawyer? : homilies, witnesses, and
    reflections / edited by Thomas E. Baker and Timothy W. Floyd.
        p.   cm. — (Notre Dame studies in law and contemporary issues :
    v. 5)
    Includes bibliographical references.
    ISBN 0-268-00825-6 (alk. paper). — ISBN 0-268-00826-4 (pbk. : alk.
    paper)
    1. Religion and law—United States. 2. Christianity and law. 3.
    Christian lawyers—United States. I. Baker, Thomas E. II. Floyd,
    Timothy W. III. Series
        KF389.C25 1998
        340'.088'204—dc21   97-37197
                                                                        CIP

∞The paper used in this publication meets the minimum requirements of
the American National Standard for Information Sciences—Permanence
of Paper for Printed Materials, ANSI Z39.48-1984.

We dedicate our work on this book to our parents,
who gave us the most precious gift of our Faith.

T.E.B.
T.W.F.

Table of Contents

Acknowledgments

We are more-than-we-can-say grateful to the authors of the individual essays for their inspiration and effort but most of all for their patience with us. We also want to thank James R. Langford and the staff of the University of Notre Dame Press for helping to see this book through to publication. These essays appeared as part of the Faith and the Law Symposium in the *Texas Tech Law Review*, volume 27, number 3, as what was described somewhat understatedly as "not the typical law review symposium." That Symposium was made possible by the leadership and work of the Board of Editors and Staff Members for 1996, especially Eric P. Gifford, Gene J. Heady, and Heather D. Webb. We appreciate the secretarial assistance of Donna B. Jones, Norma Tanner, and Leona Wyatt.

This is an appropriate place to acknowledge our deep gratitude to all the authors who participated in the Faith and the Law Symposium. The Symposium included persons of many varied and different religious traditions. Those forty-five essays covered more than five hundred pages. This book is derivative of that Symposium, to be sure, but we selected only essays from the Symposium written by followers of Jesus Christ—and even then not all of them. The two of us understand that there are many paths to the Divine, but we decided to emphasize the intersection between our shared Christian faith and our shared vocation of the law. Furthermore, we put together this book under publishing constraints that did not apply to the Symposium. Thus, numerous valuable essays by valued colleagues are not included here. We wish to acknowledge our deep respect for those other traditions and our high regard for those colleagues. We trust that they and our readers will appreciate the difficulty of these decisions and understand the spirit in which we reached them.

Editors' Preface

The intellect of man is forced to choose
Perfection of the life, or of the work,
And if it take the second must refuse
A heavenly mansion, raging in the dark.

When all that story's finished, what's the news?
In luck or out the toil has left its mark:
That old perplexity an empty purse,
Or the day's vanity, the night's remorse.

This poem, entitled "The Choice," was written by William Butler Yeats in 1928. Yeats was echoing a New Testament theme found both in the Book of Matthew 16:26 and Book of Mark 8:36. Jesus warns that we should value the things of God over the things of man. Mark has him say these words:

Whosoever will come after me, let him deny himself, and take up his cross, and follow me.

For whosoever will save his life shall lose it; but whoever shall lose his life for my sake and the gospel's, the same shall save it.

For what shall it profit a man, if he shall gain the whole world, and lose his own soul?

Or what shall a man give in exchange for his soul?

It is a leitmotif in the literature about the legal profession, in writings by those inside and those outside the profession, that we lawyers fail to heed this warning—that the practice of law for too many lawyers presents either a Faustian bargain or a Godfather's offer.

Our own faith and experience tells us otherwise. We think that lawyers might be described as people of average morals who must deal with above-average temptations. At the same time, a lawyer called to live the Gospel of Jesus Christ must reconcile the secular calling of being a lawyer with his or her faith. Sometimes the two callings take us in the same direction. Other times they pull in opposite directions.

We asked members of the legal profession—lawyers, judges and law professors—to reflect on how they have reconciled their professional life with their faith life. We asked them to write essays in the nature of personal narratives, exercises in story-telling, which might inform and perhaps inspire others.

The roster of authors includes prominent persons from all sorts of legal specializations, professional roles, and career experiences. Along the ecumenical axis, we invited authors from many of the different branches of Christianity.

We asked our authors to consider such thematic questions as: What do your religious beliefs teach you about how you should perform your life's work? Comparing your faith life and your professional life, would you describe them as being in harmony or in conflict? How has your faith contributed positively to your career, at times of crisis and success? What advice do you have for someone else attempting to rhyme a legal career with his or her religious beliefs?

These authors describe how their religious beliefs oblige them to practice the profession of law, perhaps, though not necessarily, in a manner differently from someone who might not share their beliefs. We did not expect them to reach any unified, final consensus, although they have shared their own deeply held convictions. The two of us believe that faith, and life itself, is more like a great journey—a pilgrimage of being and becoming, complete with adventures along the way. Each of us is very much a "work in progress."

Our primary intended audience is lawyers, but these essays speak to all persons of faith who have struggled to live out their beliefs in their work. What we hope for our readers is that this collection of essays will provide them with something akin to a map of others' journeys, including their wanderings and their arrivals.

The legal profession is enriched with the personal narratives of others' successes and of their failures overcome. We are all inspired by such accounts to be better lawyers and better Christians. So our editorial answer to the rhetorical title of our book, "Can a Good Christian Be a Good Lawyer?" is "Yes! But only with the grace of God and the example of others."

This book of homilies, witnesses, and reflections is our prayer for our profession, our readers, and ourselves on this Ash Wednesday in the year of our Lord one thousand nine hundred and ninety-seven.

Thomas E. Baker
Timothy W. Floyd
Lubbock, Texas

Part I.
HOMILIES

All That We Do . . .[1]

Stephen L. Carter[2]

A book on faith and law suffers at once from the problem of dissonance, because we live in an era when many perfectly sensible people doubt that there exists any connection between the two. And although I am a lawyer—still worse, a law professor—I confess that I sometimes share the doubts.

Why the doubts—including mine? The surface reasons are obvious: dissatisfaction with the work of the federal courts, popularly, and inaccurately, charged with banishing God from the nation's classrooms; apprehension about the perceived moral decay of the society, combined with a growing sense that the law (particularly the proliferation of "rights") is somehow to blame; and, not least, the strangely widespread notion that in a nation where more than three quarters of adults identify themselves as Christians, Christianity (with the connivance of lawyers) has come to be treated as a second-class religion.

These surface reasons are not at all silly, but they are certainly wrong. If so certainly wrong, why, then, are they not also silly? Because the reasons are all on the track of a point of great importance: religion in America is in crisis. In particular, religion is under pressure from within and without to be something different from what it has been at its best. Crises, of course, can be marvelous opportunities for growth, and this crisis is probably of that type.

Where do lawyers and the law stand in this crisis? Actually, better than our reputation. Indeed, among the best kept secrets in American law is this one: lawyers turn out to be just about as religious as anybody else. If you spend much time talking to religious people who are not lawyers (especially, but not exclusively, Christian evangelicals), you will likely hear sincere and pained accusations that the law has taken sides against religion, against God. Although one piece of evidence supporting the charge will be the still-unpopular classroom prayer decisions, there are others—the public school that refused, on advice of counsel, to rent its facilities to a religious group during off-hours; the child who was told she could not talk about her religious camp in describing her summer vacation; the teacher who was disciplined for reading his Bible silently as his students sat doing other work—the bizarre public policy detritus of our national misunderstanding of the separation of church and state.

Happily, the charge is untrue. Practical experience yields some of the evidence. This book, in which lawyers and law professors speak from their hearts about some of the connections between their own faith and their work, provides still more. And as lawyers and law professors work to make those connections more obvious, the charge that law is somehow anti-religious will lose what little validity it has—both because the constitutional law of religion will change in certain ways and, far more important, because the laws themselves will take on a bright, hard moral edge. This does not mean that the law will wind up reflecting the moral vision of one true "American religion"—at least I hope not. Rather, it means that the law increasingly will be infused with the rich ethical insights that have been a principal product of America's religious traditions.

For me, these essays are particularly heartening, because one of the weaknesses I have long detected in my own effort to be fully a legal scholar and fully a Christian has been my post-Enlightenment suspicion that a contradiction lurks somewhere between the two. Perhaps (I have told myself in the past) I should do more to link my faith and my work; but no (I have told myself an instant later), to do so would be unprofessional. I struggle against the second instinct, and struggle to follow the first.

To be sure, there are people who need never engage in this struggle, who are sure that faith and work are entirely separate. But I find them significantly less interesting than the people who are sure that faith and work are entirely connected, and whose struggle is to figure out just how. The struggle is often particularly tough for lawyers, who are, in important but unfortunate ways, the guardians of national morality. This is so, first, because of our national preference for legal argument over moral questions, and, second, because (in consequence of the first) so much of what the law does is express moral choices. In fact, with the exception of a handful of purely arbitrary administrative choices (driving on the right, for example), *every* law expresses a moral choice, because it either prohibits us from doing what we would like to do or forces us to do what we would not.

Part of the trouble with moral lawyering today is the weird steady drumbeat, in some parts of our politics and most parts of our law, that there is something troubling or even wicked about the explicit (or maybe even implicit) import of religious values into the public square, the place where we hold our public policy debates. I have argued against this vision at some length,[3] and will not rehearse those arguments here. I should confess, however, that my ability to array intellectual argument against this form of anti-religious neutrality does not mean that I never fall victim to it. On the contrary, I am in the need of constant reminders that my religious understanding of moral truth is not forbidden in the public square; and, indeed, that the public square is in desperate need of religious voices.

When the mood of post-Enlightenment emptiness strikes, I often turn, for inspiration, as well as for clear, no-nonsense answers, to the work of Martin Luther King, Jr.—or, more properly, the *Reverend* Martin Luther King Jr., leader of the Southern *Christian* Leadership Conference—because so much of his public ministry focused precisely on this question. It has become a commonplace of our revisionist times to insist that Dr. King's public ministry was actually something else: for example, a secular political crusade dressed up with the trappings of religion. This description strikes me as historically inaccurate, as well as an insult to the many religious and nonreligious people who were so moved by Dr. King's appeals to the word of God that they took up the cross and followed him, often at significant personal cost. Dr. King's public work was the same as his private work: to preach the word of God, making his life a witness to God's will, in the hope and the faith that others would be inspired to follow.

It is useful here, however, to remind ourselves of human frailty. Dr. King was not perfect; he was a man, he had flaws; but that is the point of the story, and, in a sense, the power of his example. Since Aristotle, the Western tradition has accepted that God is perfect. But man has always been considered at best perfectible and, for Christians, not even that. Human beings are mortal; in the Christian vision, human beings are *fallen*. The significance of this point is that we cannot reasonably expect anybody to live the life of perfect obedience to God, because to do so would be *inhuman*. What we can reasonably expect is a life of striving, falling, and striving again.

This understanding frees human beings of what would otherwise be the unbearable guilt of knowing how our own imperfection falls short of God's perfection.[4] For democratic citizens, it frees us from what would otherwise be the unbearable contradiction of fearing to preach God's word to others because of an inability to live it perfectly ourselves. And for believing lawyers in search of ethical norms around which to build their careers, it frees us from what would otherwise be the unbearable emptiness of concluding that the only guide to the proper law of man is to be found in the human mind.

This is not at all to say that the life of the religious lawyer is a life spent trying, willy-nilly, to capture the apparatus of the state in order to bring about by force a nation whose laws mirror the laws of God. Sometimes the believing lawyer will do just that—that is one way of looking at the civil rights movement—but the believing lawyer's goal is not necessarily theocracy. Rather, the goal is to live his or her own life, to spend his or her own career, exemplifying, as nearly as possible, the way that God wants us to live. There will be moments when that will lead the lawyer to twist case and doctrine to enable the state to do better justice; but it is hubris to imagine that most of what we learn from God we learn in order to make rules for others. Most of what we learn from God we learn instead in order to live as God desires; and if, in so doing, we inspire others to follow our example, so much the better.

Perhaps this is another way of saying what believing Christians, Jews, Muslims, and members of most other faiths necessarily believe: God is transcendent, and the obligation of the believer to discern God's will and then do it is unaffected by the particular job that the believer might hold.

The thirteenth-century sage Moses Maimonides put it most simply: "All that you do, do for God."[5] That "all" must include the practice and teaching of law, and an open recognition of that fact is useful, even if the problems the recognition poses are perplexing.

Lawyers, by training and inclination, want to uphold the law—that is, the law of the state. Religious people, by training and inclination, are sensitive to the possibility that there is a higher law than the law of the state—that is, the law of God. That Divine Law is superior to secular law is virtually an axiom of theistic religion, religion's own version of the Supremacy Clause. Some theorists, notably Stanley Fish, have rather mischievously used this axiom to question whether a religious person can truly be committed to the rule of secular law. So have some theologians, among them John Courtney Murray, who argued almost four decades ago that instead of asking "whether Catholicism is compatible with American democracy," a Roman Catholic should ask "whether American democracy is compatible with Catholicism."[6] And although Murray thought there was no conflict between the two, from the very form of the question, it is plain, in the event that some conflict should arise, which law is superior to which. The hard question, and not only for the religious lawyer, is what obligation a religious person has, and to whom, when the two forms of law come into conflict.

Although the religious have struggled with this question for ages, secular law has lately preferred to pretend that the question does not exist—or rather, that the answer is obvious. *Of course* one's first allegiance is to the secular sovereign; *of course* the laws of that secular sovereign trump any religious principles with which they come into contact; *of course* reasonable religious people understand this hierarchy and abide by it. Anybody who believes anything else, we dismiss as a fanatic.

Not only do we nowadays dismiss such unreasonable people as fanatics, we may even send them off to jail. This is the import of the Supreme Court's free exercise decisions since the mid-1970s, which take as their basic theme the statist assumption that when the laws of the state and the religious needs of the individual conflict, the state wins. The Congress tinkered with the margins of this line of cases in 1993, when it enacted the Religious Freedom Restoration Act, but the legislative history made plain that RFRA was not intended to overturn the most egregious of the Court's errors.[7] For example, the *Lyng*[8] case, in which the Justices allowed the Forest Service to destroy the pristine condition of a national forest and thus to "devastate" (the Court's word!) the religious traditions of three Indian tribes, was mentioned in the committee report as the kind of case that RFRA would not overturn. So, too, was *Goldman v. Weinberger*,[9] in which the Justices gave short shrift to the claim that forcing an Air Force officer who was also an Orthodox Jew to uncover his head (in order to follow military uniform regulations) violated his First Amendment rights.

But such secular pressures are an insufficient excuse for shying away from our duty to do the will of God. As believers, we are called to do God's will in all that we undertake. We are called, in that sense, to be perfect. Of course, we cannot do it. Nor, I think, does God expect us to do it. Human beings are imperfect images of God. We are mortal; we are fallible; and so our strivings do not match our aspirations. We are not thereby hypocrites; rather, this failure to meet all our moral and spiritual goals is, in a sense, the very definition of mortality. What God expects of us—demands of us—is not that we never fail, but that we never fail to try.

That is as hard a lesson for the lawyer as for anybody else. It is too often the conceit of our profession that it is harder, that somehow, because our vocation requires us to live in the interstices and divisions of society, we are exempted from the binding force of ordinary human morality. So we can, for example, take professional pleasure in our ability to persuade juries not to convict vicious killers, or to persuade the Congress to exempt our clients' dangerous products or workplaces from the regulations that apply to everybody else. One is reminded in such cases of the old ditty from the labor movement: "Mr. Businessman, he went to church, he never missed a Sunday./Mr. Businessman, he went to Hell, for what he did on Monday."

I certainly am not arguing that we as lawyers should not defend clients who are very despised or very rich or both. I could not spend my working hours training lawyers if I thought that. But I think we do little good, and much harm, when we pretend that it is possible to craft a vision of legal practice from which the moral vision of the lawyer is entirely submerged beneath the moral vision of the client.[10] A number of the essayists in this volume make this point, Thomas Shaffer perhaps foremost among them, as he has been for decades. For religious lawyers, the freedom to follow God even into the practice of the profession is of first importance, and clients who do not like it are free to shop for legal services elsewhere.

What about judges? Should they, too, allow religious principles in any sense to guide their work? The temptation, of course, is splendid—and why not yield? In his recent symposium essay, retired Judge James F. Nelson writes of his early years on the Los Angeles Municipal Court bench, when, moved by his Bahá'í faith, he would sometimes intervene to correct imbalances in the skills of the advocates before him. "This naturally raised the ire of the lawyers," Judge Nelson writes, "who, quite properly, did not see this as my role."[11] Perhaps the lawyers were right to object, as Judge Nelson suggests. But would the world really be so terrible if religious judges, moved by their faith-inspired visions of justice, were to find it intolerable that the side that can buy the better lawyers tends to win? Monroe Freedman has reminded us that a footnote in *Miranda v. Arizona*[12] quoted Maimonides for the proposition that "the principle that no man is to be declared guilty on his own admission is a divine decree."[13] The Court did not, of course, cite Maimonides as authority; but suppose that a religious judge, familiar with Maimonides and influenced by him, had been led by religious sensibility to ponder the self-incrimination problem and thus to see the wickedness of coerced confessions in a way that a more secular judge did not. Would bringing this perspective to bear on the case imply that the judge was acting unethically? I suppose it might, but only if we would reach the same conclusion were the judge to bring to bear any other moral perspective external to the law itself.[14] Otherwise, we send the message, not that church and state are separate, but that religious ways of gaining moral knowledge are inferior to others.

Of course, in contemporary American society, we too often send precisely that message:[15] and, when we do, we add to the pressure on religious people (including religious lawyers) to pretend to be less religious than they are. Moreover, we shove underground an instinct that we should be celebrating: the very human desire to know and follow God.

Having said this, I should hasten to add that we live in a nation that is, admirably, attempting to preserve a degree of religious pluralism that the world has never before seen. In consequence, it would be, in a sense, literally un-American for any one of our religions to suppose an inherent (God-given?) right to re-order American law and American life in accordance with any particular vision of divine will. This is pluralism, not relativism: it is not that all paths to God are equally valid, but that we have the good fortune to live in a nation whose constitutional traditions recognize that the state has no advantage over the rest of us in figuring out which ones are good and which ones are bad. For this reason, it is important to distinguish between the religious group that is pressing its moral positions on a skeptical nation—perfectly democratic behavior, whether the group is the Christian Coalition or the Southern Christian Leadership Conference—and a religious group that is pressing its theological position concerning the one true path to God. It is sometimes difficult to distinguish the two, but if we refuse to make the effort, we have no ground for distinguishing the religiously motivated activism of a Martin Luther King Jr. from the religiously motivated effort in the 1950s to declare, as a matter of law, that ours is a Christian nation.

In drawing the distinction, we recognize the important difference between religious and the secular notions of "freedom." To the secular mind, freedom is an end in itself; to the religious mind, freedom is a gift from God, and is to be used to help each of us move closer to God. Even the great philosophers of the Enlightenment understood this idea, that the gift of human freedom was a gift that was granted better to enable human beings to follow the will of God. Locke was quite explicit on the point, and although secular philosophers have lately forgotten it, the theologians never have. The great Western religions have this in common: the first duty of the believing Christian or Jew or Muslim is to discover the will of God and do it. Why should this be any less true for the believing individual who happens to be a lawyer? "The law of the Lord is perfect," says the Psalm.[16] It is hardly the place of the religious lawyer, then, to say: I like this law of

God but not that one, so this one, not that one, will influence my ethical universe. This is a hard rule, and none of us can follow it entirely. But we must overcome our weaknesses where and as we can; and, in particular, when great moral issues arise, we as lawyers must not shrink from consulting our religious moral understandings in discerning just and good and true solutions. The fact that many of today's religious movements reach moral answers that some of us may regard as wrong does not free us from our obligation to proclaim openly the religious reasons (when they are present) for our disagreements. And when the values on which a religious leader bases an argument are truly as universal as most like to pretend, the movement will progress—as, in a democracy, it should.

This was precisely the appeal that Dr. King offered: No matter what your prejudices, no matter what your preconceptions, look at the law of the Lord and see if you think racial segregation morally right! And although some clergy of his day offered answers different from his, those different answers, in a great redemptive movement, have fallen away, until even the Southern Baptist Convention, originally founded in order to preserve slavery against the interference of northern Baptists, has recently adopted a resolution apologizing for its century of racism. The will of God became the law of the land.

Maimonides is still right: All that we do, we must do for God

.

Endnotes

1. Copyright 1996 Stephen L. Carter. All rights reserved.
2. Episcopalian. William Nelson Cromwell Professor of Law, Yale University. B.A. 1976, Stanford University; J.D. 1979, Yale University.
3. See Stephen L. Carter, *The Culture of Disbelief: How American Law and Politics Trivialize Religious Devotion* (1993).
4. Alert readers will recognize my debt to Jesuit theologian Karl Rahner, who has pointed out that only our acceptance of God's infinite love can free us from the unbearable guilt of knowing how far we really are from the creatures God would like us to be. See generally Karl Rahner, *Foundations of Christian Faith: An Introduction to the Idea of Christianity* (William V. Dych trans., 1986).
5. Abraham Joshua Heschel, *Maimonides: A Biography*, 203 (Joachim Neugroschel trans., 1991) (1935).
6. See John Courtney Murray, *We Hold These Truths: Catholic Reflections on the American Proposition* at ix–x (1960).
7. And now the Supreme Court has held that RFRA is unconstitutional. *City of Boerne v. Flores*, 65 U.S.L.W. 4612 (1997).
8. *Lyng v. Northwest Indian Cemetery Protective Ass'n*, 485 U.S. 439, 451 (1988).
9. 475 U.S. 503, 510 (1986).
10. For a powerful argument on this point, see Anthony T. Kronman, *The Lost Lawyer: Failing Ideals of the Legal Profession* (1993).

11. James F. Nelson, "The Spiritual Dimension of Justice," 27 *Tex. Tech L. Rev.* 1237, 1243 (1996).
12. 384 U.S. 436 (1966).
13. *Id*. n. 27, quoted in Monroe H. Freedman, "Legal Ethics from a Jewish Perspective," 27 *Tex. Tech L. Rev.* 1131, 1131 n. 2 (1996).
14. I discuss this proposition in Stephen L. Carter, "The Religiously Devout Judge," *Notre Dame L. Rev.* 932, 935 (1989).
15. See Carter *supra* n. 3, especially at chs. 1–4.
16. Psalm 19:7 (New Revised Standard).

Public Lives and Private Virtue

Mark E. Chopko[1]

> You are the light of the world. A city set on a hill cannot be hidden.
> Nor do they light a lamp and then put it under a bushel basket; it
> is set on a lampstand, where it gives light to all in the house. Just
> so, your light must shine before others. . .
>
> —*Jesus Christ*[2]

This book is an appropriate occasion to reflect on the authenticity of our
professional lives and how we might more humanely serve our communities and our homes. Thus, the title of this essay, "Public Lives and Private
Virtue." Briefly, I propose to explore the interaction between and integration of the public and private sides of our lives as lawyers. My basic thesis
is that, without integrating our public lives and our private virtues, we
trivialize our private lives and we make a facade of our public personae.

A Public Profession

Unlike occupations which ply their trade aside from the public's eye, the
trade of lawyering exists only in the public. Without interaction with our
public—clients, corporations, governments, and courts—lawyering will be
ineffective in filling its own mandate: serving the needs of the community.
Aside from our "paid" work, we also serve our neighborhoods, schools, and
community groups. We call ourselves members of a profession. We profess
an oath of service and commitment to the most radical of all ideals—one
which pervades both religious and secular thought—the idea of justice. Our
public trials are searches for the truth in order to do justice. Our private
trials, however, may result in something more or something less. This
essay is not so much about "professionalism" but about "personalism."

The impetus for this essay came out of an argument that I had, years
ago now, with one of my friends. I mentioned to him that I had noticed a
bumper sticker that proclaimed: "If you want peace, work for justice" (a
quotation from Pope Paul VI).[3] My friend indicated that he thought that
was a great idea, but he questioned how many of us live that out in our
private lives. The point of the discussion, as I recall it now, was whether
lawyers as professionals had neglected their "community" in their private
lives. I, of course, was defending the profession. But the point stuck. That
encounter got me to thinking about how *we do* live our private lives. Do we

reflect the same principles that we aspire to in our legal and public work, in our marriages, families, and communities?

When I was licensed to practice during the post-Watergate phase of American jurisprudence, lawyers were often in the public eye in a very negative light—so many, it seemed, went to prison or were otherwise punished. But aside from ethics, there was a good deal of concern in the nonlegal community about the *humanness* of lawyers. Somehow, it seemed, public lives and private virtue had gotten separated from each other.

Unintegrated Private Lives

When our private virtues do not fuel our public lives, we become unintegrated. What the public sees and who we really are do not coincide. This negatively affects lawyers in two ways that I will deal with in turn.

The first undesirable situation occurs when a lawyer's private life never surfaces. For those of us who might fall victim to this tendency, our private lives are inspired and enriched by private virtues. We hear in the message of the Gospel, "[W]here your treasure is, there your heart [will be] also."[4] But there it stops; there is no growth or movement. There is a failure to live fully in communion even with ourselves,[5] a failure to share our true gifts and graces with others. Denied the benefit of this richness, the public life appears frail and indecisive, almost too "politic."[6] It also appears to be common.

Too much of the current political debate in the United States merely purports to speak to "values." Both sides in recent Presidential campaigns have focused almost incessantly on that word. But persons in public political life, at least what I see in Washington, rarely seem to reflect their *own* values. Nobody seems to be saying, "This is what I believe and what I stand for. Your vote should be cast accordingly." Rather, what we see is people doing always what is politic, not necessarily what is right. For these people, private virtues—honesty, dedication to truth, liberty, and a strong desire to serve the common good—may still exist, but go unannounced. The leader's "public life" announces he or she is personally opposed to something or in favor of something, but wouldn't want to *impose* those values on other people. But talk about imposition of values misses the point: I question how many lawyers in public life are willing to be publicly honest about what they believe and let their private virtue develop and direct public lives. They perhaps believe that if their own private virtues were really known, they would be rejected for public office or denied even public respect.[7] In this, I submit, private virtue has been trivialized. One's public life exists as a shell, used as a front for fear that their private sides might truly be known, for which one must account and be held responsible.

The second undesirable outcome of a lack of integration, somewhat paradoxically, is precisely the opposite—a public life that not merely ignores but suppresses a private side. The public persona as "lawyer" appears to exemplify the best of our tradition. But that too often is a facade, masking the fact that our private virtues have somehow not sufficiently developed. We hide our brokenness in the shadows of our lives, therefore deceiving ourselves if not others. We who have professed a lawyer's oath understand that our commitment will be measured by the standards of our own professional communities. We are subject to state regulations and licensing. If we disobey those standards, we are punished, even disbarred. By contrast, there is no enforced standard for our private lives—no mechanism for measuring our performance, except our own consciences. Perhaps when the struggle becomes too great, our private virtue gets lost; only the public side shows. When that occurs, how is it possible to seek justice in what we do?

These lawyers may be unwilling or unable to let their own struggles for humanness ignite their public lives. This is not an easy task, as I know. They are not willing to see themselves in the humanness of clients or courts, or their own quests for private justice as a part of a greater struggle shared by all. When this occurs, I submit, our private lives become shams. I would hardly suggest that we parade around our private hurts and imperfections as if we were appearing on some tawdry talk show. Our public lives—which aspire to so much that is good and so much that is decent—must allow that side of us that doubts and struggles to infuse us with humanness in order for us to see how our own public lives necessarily must reflect our private virtues.

Lawyerly Temptations

Nikos Kazantzakis wrote a book in the 1950s called *The Last Temptation of Christ*.[8] It was made into a rather controversial, some would say dreadful, movie.[9] It does, however, offer some insight into this situation.

What I want to recount for you is not the *last*, but the *first* temptations of Christ. As you know, Christ went into the desert to fast for forty days prior to His public ministry. In the Gospel accounts of Matthew and Luke, He is tempted by the devil three times.[10] He is asked to turn a stone into bread, He is offered earthly dominion, and He is asked to tempt God. In the movie, He seeks to know God's will in the desert. The devil presents three similar choices to Jesus. The first is to live life as an ordinary man, which I will call "ordinariness." The second is power or dominion. When that, too, is rejected, the devil offers a third temptation. In the form of fire, calling to mind the Biblical images about God appearing in the burning bush,[11] the third temptation is arrogance or conceit. The fire taunts: "So—you would be God?"

Most commentators focusing on the humanity of lawyers deal with the uses and abuses of power, both in our practices and in our public lives. These public ethical trials characterize much of the common reporting of lawyerly faults and human foibles, from Watergate to Waldholtz. My focus concerns the other two temptations because we all face them in our own lives and because they merit attention—whether we are going to be ordinary and whether we think we are above it all.

Previously, I described two types of lawyers whose public lives were separated from their private virtues. The first type—a private life which had been unable to inspire a true public life—reflects the temptation of ordinariness. Those who avoid the inner truth of their private lives, refuse to let their lights shine. As stated in the Sermon on the Mount,[12] By contrast, the second situation—lawyers who refuse to allow their public lives to be touched by humanness—illustrates the third and perhaps the most dangerous temptation: arrogance or conceit. In this we have lost touch with ourselves. We exist *only* as the public personae. While the first temptation of ordinariness reflects "fear," the latter, by contrast, shows a tragic lack of wholeness. We exist only in the public eye, a two dimensional figure.

Personal Integration and Authenticity

To a certain extent, I am the least among you to make these observations. My observations reflect lawyers that I have known and temptations that I have felt in my own professional life. My own personal struggles through the throes of civil divorce and the long process of church annulment are enough to remind me of my limitations and limits. Yet, I draw courage from those of our profession who have more years of experience in the life of their community and service to the people. They have known their own struggles, both in public lives and with their own private virtues. Those are struggles that I cannot know. I commend those lawyers to you today only as observations on the life of a lawyer.

The questions I pose are: If lawyers must work for justice, how do we know when it is achieved? How do we do justice unless we know it in our own lives? One of the most popular books ever written in this country, at least as measured by the various trade publications, was published in 1978 by a psychiatrist, Dr. Scott Peck, called *The Road Less Traveled*.[13] That is true. But it will not get easier if we either refuse to acknowledge our own humanness or provide a false shell for public (and private) display.

The Challenge

As we lawyers serve our communities and interact with various aspects of people's lives that we may touch, our challenge is to strive for authenticity. We cannot avoid the hard questions that come when public lives are open to being molded by private virtue. Just as Joshua demanded of the tribes,[14] every day we must choose whom and what we will serve. If it is time to take a stand, let us stand for the things we believe and not for the things we read or for things that might be expected. Finally, I would ask that as lawyers we resist the temptation to arrogance and conceit. Our obligations as lawyers can best be discharged with value and meaning only if we are willing to acknowledge the private virtues in our own lives and the lives of those with whom we must work whether we be judges or lawyers. The most difficult—but the most important—thing that I can do as a lawyer is to allow the shadows of my own life and my own imperfections to humanize me in my daily interaction with the people I must serve.

Shakespeare once said, "[T]o thine own self be true, [for t]hou canst not then be false to any man."[15] To me, that is what my essay is all about: To be fully human, to be alive, to be fully integrated, to have one's values and humanness touch and infuse one's life in service to the community and ultimately to serve one's own life.

Endnotes

1. Roman Catholic. General Counsel, National Conference of Catholic Bishops & United States Catholic Conference, Washington, DC. B.S. 1974, University of Scranton; J.D. 1977, Cornell University Law School.

   This essay is adapted from a speech delivered at the 21st Annual Red Mass, St. Vincent Archabbey, Latrobe, Pennsylvania, on October 28, 1988. The author wishes to thank Bishop Robert N. Lynch of St. Petersburg, Florida, for his encouragement in the preparation of this essay.
2. Matthew 5:14–16 (New American Bible).
3. Slogan on bumper stickers distributed by the Campaign for Human Development, United States Catholic Conference, Washington, D.C. See generally Address of His Holiness Paul VI to the General Assembly of the United Nations (Oct. 4, 1965), in *The Gospel of Peace and Justice* 379 (J. Gremillion ed., 1976).
4. Matthew 6:21.
5. See Ephesians 4:4–14.
6. Here, I pause to interject my own rather public and political life even as the General Counsel for the Conference of Bishops. I do not mean to suggest that it is never inappropriate to consider the consequences of one's actions. For myself, I routinely confront the problem of having to balance the various constituent pieces of the whole fabric of the Church's public policy program. I am, on the contrary, suggesting that frequent use of the politic response as one's only benchmark will, it seems to me, result in losing one's authenticity to one's politics.
7. Pope John Paul II identified this phenomenon in his encyclical letter, *Evangelium Vitae* ("the Gospel of Life"), as a reason to be concerned for the political life of a country. Pope John Paul II, *Evangelium Vitae*, ¶ 69–70, 90 (1995) (one cannot renounce one's obligation to follow one's conscience and work for the common good).
8. Nikos Kazantzakis, *The Last Temptation of Christ* (P. A. Bien trans., Simon & Schuster 1960). The novel is called by Encyclopaedia Britannica a "revisionist [psychology] of Jesus Christ." 6 *The New Encyclopaedia Britannica* 776 (15th ed. 1992). It is supposed to reflect, in part, Mr. Kazantzakis's own struggles with his personal faith.
9. The 1988 Martin Scorsese movie of the same name as the book was called a "[d]eeply flawed screen adaptation" by the United States Catholic Conference Office for Film and Broadcasting. Office for Film and Broadcasting,

United States Catholic Conference, *The Family Guide to Movies and Videos* 312 (Henry Herx ed., 1995).

10. Matthew 4:1–11; Luke 4:1–13.

11. Exodus 3:2–4.

12. Matthew 5:1–7:29.

13. Matthew 5:14–16.

14. M. Scott Peck, *The Road Less Traveled: A New Psychology of Love, Traditional Values and Spiritual Growth* (1978).

15. *Id.* at 1.

16. Joshua 24:14–15.

17. William Shakespeare, *Hamlet* act 1, sc. 3, lines 78, 80 (Harold Jenkins ed., Methuen 1982).

Reflections on Three Stories: "Practicing" Law and Christianity at the Same Time

Dan Edwards[1]

The Jesus Prayer and *United States v. Alejandro*

My secretary took the call from the Clerk of the Federal District Court. I had been appointed to represent an indigent defendant in a criminal case. The phone message gave me the arraignment date and time, the name of the defendant (I'll call him Juan Alejandro), and the charge—illegal re-entry. This offense consists of re-entering the United States without permission from the Immigration and Naturalization Service after having been previously deported. It isn't a terribly serious crime, but it does carry prison time.

I knew two things from the nature of the charge: First, the defendant must have come here numerous times. Ordinarily, in those days, one was given a voluntary departure the first few times, then deported, then deported again and threatened before such a charge would even be considered. Second, there was something more offensive about this defendant than being in the country without a visa. Even habitual illegal re-entry was, at least then, so common and relatively harmless that it hardly justified the expenditure of resources to prosecute and incarcerate an illegal alien unless there were serious aggravating circumstances.

On the way to visit my client, I stopped by the Federal Probation Office to pick up his rap sheet. When I saw that it was three and one-half pages long, I began to suspect why the government was prosecuting Mr. Alejandro instead of simply sending him back across the river. When I read the rap sheet, it left no doubt. The charges ranged from murder and attempted murder to child molesting. The convictions were mostly in the arenas of armed robbery, aggravated assault, and drug possession. The main reason illegal re-entry is rarely prosecuted is that the perpetrators are usually such good people. Apparently, Juan Alejandro was not.

Now you know something about Juan Alejandro, but you still know nothing about his new lawyer. I might tell you about my legal education, my family, or the nature of my practice. But for purposes of this essay, I'll tell you about the state of my faith when I took on *United States v. Alejandro*. I had given up Christianity during college and had dabbled in Eastern religions since then. But my real religion had been a commitment to social justice. Then, for reasons that I'll describe later in the course of reflecting on another case, I had returned to the Church essentially as an experiment. I was looking for a God I'd never known, and I was exploring the sacraments and prayer disciplines of Anglican Christianity to see if God might be found that way. I still didn't know what I believed. I just started going to Church. Then I began praying the traditional prayers of Christianity to see what would happen.

Not much was happening. I sometimes got a faint intuition of something when I received the Eucharistic bread and wine. But the prayers felt false to me. I had the distinct sense that I was repeating meaningless sentences to myself—that I was the only one listening. About this time I took up the "Jesus Prayer," the ancient prayer practice of the Eastern Orthodox Church, popularized in America by J. D. Salinger's novel, *Franny and Zooey*.[2] The Jesus Prayer is an attempt to follow seriously the admonitions of Jesus and Paul to "pray without ceasing." Practitioners recite the prayer like a mantra, "Lord, Jesus Christ, Son of the Living God, have mercy on me, a sinner." One plants these words in one's consciousness by meditating with the prayer for a protracted period of time, then continues rolling the prayer through one's mind constantly throughout the day. Usually, one links the words to the pattern of one's breath or heartbeat. So, I was saying the Jesus Prayer in those days, methodically, by rote, but not really getting anywhere with it. I was thinking the prayer over and over as I drove from the Probation Office to the jail.

One of the reasons I rejected Christianity in my college days was that I couldn't find much connection between the way of life taught in the New Testament and the lives lived by any professing Christians I knew. I didn't see them abandoning their families, giving all their goods to the poor, considering the lilies, and getting persecuted for radical obedience to their faith. Nor was I particularly inclined to such a lifestyle myself. Now, I was a professionally ambitious lawyer in the 1980s American West, trying to build a law practice while raising two children. Whether I could reconcile my life with the radicalism of the New Testament was even more dubious now than before.

I approached this question in a fairly gentle, perhaps self-serving way. Instead of asking whether I could reconcile all of my life with the New Testament, I asked whether there was anything in my life, particularly in my legal practice, which partook to any degree of Biblical faith. I was searching for sparks of Christianity in my life, hoping I might be able to blow on them and perhaps kindle something. So as I drove into the parking lot of the jail, I recalled the "sheep and goats" passage from St. Matthew's Last Judgment. That's the story in which the Lord divides the good folks from the bad ones, and says to the good, "I was hungry and you gave me food, I was thirsty and you gave me drink, I was a stranger and you made me welcome, lacking clothes and you clothed me, sick and you visited me, in prison and you came to see me."[3] The people who'd done these works of mercy did not recognize the Lord as the recipient of their mercy; but the Lord said, "In so far as you have done it to one of the least of these brothers of mine, you did it to me."[4] So perhaps here was something that smacked of Christianity in my practice. I was visiting Juan Alejandro in prison, or at least in jail, and he was surely one of "the least" of Christ's brothers measured by any standard—political, economic, or moral. That much was clear. Perhaps I was, in some spiritual sense, visiting Christ, notwithstanding the rap sheet. So I thought, but didn't truly believe it. I just entertained the possibility.

Within a few minutes, I was sitting in the attorney visiting room, a tiny cinder block cubicle with a stool under a naked light bulb. There was a barred window through which I could speak with my client when he arrived. Eventually, Juan Alejandro came to the other side of the barred window, nodded and sat down. He was a small man, thin, about thirty years old, with dark skin and a black beard. When I saw him, the first thing I thought of was his rap sheet. I remembered all the things he had done. But I forced myself to balance that thought with a recollection of the Matthew text. I tried to think of my client as having something of Christ in him.

We discussed the case, but we conversed with difficulty because he had little English and I had less Spanish. There were long pauses as one of us would try to think of the words, and the other would watch and wait expectantly. I don't remember what I'd asked, or even if it was the answer to a question I was waiting for. I only know that Juan Alejandro was silent, and was looking at me quite openly and honestly, and I was watching his face closely and expectantly. Then I noticed the words rolling spontaneously and uninvited through my mind, "Lord, Jesus Christ, Son of the Living God, have mercy on me, a sinner." I was staring silently into the face of this prisoner with the three and one-half page rap sheet, praying to Christ in him to forgive me.

A decade later, in a Jesuit retreat center across the continent from that Western jail, I had an equally powerful sense of Christ's presence. But at no other time in those ten years did I have such an experience. At no other time did faith materialize into such a palpable reality.

Evil as Springboard: *State v. Selby*

Several months before I met Juan Alejandro, my spiritual life took a sharp turn, the turn which led me to try the Church as an experiment. A case, *State v. Selby* (another pseudonym), was a major part of the impetus for my experiment.

Five years of legal practice had exposed me to a broader spectrum of life than many nonlawyers experience. I'd represented and otherwise dealt with quite an array of people. However, the *Selby* case was different. It was drenched in evil. It wasn't just that my client was alleged to be a contract killer. The evil was pervasive. It manifested in stories of political corruption, police brutality, people willing to sell their families and supposed friends for rewards, contracts to kill business associates and contracts to

kill those who had hired the first killers, adultery, prostitution, embezzle-
ment, tax fraud, and blackmail. Some of the moral malignancy, I could see
directly. Most of it, I only heard about. But it was as if I'd been caught up
in a large-cast drama in which no one could be trusted, no one was good.

Somehow the encounter with this evil, not just the banal evil of sadistic
debt collectors or juvenile sociopaths, or the pathetic evil of family violence,
but a sinister spirit permeating the legal and business dealings of so many
people, took me aback. I had no framework within which to understand
such a moral morass. When I returned to the Church, I was looking for the
answer to a question obliquely asked by my legal practice. It was nothing
so simple or merely curious as, "Why is there evil?" It was more a quest for
a world view which made sense of the senselessness. A narrative theorist
would say that I was looking for a story that was big enough to include
such a cruel and cynical chapter without collapsing into chaos and despair.
The Christian narrative, climaxing as it does in the grim victory of evil on
the cross juxtaposed with the joyful mystery of Resurrection, became that
story for me.

In my tradition, we speak of certain theological and cardinal virtues[5]
which are the foundations for all other virtues or excellences of character.
The first of the theological virtues is "faith" by which I mean the existential
posture of investing the value of one's life in a particular world view or
narrative. Faith came to me only when I went looking for it; and I was sent
looking by the first of the cardinal virtues—"the mother of all virtues"—
"prudence," by which I mean seeing reality directly and clearly as it is. The
law taught me prudence, not just in the Selby case, but over and over, day
in and day out. Prudence was knowing the good and the bad in human
characters, the risks and possibilities in human life. The encounter with
reality, stripped of illusions, provoked my search for faith. Without faith,
without trust in a world view sufficiently comprehensive to embrace the
diverse realities uncovered by prudent consciousness, life is not only too
painful, but too complex, too mysterious, too provocative to endure.

The Foot of the Cross: In the Matter of _____

A year after I met Juan Alejandro, the *pro bono* panel of the state bar
association asked me to take the case of Giles Woods (a pseudonym). Mr.
Woods was in jail too, but his criminal defense wasn't to be my job. I
represented him in a proceeding to decide the guardianship of his two small
children.

Mr. Woods had been in the Canadian navy and had been a camp cook
for loggers. When he came to the States, he fell in love with a wholesome,
amiable, small town, young lady. They were married, had two children,
and things were going well enough. Then, for no reason Mr. Woods could
understand, his wife became wildly promiscuous, taunting him cruelly
with her sexual exploits. Soon they were divorced, and there was a custody
fight, which Mr. Woods lost. The day after the divorce, he went to visit his

wife. Eventually, she told him it was time to leave. He pulled out a fishing knife. She said, "I love you." Then he fatally stabbed her in the chest, and immediately called 911.

The criminal trial was still pending when the guardianship proceeding occurred. The dead mother's sister and brother-in-law sought custody of the children. Obviously, Mr. Woods couldn't take care of the children. But he didn't want his in-laws to have custody because they'd hated him even before the divorce and homicide. He felt sure they'd destroy any hope he might have of ever restoring his relationship with the children. He had urgently prevailed upon his aging parents to consent to serve as guardians if appointed.

So we went to hearing on the petition. The in-laws weren't the best parents in the world, but they were no worse than average. Mr. Woods' parents were more candid with the court than they'd been with either their son or with me about their reluctance to take on such a responsibility at their age. In short, we didn't have much of a chance from the beginning, and that chance had flickered out well before we came to closing arguments.

As we waited for the judge's ruling, I felt absolutely empty and helpless. My client had done a horrible thing. And yet, he genuinely loved his children. In a sense he had loved his wife, albeit with a destructive passion. He was certain to spend years in prison; and the most essential thing for spiritual survival in prison is hope for a better life outside someday. He desperately needed some hope of reconciliation with his son and daughter. But when all was said and done, I had no case. I'd failed.

The judge pulled no punches in announcing his decision. He told the new guardians not to encourage any contact between the children and their father. He told my client the best thing he could do for his children was to cease to exist in their lives. Maybe he was right. But each of his words was a nail in my client's hands and feet. All I could do was sit with him at the same table, to be his advocate and in some sense his friend. If no lawyer had taken his case, the result could not have been worse. But there was one difference. I was with him when it happened. I shared his experience. A priest once told me, "The foot of the cross is the hardest place to be." Most lawyers spend more time there than they'd choose, but perhaps not more time than compassionate ministry requires.

Christian Practice and Legal Practice: Reflections on Three Stories

Eventually, I became a priest. Since then many people have asked me to explain the change in my vocation. They have often expected me to say that I left the practice of law because it was too immoral and unspiritual for a genuinely committed Christian. That assumption reflects a very different concept of the practice of law from the one I have long held, and a very different concept of Christianity from the one I began to discover in jail with Mr. Alejandro. The idea that there is a tension between the values of legal practice and the values of Christian spirituality is not altogether wrong. There is a tension. Christianity places its practitioners a bit out of step with all human culture, and yet Christianity is a faith lived in the horizontal dimension of community as well as the vertical dimension of striving toward the transcendent; so the Christian must be intimately involved with the same culture in which he or she does not quite fit.

Law and Christianity are both said to be "practiced." We say someone is a "practicing" lawyer or a "practicing" Christian. This terminology suggests that Christianity and law are enterprises which are done. The word practice may even imply that law and Christianity are done repeatedly in the hope of developing proficiency at them. It is commonly held that law may be practiced with greater or less proficiency. Some may object that proficiency at Christianity is nonsense. Their argument rests on the premise that Christianity is grounded in faith rather than works. This premise is certainly true; but, with the exception of a few heresies such as Quietism, Christianity advocates a "living faith," meaning not only trusting in a particular world view, but also acting in accordance with and in response to that trust. Hence, we have a field of inquiry known as moral theology or "Christian ethics," just as we have "legal ethics." Each system of ethics purports to guide practitioners in how to practice rightly, how to do well.

The question arises what these two practices may have to do with one another. Are they compatible, complementary, mutually exclusive, or paradoxically poised in a dialectical tension? I have told three stories to illustrate three ways in which Christian practice and legal practice have come together for me.

First, Christianity is not an abstract doctrine of reality which one simply adopts as a convenient way of understanding, which one swallows as an intellectual sedative to quell curiosity. It is an experience born of our conscious encounter with real life. I say "conscious" encounter because the anesthetized life of superficiality, relying on platitudes and banal optimism, does not give rise to the Christian experience, or for that matter the spiritual experiences embodied in any major world religion. It is most often painful experience that wakes us up and sets us searching for authentic meaning. In Buddhism, the first noble truth is *dukkha* or suffering. A metaphor for *dukkha* goes, "The world grinds on its axle." The Anglican theologian, better known as a poet, Samuel Taylor Coleridge, called it "the tears in the nature of things."

The moral dimension of this "axle grinding" is called "sin" in our tradition. "Sin" is the English translation of a Greek archery term used in the Scripture. Literally, it means "missing the mark." Things are somehow not right, not on target. If one practices law without working very hard to keep one's blinders in place, one encounters the sharp edges of reality that prompt consciousness. Suffering, evil, injustice and the whole axle-grinding not-rightness of the world are laid bare in the practice of law. And so we are pricked into consciousness; but consciousness can endure only ephemerally without faith, without a sustaining trust in a narrative or world view sufficiently comprehensive to preserve consciousness from falling into despair in the face of the absurd and wrong. My experience in *State v. Selby* was not the only force that put me on the road to faith, but it was the strongest force.

The central spiritual theme of Christianity is personal reconciliation with the core of reality, the essence, the source, and the destiny of Being. The doctrines of the Incarnation, of God's immanence and omnipresence, and of spiritual co-inherence[6] mean that the core of reality, perfectly expressed in the person of Jesus of Nazareth, is somewhat present in all things and all people. That core reality confronts us through each other. The Christian response seeks reconciliation. Such a personal reconciliation was my unexpected experience in *United States v. Alejandro*.

The "living faith" taught by Christianity as the way to live in a world simultaneously fallen and drenched in divinity is a life of service. There are many ways to serve. To stand for justice against injustice, for mercy against cruelty, for truth against falsehood are all authentic ways to serve. But the key element of Christian service is that it is personal. It is service grounded in genuine care for the person served. In fact, the care is really the heart of the service. A "client satisfaction survey" conducted by a state bar association some years ago revealed a surprising value held by our clients. Their satisfaction with their lawyer depended not so much on the successful outcome of the case as on their lawyer's care for them and commitment to them. I was not able to win Giles Woods' case; but I was able to care for him when so many people hated him, and I was at his side when he lost. The narrative of my faith made sense of that experience for me; and, in fact, enabled me to play my part in Mr. Woods' story.

It has never seemed to me that lawyering was inherently "unchristian." Rather lawyering was the context which set me in search of faith, the context in which I found faith, and the context in which I practiced faith. Jesus anticipated that faithfulness to him would entail being rejected and reviled by society.[7] I have occasionally experienced such animosity as a result of being faithful in my priestly vocation, but I experienced it far more often and more intensely as a result of being faithful in my lawyerly vocation. It has seemed to me that the law is an ideal arena for the practice of a living faith.

The Devil's Due: The Real Conflict between Legal Practice and Christian Practice

The common assumption that law practice and Christian practice are incompatible rests on misconceptions of both practices. The proper practice of law is not unrestrained advocacy for hire, but rather faithful advocacy and counsel grounded in a commitment to obtaining the goods of justice, mercy, reconciliation, peace, and liberty for one's client. The practice of Christianity is not a legalistic niceness lived in docile obedience to the political and economic powers that shape the law. Rather, it is the sharing of the common lot of humanity, participating in the fallen world—yet participating as people who are faithful to God and to those whom God gives us to serve. So the essential natures of the two practices go quite well together.

Yet, because the world grinds on its axle, there is a tension between these practices. The first source of the tension is that lawyer culture is seductive in its promise of rewards for the successful. Money, power, and prestige are available in legal practice, and are commonly regarded as valuable, not only in themselves, but as indicia of professional skill and accomplishment. However, the deliberate accumulation of money, power, and prestige run counter to the Christian values of apostolic poverty, vulnerability, and humility. The adversarial process and the aggressive ethos of the profession may not be problematic in themselves; but they aggravate the drive toward success measured by victory rather than by faithfulness, integrity, and the genuine excellences of good lawyering.

The second source of tension is the desire and financial incentive to please our clients. Subservience to the client's will is a problem for several reasons. Our clients' goals are often meanspirited, vindictive, greedy, or otherwise contrary to a healthy spirituality. Moreover, the goal of pleasing the client not only separates us from a single-minded devotion to the will of God, it also impairs our ability to serve our client's interests, since client goals are often contrary to the client's interests, even when judged by objective economic criteria.

A third source of tension is that legal practice is often morally ambiguous. The most common moral ambiguity is the situation in which one keeps the secrets of a client rather than exposing them in the interest of truth. Those who suggest that Christians are out of place in legal practice assume that Christians honor truth-telling above honoring the privacy of confidential communications. However, clergy function under similar obligations of confidentiality; and Christian support and study groups routinely bind themselves to pledges of confidentiality. The law has no monopoly on moral ambiguity, but law practice does present the issues of morally problematic situations more often than many other pursuits.

The final, and perhaps most difficult source of tension, is that Christianity is often held to eschew the use of power as a way of confronting the world, even when confronting evil, in favor of the vulnerable assertion of truth.[8] Law, on the other hand, is ultimately a power game.[9] The judgment is ultimately enforced by uniformed people carrying guns. Lawyering is invoking the power of the state rather than trusting in the power of truth. Arguably, resort to legal action is an act of despair rather than hope.

The practices of law and Christianity are not perfectly compatible, not comfortably complementary. Just as there are opportunities to practice

Christianity in the midst of practicing law, so there are opportunities to betray either practice in the interest of the other. But it may well be the opportunities, even the temptations of betrayal, which make each practice helpful to the other. In the early years of the Church, martyrs submitted themselves to persecution as a test of their faith, because only when faith is tested can it be proven and convincingly professed. After the era of persecution ended, the Desert Fathers practiced eremitic monasticism in the Egyptian desert to subject their faith to testing in the trials of loneliness and asceticism. The practice of law is an opportunity to meaningfully practice faith precisely because it is simultaneously an opportunity to betray faith.

The School of Virtue: Legal Practice and Spiritual Formation

The field of inquiry known as Christian ethics does not deal with what one must do in order to stand justified before God, because in Christian theology justification is a divine gift rather than a reward. Rather Christian ethics is concerned with our response to that gift. The basic metaphor of Christian spirituality is a gift exchange. Because God has given Godself to us and for us, we give ourselves to God and for God. Our gift is accomplished by the transformation of our souls through a variety of means, but most importantly through the cultivation of Christian virtues. I have previously referred to the three theological virtues—faith, hope, and love; and to the four cardinal virtues—prudence, temperance, fortitude, and justice.

What kind of a lawyer would a person be who had acquired proficiency in these virtues? Consider first the cardinal virtues. Prudence, seeing things realistically, facing facts, is essential to competent lawyering. Temperance means a reasonableness born of detached impartiality. Temperance is essential to all aspects of lawyering from case evaluation to negotiation. Fortitude is moral courage. Lawyering requires a deep store of such courage. Lawyers must have the courage to do battle with their adversaries, even withstanding personal attacks. They must have the everyday courage required to deal with the business at hand, rather than lapse into the patterns of avoidance which doom many legal careers. Finally, justice is a commitment to the right ordering of things, to giving each person what is due to him or her. That is, of course, the first concern of the law. The effective advocate is one who is visibly committed to justice and who knows it when he or she sees it.

Does lawyering also require faith—not necessarily a particular theological articulation of faith—but trust in a sufficiently comprehensive narrative or world view to make sense of the realities one confronts in legal practice? Does lawyering also require hope that out of the turmoil in which we are endlessly engaged something of value may be born? I think the answer is "yes" to both questions. Does lawyering require "love" or something like it? I don't know. Certainly lawyering does not require sentimental attachment to our clients or anyone else. But "sentimental attachment" isn't really what the virtue of love means. It has at least seemed to me that the best lawyers have the capacity to care for others.

Conclusion

Am I saying that being "good at Christianity" makes one better at lawyering than would be the case if one were of another faith, or if one practiced no faith at all? No. I am not comparing the spirituality of Christianity to that of Islam, Judaism, or Buddhism. Other religions would also influence legal practice, probably in ways somewhat different from, and somewhat the same as, the ways in which Christianity influences lawyering. As for those who "practice no faith at all," I don't think that is a real category. Everyone has a world view in which he or she invests the value of life. Secularism is such a view. I am saying that being bad at Christianity, if that is one's religious vehicle, will make one a worse lawyer than one would be if one were good at Christianity, meaning proficient in the Christian virtues.

However, the foregoing answers skirt the fundamental question beneath the question of this section. Are all world views equally sufficient to make sense of the senselessness? Are all narratives sufficiently comprehensive to face the hard truths of life without collapsing into despair? In my experience, such a grasp on the sustaining meaning and value of life is hard to come by, even if one nominally adheres to a religious tradition which contains such a view, and tells such a story. Whether any particular belief system is sufficient to the task of faith requires testing through reason and experience. Without an adequate religious tradition, it seems to me that any lawyer's practice of law will be fatally flawed. And that is the good news in the relationship between lawyering and any living faith. The demands of legal practice test our world views and narratives, sifting the wheat from the chaff.

Endnotes

1. Episcopalian. Rector, St. Francis Church, Macon, Georgia. B.A. 1972, J.D. 1975, University of Texas; M.Div. 1990; S.T.M. 1992, General Theological Seminary.
2. J. D. Salinger, *Franny and Zooey* (1953). This mantric prayer practice is part of the hesychast tradition and is best set out in the anonymous spiritual classic, *The Way of the Pilgrim* (R. M. French trans., 1965).
3. Matthew 25:35–36 (New Jerusalem Bible).
4. Matthew 25:40.
5. The theological virtues repeatedly referenced by St. Paul are faith, hope, and love. The cardinal virtues in medieval moral theology are prudence, temperance, fortitude, and justice.

6. This is the doctrine that God is present in Jesus, and Jesus in God; that Jesus is present in all believers, and all believers in Jesus; and hence God dwells in believers. Cf. The Gospel According to John, Chapters 14–15.

7. Matthew 5:11–12; John 15:18.

8. Matthew 5:38–46; 1 Corinthians 6:1–7. See generally Walter Wink, *Engaging the Powers* chs. 7–17 (1992).

9. Robert Cover, "Violence and the Word," 95 *Yale L.J.* 1601 (1986).

On Maintaining Spiritual Sanity in a Secular Vocation

Nancy Miller-Herron[1]

Introduction

Once, when my husband, Roy Herron, and I were students in Vanderbilt University's joint divinity and law program, he traveled to New York City. On the plane, he met two of our professors, Robert Belton from the law school and Kelly Miller Smith from the divinity school; and the three men decided to share a cab from LaGuardia.

As they rode to their hotels, with Roy in the middle, law professor Belton pointed to himself and announced, "Here we have pure law." Pointing to Professor Smith, he added, "And here we have pure theology." Then, pointing to joint divinity-law student Roy Herron he asked, "But what do we have here in the middle?"

Divinity professor and Baptist preacher Kelly Miller Smith replied, in his great booming voice: "I *fear* . . . we have . . . POLLUTION!"

Law and Divinity

Some would say pollution is a charitable characterization for those who mix theology and law. During five years in Vanderbilt's joint divinity/law program, someone said to me almost daily: "Law and divinity, aren't those contradictory?" That question was often followed by a clever quip like, "What do you do, marry people and then divorce them?" Although I almost always laughed as I responded, I remember one early morning in the Vanderbilt Law Library, before my first cup of coffee, when I did not. A fellow law student, a member of the Christian Legal Society, said: "Law and divinity, aren't those contradictory?" I demanded, "Then why are you in law school? If you really think you can't be a Christian and a lawyer, then you should drop out this very day."

The questions raised about my schizophrenic professional life, a light-hearted expression of peoples' distrust for unscrupulous cutthroat lawyers, grew tiresome during student days. But I think what many people were asking is this: How do the different parts of your life fit together? During seven years as a United Methodist pastor, I discovered that many people were similarly struggling with one version or another of this central issue: how does the fact that I am a person of faith affect the rest of my life?

This question suggests a desire to be whole, to have a life not compartmentalized into work, play, family, civic activities and religious practice. Those of us who ask it express a deep longing for vocation, a life woven together, one in which we are the same person, no matter what setting we happen to be in at the time.

Father William Barnwell recounts Jesse Jackson's story about growing up on a farm in South Carolina.[2] His family accumulated a little money and was able to buy a new wood stove. They put the old wood stove outside in the chicken yard. One day a female cat found her way into that old wood stove and gave birth to a litter of kittens. "Now," said Jackson, "just because those kittens were in the stove, it didn't mean they were biscuits. They were still cats."[3]

For Barnwell, this story underscores that "whatever work we do, we need always to be clear about who we are and what we are, like cats in a wood stove."[4]

Many of those who question me assume that lawyers are merely "hired guns," and thus are daily faced with tough moral choices about whether to represent their clients vigorously or to maintain their personal integrity. So far, I have not found it particularly problematic to remember who I am and what I am in my small town practice, at least not any more problematic than when I was a pastor. And, my practice has not been fraught with moral peril, or even been terribly contradictory.

In fact, most of the time, being both a lawyer and a minister, or a minister and a lawyer, has been quite useful. For one thing, the roles are often the same. Roy and I identify four roles common both to the lawyer and the minister: Counselor. Organizer. Conciliator. Advocate.

For example, recently a young man whose wife had unsuccessfully battled cancer came to our office a few days after her death to open an estate. The skills I used in our encounter were primarily those learned in seven years as a pastor. Not more than a few minutes of our hour and a half conversation were about legal matters. We talked instead about how one can grieve while he is standing next to his children as they grieve: "counselor" is often an appropriate title for both minister and lawyer.

Roy similarly played many roles when representing a sixty year-old woman with severe heart problems. The woman's insurance company had refused to pay disability benefits, even though each of the three physicians to whom the insurance company sent her had determined she was disabled. The adjuster maintained that she could do some housework; therefore, she was not disabled. But she had been a farmer.

Roy asked the adjuster if the company would pay his disability claim if he could not practice law but could do a little housework. "Why sure!" the adjuster said.

"So what is the difference between my client and me," Roy wanted to know, "except that I am a man and she is a woman?" The company eventually paid in full. And Roy played several roles: he was a counselor to the disabled woman, her advocate to the insurance adjuster and a conciliator between the two. Roles that ministers—and lawyers—play all the time.

For several years at West End United Methodist Church in Nashville, my charge was to help equip the congregation for *diakonia*, service. The congregation asked me to help them struggle with the question, "How can we weave together our common life with what God is calling us to do in the world?" Or, as my friend Tara Seeley frames the question, "How is our common life good news for the poor?"[5] Although they did not really need someone with legal training, West End deliberately chose a pastor-lawyer because they *did* need someone who could play counselor, organizer, conciliator and advocate. As the local church faced mundane questions such as whether we should open our doors to serve as an emergency overflow shelter for the homeless during winter, or how our congregational life could become more hospitable to people of different races, cultures or economic backgrounds, I played each of these four roles.

Yet when I took a leave of absence from the church for mothering and lawyering, some of my friends worried about moral dilemmas I would face "out there in the real world." But I rarely struggle with being asked to do something unethical or immoral. I mostly help meet the needs of individuals, families and small businesses. But when I represent large corporate clients I find, for example, that whether one large company or the other wins a contract dispute often has a certain moral neutrality that actually reduces anxiety. God forgive me for the times I am in denial, but whether I should succumb to the temptation to an obviously immoral act is not a major struggle in my professional life.

Instead, the central spiritual struggles in my life are two-fold; they are shared by many lawyers and many ministers, and perhaps by most people of faith. The first struggle is to recognize and accept my limits, or in theological language, to recognize that I am a creature of God, but *not* God. The second struggle is not to let the "urgent" in my life eclipse the "important." Theologically, I must work hard not to let what "must be done today" cloud my discernment of what God is calling me to do with each moment of my life.

As to accepting my limits, I made a major step forward in the spring of 1990, when Roy and I found out we were going to be parents.

"See the little heartbeat," the doctor said as we looked at the videoscreen during the first ultrasound (and we did see sort of a pulsation—the heart of our firstborn to be).

"And look, there's a second heartbeat," the doctor stated almost matter-of-factly. Roy started laughing. I gasped for breath. Then the doctor got excited and she asked the nurse, "What's that over there? Are there *three*?"

After the longest twenty minutes of my life, the doctor finally announced, "I think there are *just two* babies." We left the office relieved that we were having *just two* babies.

Ten weeks later we went for another ultrasound. A specialist in high resolution ultrasounds told us there were two little boys, almost certainly identical. Roy joked about naming them Roy, Jr. and Roy, III.

Then suddenly, the doctor told us there was a rare complication with twins that he had seen only sixteen times. In fifteen of those cases, both twins had died; in the other case, one twin had died. Thirty-two babies. Thirty-one dead. He recommended an abortion.

"How certain are you?" Roy asked the doctor. The doctor said he was pretty sure.

"Like 90, 95, 98 percent certain?" Roy demanded.

The doctor looked down and replied, "Yes."

In the next twenty-four hours, we had six consultations with three doctors in two different hospitals. Roy had to ask all the questions; I was too grief-stricken to talk. Further tests and a visit with a high-risk pregnancy specialist produced a more hopeful prognosis. If I could carry the boys a few more weeks, we *might* take home two babies in late summer.

I went on bedrest, and began the most incredible spiritual journey of my life. In the words of Isaiah, I was accustomed to soaring, *to mounting up on wings like eagles*.[6] But I did not soar through this: now the idea of running and not being weary was almost laughable. Even walking and not fainting was a stretch. I was used to juggling many things at once; now, all of a sudden, I had to focus on just one thing: the health of my unborn children.[7]

Spiritually speaking, I bumped up against my limits. I had to deal in a major way with my finitude—I could not fix my own meals or do the laundry. I was not able even to pray for myself. But, providentially, I did not have to. The Sunday after our visit with "Dr. Doom," my Bible study group came to our apartment for its regular meeting. Upon hearing about our week, one person asked me, "How can we be a part of your prayers?"

I cried as I explained that my prayers had been mostly "sighs too deep for words." My friends formed a circle around me and added their prayers to my sighs. Over the weeks that followed, people around the country joined the circle of prayer. My thoroughly Methodist mother even befriended a nun, who talked her entire order into praying for us. I don't know exactly what all of those people prayed for, but I do know that after weeks flat on my back and four weeks in the neonatal intensive care unit, pushing the limits lost some of its glow. During those weeks on bedrest, I was given the incredible gift of space to listen to God's call. It is a gift I continue to fall back on five years later, especially when there seems to be no space for God in my life at all.

In contemplating my topic, "Spiritual Sanity in a Secular Vocation," I do not miss the irony of the fact that many asking these questions are trying to keep up with at least two professions. In my own case, I have two part-time jobs, one as a lawyer and one as the chair of a bank board; I also have a commitment to co-author a book, and three children ages five and under. Fortunately, I am married; unfortunately, my husband, who holds elective office, has more jobs than I do.[8]

Despite a healthier regard for my limits, I remain baffled about "the tyranny of the urgent." The problem of Saint Paul, "the good that I would I do not . . . ."[9] is more often eclipsed by another issue in my life, "the better I would do I do not . . . ." The urgent matters which threaten my vocation tend not to be intrinsically evil, but basically good: the business organization documents which must be done today so the sale can close tomorrow or the adoption petition that must be filed before school starts next week so a first-grader can share a name with the man who always has been his daddy or the auto accident complaint which must be filed the day the client first comes to the office to beat the statute of limitations.

Things that have seemed urgent to me lately are:

1. Clearing off my desk, which gets cluttered anew every day with mail, periodicals, journals, notices of professional meetings, newsletters—from two (or more) disciplines;
2. Dealing with some fairly fallen powers and principalities: the Courts, Wall Street, the U.S. Government and the Church.
3. Clearing off my desk.
4. Writing this essay.
5. Clearing off my desk.
6. Coordinating child care.
7. Clearing off my desk.
8. Changing diapers.
9. Billing hours.
10. Clearing off my desk.
11. Collecting for the hours I billed.
12. Clearing off my desk.
13. Going with my seventy-two year old father from doctor to doctor as he makes a decision about prostrate cancer treatment.
14. Clearing off my desk.

Things which seem important, but which lately have been usurped (or at least curtailed) by the above urgent matters include:

1. Working on a writing project I've felt called to for more than three years.
2. Cultivating a community of women friends where I now live.
3. Just hanging out with my five-year-olds.
4. Spending time with my parents—when we're not in the presence of doctors.
5. Praying.
6. Making entries in what I call "A Mother's Journal."
7. Being alone with my husband. Or, as Roy puts it as we survey the two or three little boys piled in bed with us, "I remember when I was the only guy you slept with."

Luckily, at least for the most tyrannical urgent matters—the mounds of paper that daily appear on my desk—I have a system. On my desk are piles, affectionately known as "truly urgent," "sort of urgent," and "will wait." I probably need an entirely separate stack for "really important." But then again, the most important things in my life don't tend to be stackable.

As I approach my fortieth birthday, I continue to feel tyrannized by the urgent. Once, responding to a definite, unambiguous call seemed to be the easy part; the process of discerning what I was being called to do in the first place was the hard part. But now I'm not so sure. Now, I am struggling with a very definite call I feel to take a sabbatical from practicing law to make room for other things God is calling me to do. In part because lawyering is good work and in part because it offers financial security, being a lawyer is hard to let go, even for a while. In addition, a law practice, like any other small service business, has a life of its own: the well-being of employees and needs of long-term clients contribute to my reluctance to make a change. Yet, it is hard to run a law practice in a different way, one that does not always put the work first.

Even if I do take my overdue sabbatical, however, I'm keenly aware that I will still have to wrestle with that familiar devil, the "tyrannous urgent." As my multifaceted career has taught me, the tyrannous urgent is not a plague which victimizes only lawyers—any honest pastor will admit that it also tyrannizes the church, sometimes at the expense of the truly important. Stay-at-home moms and free-lance writers testify to the same struggle.

Recently our youngest son, Benjamin, was baptized—twelve months after Roy and I had planned. Benjamin's baptism moved from the "important" list to the "urgent" list when my father's cancer surgery was scheduled, and we wanted to be sure he could be present. As I planned the baptismal liturgy, I thought of Martin Luther who, at times of great stress would touch his forehead and say to himself, "Martin, be calm, you are baptized."[10] The story is told—perhaps apocryphally—that Martin Luther once said he had so much to accomplish that he could not possibly pray less than three hours a day.

Conclusion

Martin Luther had his foibles, probably including an inability to accept his own limits; but at least in his spiritual life, he seemed to have put the truly important ahead of the merely urgent. And he regularly reminded himself that he had been baptized into a community with a vocation.

For many of us who are trying to be faithful people, including attorneys, the challenge is not finding important work to do and pressing needs to address. For us the challenge is to move past the *urgent* to be about the *important*.

Endnotes

1. United Methodist. Partner, Herron & Miller-Herron, Dresden, Tennessee, and ordained clergy, United Methodist Church. B.A. 1978, Lambuth College; J.D. 1983, M.Div. 1983, Vanderbilt University. A substantially similar form of this essay appeared in 21 *Journal of Law & Religion* (1995) and is reprinted here by permission.
2. William H. Barnwell, "Cats in a Wood Stove: Reflections on Building a New Social Gospel Movement," 96 *The Christian Century* 585, 588 (1979).
3. *Id.*
4. *Id.*
5. Tara Seeley is a 1986 graduate of the law-divinity program at Vanderbilt. After two years in a traditional law practice and a stint at a Roman Catholic parish in Maryland and the Archdiocese of Washington, D.C., she now writes and spends time with her three young children.
6. See Isaiah 40:31.
7. Isaiah 40:27–31 inspired me throughout the pregnancy along with a sermon by William Sloane Coffin, Jr., which interpreted the passage to mean that soaring like an eagle, running without getting weary, and walking without fainting, were three different ways of divine renewal. Allowing us to soar is not the only way God gives us strength. William Sloane Coffin, Jr., *Not Self-Control But Self-Surrender*, Sermons from Riverside (Feb. 27, 1983).
8. See Roy B. Herron, "Making Laws and Protecting Lives," 27 *Tex. Tech L.Rev.* 1177 (1996).
9. Romans 7:19 (King James).
10. William H. Willimon, *Peculiar Speech: Preaching to the Baptized* iii (1980).

What Doth the Lord Require of Thee?

Thomas A. Wiseman, Jr.[1]

As a Methodist by birth and a Presbyterian by marriage, religion has played an important role in my life since childhood. As a rational and curious being, I have experienced agnosticism and doubt, only in maturity to resolve that doubt through faith. As a lawyer by profession and a Federal Judge by political good fortune, I have had a unique opportunity to apply that faith and that religious training to human affairs and, hopefully, to be an influence for some good in the implementation of God's plan for the world.

The question we are asked to address is: How does my religion impact the performance of my job as a judge? My answer may be more the ideal than real, as is the case with most sinners.

The Hebrew Bible speaks eloquently of desirable characteristics of judges and gives specific instructions on how to perform the job. "Moreover choose able men from all the people, such as fear God, men who are trustworthy and who hate a bribe. . . ."[2] "You shall appoint judges and officers in all your towns . . . and they shall judge the people with righteous judgment. You shall not pervert justice; you shall not show partiality; and you shall not take a bribe. . . ."[3] "You shall do no injustice in judgment; you shall not be partial to the poor or defer to the great, but in righteousness shall you judge your neighbor."[4]

The admonition of Micah is especially poignant to a lawyer or a judge. Micah asked the rhetorical question: "What must I do to please the Lord?" His answer: "He hath shewed thee, O Man, what is good; and what doth the Lord require of thee but to do justly, to love mercy, and to walk humbly with thy God."[5] I have adopted this as a personal creed, but I experience occasional conflict between it and the secular demands of my job. I will explore and try to resolve those conflicts here.

Doing Justly

What does it mean to "do justly?" Aristotle said it was the practice of virtue toward others.[6] A dictionary definition of "just" is "the quality or characteristic of being impartial or fair; fairness, integrity, honesty; the principle or ideal of just dealing or right action."[7] Another dictionary definition is "acting in conformity with what is morally right or good."[8] None of these is very precise. One abstraction is defined by four or five others. Legitimate debate could be made over what is "fair," what is "right," what is "honest" or "good" in many daily examples of human interaction. Where does one look for a more precise definition? As is often the case, it is easier to define something in terms of what it is *not*. Examples of what is unjust, of injustices, of moral wrongs and unfair actions, come immediately to mind.

The prophet Amos condemned the people of Israel for their sins and rebellion against God. He indicted them for their violation of the most elementary principle of righteousness—their denial of justice to the poor. He cited the fraudulent commercial practices of the day such as using smaller than proper measures for selling the wheat, stretching the size of the measure for the money, selling the refuse of the wheat, and generally taking commercial advantage of the poor and needy.[9] In some of the most stirring language of the Bible, Amos called for judgment to "run down as waters, and righteousness as a mighty stream."[10]

There was a time in the law when we had a doctrine of *caveat emptor*— "let the buyer beware." The law simply said that it was not the place of government to hold the buyer's hand in the marketplace. The day of *caveat emptor* has been replaced by the age of consumerism and Ralph Nader and his raiders. The Federal Trade Commission and the Food and Drug Administration would get into the act very quickly if you started selling the refuse of the wheat, or making the ephah small or the shekel great. The examples of Amos are still valid, however, in defining the principles of commercial fair dealing integral to "doing justly."

But Micah's injunction goes beyond what the law requires. For a Christian, it is not enough to do only what is legal. We must do what is morally right, what is honest, what is just. Jesus Christ both simplified and complicated the inquiry into what is just. He turned the searchlight inward and made the inquiry almost totally subjective. If you would like someone to treat you in a particular way, that is the way you should treat him. If there is something you would not like someone to do to you, then you must not do it to her. Christ simplified the law and the prophets into this one golden rule.[11] But it also complicates the definition in that it puts the burden of definition back squarely on each of us.

Under this "golden rule" formulation, one must look to his own conscience, his own sense of right and wrong, put himself in the other person's shoes and make that decision. One must find that definition of justice, of what it means to do justly, to a large extent, within himself.

If I applied this method of decision-making to my daily job of judging, I would confirm the accusations of the Legal Realists that the law is what the judge says it is; I would support the cynicism of critical legal studies devotees that it is only the law because a judge says it. The extent to which each of us participates in the Divine Reason, if at all, certainly varies. Judicial decisions based only on the value choices of judges is judicial activism, judicial anarchy at its worst. Justice Cardozo put it well:

The judge, even when he is free, is still not wholly free. He is not to innovate at pleasure. He is not a knight-errant, roaming at will in pursuit of his own ideal of beauty or of goodness. He is to draw his inspiration from consecrated principles. He is not to yield to spasmodic sentiment, to vague and unregulated benevolence. He is to exercise a discretion informed by tradition, methodized by analogy, disciplined by system, and subordinated to "the primordial necessity of order in the social life." Wide enough in all conscience is the field of discretion that remains.[12]

The great theologian, Paul Tillich, describes the usual understanding of justice as proportional, that is everything receiving proportionally what it deserves, either positively or negatively. Attributive justice gives to beings the tribute to which they are—and claim to be—entitled. Distributive justice is economic in that it gives to each the proportion of goods due; retributive justice gives to each negatively what is due.[13] Tillich goes on to suggest that the justice of God is more than proportional. God changes the proportion in order to fulfil those who, according to strict proportionality, would be left unfulfilled. Divine justice may appear to be plainly unjust—it justifies the unjust. As the Apostle Paul explained, it is the paradox of justification by grace through faith.[14]

Criminal sentencing sometimes offers the opportunity to apply this disproportional justice motivated by a desire to rehabilitate an offender. Those opportunities are not as frequent now as they once were. The express intention of Congress to restrain this kind of action on the part of Federal judges spawned the U.S. Sentencing Guidelines.[15] The Congress decided that too many "bleeding heart" federal judges were being too soft on crime. The resulting legislation, along with the guidelines promulgated by the Sentencing Commission, effectively removed much of the sentencing discretion federal judges previously exercised.[16] The rehabilitation model was rejected in favor of the punishment model.

Pre-guidelines, I put about half of the people who came before me for sentencing on supervised probation. The rate of recidivism was less than eight percent;[17] the cost of supervision was about one-tenth that of incarceration;[18] persons on supervision had jobs and could pay restitution, support their families and stay off welfare. Perhaps, after we have built several thousand more prison beds[19] and warehoused several thousand more nonviolent offenders for lengthy sentences,[20] the expense will be so great that we will be forced to rethink the problem and the current "solution."[21] Perhaps we will try some new or old forms of alternatives to incarceration, such as supervised probation, suspended sentences, community service, home detention, etc. Perhaps we will once again put some faith in the rehabilitative model, and pull back a little from the "just deserts" model. Perhaps we will once again legitimate disproportional justice. This is the one area of my job where that which the law requires of me sometimes differs from what I believe, religiously and philosophically, to be the right thing to do.

Loving Mercy

The second injunction in Micah's code of conduct is like Tillich's disproportional justice. We are required to "love mercy." First, we were required to give every person at least his or her due, that is to do justly. But now he goes further and tells us to be merciful, and give every person more than what is due. This instruction did not begin or end with Micah. Mercy is an attribute ascribed to God throughout Judeo-Christian theology. In Moses' conversation with God in the book of Exodus, God said, "I will show mercy."[22] In Psalm 145 God is described as "gracious and full of compassion; slow to anger and of great mercy."[23] In the Luke version of the Beatitudes, Christ said: "Be merciful, even as your Father is merciful."[24]

Some of the most beautiful and powerful poetic lines of our language have been devoted to the quality of mercy. In the *Merchant of Venice*, Shakespeare has Portia describe mercy to Shylock:

> *The quality of mercy is not strained,*
> *It droppeth as the gentle rain from heaven*
> *Upon the place beneath;*
> *It is twice blessed;*
> *It blesseth him that gives and him that takes;*
> . . . .
> *It is an attribute to God himself,*
> *And earthly power doth then show likest God's*
> *When mercy seasons justice.*
> *Therefore, Jew,*
> *Though justice be thy plea, consider this,*
> *That in the course of justice,*
> *None of us should see salvation;*
> *We do pray for mercy,*
> *And that same prayer doth teach us all to render*
> *The deeds of mercy.*[25]

In appropriate circumstances, mercy can and should enter into the sentencing matrix. But there are other circumstances in which a judge should be merciful. Kindness in a situation where a person cannot fight back is mercy. The way I treat a witness or a lawyer, the slack I cut a young lawyer making his first appearance, the way I treat my staff—these are some of the ways in which I personally have violated the second part of Micah's injunction.

Walking Humbly

The final side of Micah's triangular formula of requirements is to "walk humbly with thy God." Most lawyers I know would say that a humble federal judge is an oxymoron; and they are probably right. I will never forget the evening of my swearing in as a federal judge. Some of my friends had given a nice party for us, and my wife and I, still basking in the glow of the day, were getting ready for bed. She looked at me and said, "All of our married life I have heard you cuss federal judges. Now you are one and you expect me to sleep with you?"

Recognition of one's capacity for error is an aspect of humility. Professionally, the appellate courts remind me of this capacity frequently. I do what I think is right, and then they do what they think is right. The system says they are right because they are last, but sometimes they are right because I was wrong. A lawyer who refuses to analyze and recognize any merit in the positions of his opponent lessens his ability to meet and overcome those positions, and lessens the likelihood of an advantageous settlement. In the act of judging, it is indeed a rare occurrence when all the right is on one side, when the correct judgment is crystal clear.

When we measure our five or six feet of height against the expanse of space and the universe, when we compare our relatively short lifetime with the infinity of time and existence, it is difficult to feel overly important. Yet my religious tradition teaches me that I am a child and heir of God, that I am a chosen beneficiary of the New Covenant in Jesus Christ. To have been chosen must mean that my life has meaning and significance. I am important.

I use an analogy that helps me understand this apparent anomaly between relative insignificance and God-chosen importance. I think of some of the Civil War battlefield cycloramas or some of the great murals of the art world. The eye can only examine the parts, and these parts must be put together in the mind. In like manner, the entirety of God's plan for the world is a giant, but yet incomplete mural. Only God knows what the final picture will look like, or can comprehend how all of the parts fit together. My life is a small dot of the brush on that mural. Although it seems infinitesimally small and insignificant when the whole is contemplated, still it is an essential and integrated part of the whole. It is my responsibility to make my dot of the brush as beautiful as I possibly can in contributing to the whole. Thought of in this way, each of us is a very, very small part, but a very important part of God's plan. This realization makes for an humble self-esteem.

My Reformed Tradition also demands of me that I continually be engaged in the reformation process. My vocation in the law has afforded a unique opportunity to be engaged, to try to make a difference. Rarely has there been a divergence between my religious belief and the requirements of my profession. Legal professionalism is the rendition of a service. Secondarily, it is a source of livelihood. Viewed in this way, the practice of law, the practice of judging, can be faith in action. It can be part of the divine artwork.

Endnotes

1. Presbyterian. U.S. District Judge for the Middle District of Tennessee; B.A. 1952, J.D. 1954, Vanderbilt University; LL.M. 1990, University of Virginia.
2. Exodus 18:21 (Revised Standard). Unless otherwise indicated, all subsequent citations to the Bible are to the Revised Standard version.
3. Deuteronomy 16:18.
4. Leviticus 19:15.
5. Micah 6:8 (King James).
6. Aristotle, *The Nicomachean Ethics*, Book V 103 (D. P. Chase trans., 1915).
7. *Webster's New Collegiate Dictionary* 628 (1976).
8. *Id.*
9. Amos 8:4–6 (King James).
10. Amos 5:24 (King James).
11. "Therefore all things whatsoever ye would that men should do to you, do ye even so to them: for this is the law and the prophets." Matthew 7:12 (King James).
12. Benjmin N. Cardozo, *Nature of the Judicial Process* 141 (1921).
13. Paul Tillich, *Love, Power and Justice: Ontological Analyses and Ethical Applications* 63–66 (1954).
14. We *who* are Jews by nature, and not sinners of the Gentiles, Knowing that a man is not justified by the works of the law, but by the faith of Jesus Christ, even we have believed in Jesus Christ, that we might be justified by the faith of Christ, and not by the works of the law: for by the works of the law shall no flesh be justified. But if, while we seek to be justified by Christ, we ourselves also are found sinners, *is* therefore Christ the minister to sin? God forbid. For if I build again the things which I destroyed, I make myself a transgressor. For I through the law, am dead to the law, that I might live unto God. I am crucified with Christ: nevertheless I live; yet not I, but Christ liveth in me: and the life which I now live in the flesh I live by the faith of the Son of God, who loved me, and gave himself for me. I do not frustrate the grace of God: for if righteousness *come* by the law, then Christ is dead in vain.
    Galatians 2:15–21 (King James).
15. "The Commission shall insure that the guidelines reflect the fact that, in many cases, current sentences do not accurately reflect the seriousness of the offense." 28 U.S.C. § 994(m) (Supp. V 1993).
16. *U.S. Sentencing Comm'n, Guidelines Manual* 7, § 1A.4(d)(1994).
    Under pre-guidelines sentencing practice, courts sentenced to probation an inappropriately high percentage of offenders guilty of certain economic crimes, such as theft, tax evasion, antitrust offenses, insider trading, fraud and embezzlement, that in the Commission's view are "serious."
    The Commission's solution to this problem has been to write guidelines that classify as serious many offenses for which probation previously was frequently given and provide for at least a short period of imprisonment in such cases.
    Id.
17. Recidivism for this purpose is defined as the requesting of a warrant alleging violation of probation/parole and revocation of supervision. War-

rant request might be the result of technical violations, rather than new criminal activity.

18. Current estimates from the Administrative Office, United States Courts, dated March 10, 1995, are: monthly cost of incarceration—$1779.33, community confinement—$1183.08, and probation—$195.30. Memorandum from Eunice R. Holt Jones, Chief, Probation and Pretrial Services Division, Administrative Office of the United States Courts, to Chief Probation Officers (Mar. 10, 1995) (on file with author).

19. In 1993, state and federal systems added 42,899 new beds to prison facilities at a cost of $1,976,682,000.00. Between 1988 and 1993 there were 302 new prisons opened in the United States. Camille G. Camp and George M. Camp, *The Corrections Yearbook 1994* (Criminal Justice Institute).

20. In 1992, of 33,622 convicted offenders sentenced to prison in the federal courts, only 2,618 or 7.7 percent were for violent crimes. *U.S. Bureau of the Census, Statistical Abs. of the U.S.* 212 (114th ed. 1994).

21. In 1970 we had 196,429 adult prisoners incarcerated for a rate of 96.7 per 100,000 population. In 1992 that number had grown to 847,271, a 431 percent increase. The 1992 figure represents 330.2 persons per 100,000 population, more than any other country in the Western world except Russia. *Camp & Camp, supra* note 18.

22. Exodus 33:19 (King James).

23. Psalms 145:8 (King James).

24. Luke 6:36.

25. William Shakespeare, *Merchant of Venice* act 4, sc. 1 (John Russel Brown ed., Harvard U.P. 1959).

On Hoping to Be, Being, and Having Been

William Bentley Ball[1]

If I am asked what my faith has meant to me in the practice of law, my gut reaction is to respond: what *hasn't* my faith meant to me? Most inadequate as a Catholic Christian, I nevertheless cannot imagine what my years of practice would have been like without that faith. I don't mean to suggest that I have descended to my knees in prayer as I filed each motion in a litigation. (I recall with horror a fundamentalist lawyer who, in a religious liberty case, descended to his knees before a judge in order to beg God to guide His Honor!) Yet I must say that prayer has accompanied at least my toughest legal endeavors. But at a deeper, more important level, my faith has been part of the larger area of my life which is not the practice of law—my marriage, my family, and simply the pursuit of daily living.

For some decades now, my legal work has been in cases involving threats to First Amendment liberties, in particular, freedom of religion. Those cases have stood in stark contrast to legal work I had earlier engaged in—the industrial real estate problems of a large New York corporation, with negotiations, settlements and occasional suits in business matters as the mill's usual grist. The law has many mansions, few of which I would find uninteresting. Real estate work had its excitements, its sometimes intriguing legal issues, its often enjoyable sparring in bargaining. While my religion counseled me in these matters in terms of ethics, it did not present itself in the very subject matter I was addressing. So I found myself placing a *lis pendens* on the Hopkins Street building, or drafting that opening phrase in property descriptions over and over again, "All that certain piece or parcel of land . . .," or making sure that the gas tank in the East River did not counter my client's riparian rights. It was all good work, often fun. But I gave that up for something which, to me, answered a deep need: somehow to serve better causes.

One must always be wary of impulses to "do good." Usually, we serve God best right where we are, accepting the place He has chosen for us and the people there, and observing, in the work at hand, the simple old rule from *The Imitation of Christ*, "*Age quod agis*"—do what you do (do it well).[2] We should always keep before us the example of the many saints who neither won nor sought exalted roles in the world. Francis of Assisi and Thérèse of Lisieux come to mind. Discontent, envy, the itching desire to be noticed can be successfully masked (and too often are) by a facade of stated noble purposes. Young Richard Rich, in Robert Bolt's *A Man For All Seasons*, begged Sir Thomas More for a position at court. More advised him to be a teacher. Rich responded, "But who would notice it?"[3] Rich had no noble purpose in seeking a position at court, no desire really to serve for the good of king and country.

Sometimes, however, we see people who have not base motives, but the highest motives, for trying to move from work which does not excite them to work which serves good causes. We should think well of them when their motives are pure but always offer sober admonition. Once a young lawyer, knowing of my work in First Amendment cases, wrote me seeking to work in that field—being so eager to "do good" in the law, or serve God in the law, that he offered to work unpaid, as an apprentice, as it were. I praised his good intention, but I let him know, first, that the "Great First Amendment Case" is a rarity. Second, though, came the even more sobering part of the advice. Most constitutional litigation is made up of a bundle of unglamorous, non-constitutional issues. Everything in that "Great First Amendment Case" may finally turn on standing to sue, or Rule 24 of the Federal Rules of Civil Procedure governing intervention. So I told him: "Follow your good intention, but you'll be able to 'do good' only by being a good master of the law's basics."

My own desire to serve "better causes" as a lawyer did not take me on any search for the means to do it. The means came to me, almost by accident, in the form of a suggestion by a former law professor of mine, then serving as the first dean of a just-founded law school. Would I be interested in coming on board the initial law faculty? Eventually, after accepting his offer, I found myself teaching Constitutional Law. Five years of that, I felt, did more for me than for my students. I had a growing desire to practice what I was teaching. Presently the chance to do just that came to me, and for three and a half decades I've been able to serve people in pursuit of their constitutional liberties. Most of those liberties have been religious liberties—and what a series of clients they have been! Catholics, Jews, Seventh-day Adventists, Baptists, Episcopalians, Mennonites, Amish—and in cases involving all manner of religious issues, even mortmain.

Because I have had a sort of instinctive concern for religious liberty as well as a reverence for religion itself, I found work in these litigations deeply satisfying. What was a Catholic doing representing all those people of other faiths? Some Catholics might have wondered. So, indeed, might some of those religious bodies which possessed a hardy tradition of hostility to the Catholic Church. But in the handling of these cases, which so often involved oppressive actions by government, I was conscious not of differences between, say, Catholics and Seventh-day Adventists, but of what things we profoundly had in common. In fighting, for example, for the liberty of Adventist Nebraska prairie schools to exist without grossly unreasonable governmental controls, I felt deeply for the good Adventists, their real faith in God, their unswerving fidelity to their beliefs. Here were people worth one's best effort. And I can properly call that best effort a personal *religious* experience. So it was in case after case for religious people in twenty-two states of this country: it was not possible to work with them without feeling myself a part of them. They were witnesses on the stand bearing witness to their faith.

My Christian faith has been my teacher and my inspiration in another important area of law, an area to which I can best pin the label, "the sacredness of human life." Activity in this area came to me in two ways: advocacy for the civil rights of black people in struggles which followed *Brown v. Board of Education*[4] and the defense of the unborn in the pro-life struggle which resulted from *Roe v. Wade*.[5] In both areas religious groups were (and today yet are) denounced for their positions as seeking to "impose their morality" on others. But (happily, I think) churches and religious leaders throughout our history have entered the public forum to defend principles they deem morally urgent to defend. For me, to try to do something constructive in these two areas was not a duty dictated to me by my Church. Rather, it was the prod of conscience in the face of opportunity. In service in both areas I had no desire to impose religious views on anyone. It was instead the image of crippling unfairness to black people and the horror of the destruction of innocent unborn children that left me, when occasion to do something arose, unable *not* to do what little I could. Justice Oliver Wendell Holmes once admitted to what he called "can't helps," actions which this pragmatist undertook out of impulses which could surely best be described as prods of conscience.[6] I cannot help but speculate that these prods ultimately were rooted in Holmes' Calvinist ancestry. For me the prods surely have been rooted in the Catholics and Protestants from whom I descended and the specific teachings of the Catholic Church about the dignity and sacredness of human life. I had no struggle to reconcile those teachings with my professional life. It all went together.

Yet always along the way a Christian lawyer is reminded of references to lawyers in the Gospels. Our blessed Lord had no good word to say for them. They appear in roles baiting Him, "tempting" Him to contradict the law of the prophets or to contradict Himself. "Woe unto . . . *ye* lawyers!," He thunders, "for ye lade men with burdens grievous to be borne, and ye yourselves touch not the burdens with one of your fingers."[7] Christ's teachings wholly condemn the greediness, deceitfulness, vainglorious self-promotion of advertising, pretentiousness and litigiousness which characterize the justified public image of too many members of our legal profession today. It is difficult for many of us to realize that Christ, in His sermon on the mount, did not preface His words by exempting lawyers from His admonitions. Rather, they too, He said, are to be peacemakers, merciful, thirsters, not after rights of self, but after righteousness.[8]

Coming to the late years of life, as now I am, my religious faith is more important to me than ever it was. And that relates, in new ways, to my continuing to practice law. At this stage of the game I can contemplate life, not in Shakespeare's seven ages of man,[9] but in three phases—hoping to be, being, and having been.

There was law school, then the years of the struggle (not merely to keep on being a lawyer but to keep on supporting a family). A good part of my religious life in those days was made of prayers that we'd all survive!

After that came the few decades of wins and losses and some degree of fulfillment, I guess you'd call it. Back then my prayers should have been daily prayers of thanksgiving merely for a life lived, for family, and for God's presence always.

But now I'm into that time of life when I must contemplate "having been." As we get to that age, I think most of us are caught by surprise. "What has happened to all those years?" we ask. A scary feeling, but a still scarier one when we peer ahead and see that there is no sure supply of future years to be had. Through all our decades we pursued horizons. Now there isn't any horizon. And we should not start imagining horizons. Therein lies a great danger to aging lawyers: hubris, the temptation to perpetuate one's self when, if one would but take time to look ahead and really see, one's best days are past. I know there are exceptions—some glorious, like Verdi's composing "Falstaff" at age eighty. But in law there is also the pitiful example of Clark Clifford.[10] And there are minor Clark Cliffords in law firms who seek desperately to cling to roles of dominance when they would do much better for themselves, their associates and their families by stepping aside or at least stepping back.

Should we aging lawyers yield to the opposite temptation (as everlastingly phrased by retirees from other businesses) to "take time to smell the roses"? While I, for one, don't want to take time smelling anything, I do get the point. Law, as Dean Acheson once remarked, while deepening the mind, narrows it. It can narrow us so closely that other knowledge, beauty—and even people—become uninteresting. Passing sixty or sixty-five presents a real crisis to some people, almost like becoming an adolescent again. They once again are faced with what to do for the future, and they even may have to face up to who they really are. Already, at this stage, friends and family members begin to die. That period of life is made livelier as we note reminders of mortality increasingly abounding, with dinner party talk among geriatric folk noting who just had a stroke, a heart attack, a hip job, the Big C or the Dread A. Don't ever ask an elderly fellow how he's doing. He will tell you, with long elaboration and great medical detail.

At this late stage of the game, with all the questions it raises, one who has a firmly rooted faith in God has the means to cope with the sad sense of one's mortality. Faith allows one to glance at the junk heap of one's sins and failures without despairing and to remember one's few successes without gloating.

Whatever is left of our time (and whatever is left of us!), our faith in God gives us the means to put life to its best possible use. Shakespeare, in a sonnet, spoke of the need, at this time of life, "to love that well which thou must leave ere long."[11] In 1914, Leon Bloy spoke in the same vein in his *Pilgrim of the Absolute*: "When you die, that is what you take with you: the tears you have shed and the tears you have caused others to shed—your capital of bliss or terror. It is on these tears that we shall be judged, for the Spirit of God is always borne upon the waters. . ."[12]—reminders of the importance of penitence in relation to one's past and of compassion in the days remaining. Those are words of warning to men and women entering life's much touted Golden Age: there is still a job ahead, but it does not necessarily consist of golf, cards, travel, TV, investing, or worrying.

Endnotes

1. Roman Catholic. Member, Ball, Skelly, Murren & Connell, Harrisburg, Pa. B.A. 1941, Western Reserve University; J.D. 1948, University of Notre Dame.
2. Thomas à Kempis, *Imitation of Christ* 34 (Leo Sherly-Price trans., 1952).
3. Robert Bolt, *A Man for All Seasons* act 1 (Vintage Int'l 1990) (1962).
4. 347 U.S. 483 (1954).
5. 410 U.S. 113 (1973).
6. Letter from Oliver Wendell Holmes to Lewis Einstein (June 1, 1905), in *The Holmes—Einstein Letters*, 1903–35, at 15–16 (James Bishop Peabody ed., 1964).
7. Luke 11:46.
8. Luke 6:20–23.
9. William Shakespeare, *As You Like It* act 2, sc. 7.
10. At least as Mr. Clifford is represented in the recent biography, Douglas Franz and David McKean, *Friends in High Places: The Rise and Fall of Clark Clifford* (1995).
11. William Shakespeare, Sonnet LXIV in *The Histories and Poems of Shakespeare* (Oxford University Press 1941).
12. Jacques Maritain, *Introduction* to *León Bloy, Pilgrim of the Absolute* 18 (John Coleman & Henry Binsoe trans., Pantheon Books 1947).

Christian Life in the Law

Kenneth W. Starr[1]

Lawyers perform so poorly in the Scriptures that it is small wonder that I frequently hear from young people of faith, "Can I in good moral conscience become a lawyer?" Inconsistency between professional obligations—the duty of loyalty to the client—and religious and moral mandates loom large in the reflections of thoughtful young men and women contemplating prospects in the legal profession.

This stems in no small measure from the powerful fact that lawyers fare so poorly in the Bible. They are seen as manipulative and deceitful, qualities that sometimes are perceived by more modern observers of the legal profession.

My own sense, based on twenty-five years as a student and practitioner of the law, is that one can live—in a religious and moral sense—greatly in the law, as Holmes opined from a secularist perspective.[2]

So frequently in daily professional life in the law, the questions genuinely are: What is right? What is fair? The moral lawyer is one who takes such questions quite seriously, because sound legal advice and legal judgments are rarely far removed from such fundamental moral perspectives. That certainly has been my sense in the world of litigation, where adversaries clash over competing positions and visions of both facts and law. This has most dramatically been evidenced in my experiences as a government lawyer—as Counselor to the Attorney General, as Solicitor General, and now more recently in a prosecutorial role. The morally-infused motto of the Department of Justice is this: "The United States wins its point whenever justice is done its citizens in the courts."

But that underlying sense of justice also holds true in representing private clients, including carrying on the battle with one's adversaries. Advising clients to do right, to do what is fair is entirely compatible with the ancient Scriptures' admonition to do justice. Indeed, the prophet Micah identified doing justice as one of the three basic commands that God has laid down for humankind.[3]

That may strike some as rather minimalist. Indeed, in a Christian perspective, it seems incomplete. We are taught to be meek and lowly, to turn the other cheek, and to rely not on our own devices but upon faith and trust in God. How does a lawyer seek to do that? Even more provocatively, how does a Christian lawyer—which I lay claim to being—seek to emulate Jesus Christ?

The Christian perspective in particular demands of us qualities and characteristics that at first blush seem inconsistent with lawyering skills, but reflection and experience convince me that the two are cheerfully compatible. Above all, Christian lawyering means treating one's colleagues and adversaries with a profound sense of respect for human dignity. It means civility and kindness in interpersonal relations, even toward one's adversaries, even when they do not reciprocate. Turning the other cheek translates into not stooping to engage in sharp or questionable practices. It means respect for truth and a singleminded commitment not to play fast and loose with the truth.

Years ago, a very great trial lawyer—with whom I was privileged to co-labor early on in my days in private practice—shared with me the secret of his fabulous success before juries. It was not razzle-dazzle or histrionics or eloquence. It was trust. "Ken, I make sure that the jury knows that everything I say, they can trust. I will have worked hard in preparing. And everything I tell them that I will prove, I indeed prove."

Now this able lawyer—himself a faithful Christian—was not bragging. Pride precedes a fall, the Scriptures teach,[4] and he was not indulging in the ancient sin of arrogance and false pride. He was, rather, describing a methodology of practice, a self-disciplined dedication to facts. Justice Brandeis dramatically changed the way modern lawyers think about law, by emphasizing the over-arching importance of facts.[5] The moral lawyer—including the Christian lawyer—will share in that Brandeisian love of facts, of reality, and respect that reality in the courtroom or counseling room.

So too for the law itself. Courts should be able to trust an advocate's scrupulous, careful treatment of law. Law has integrity, it has meaning. And courts will detect that in the Christian lawyer, who will not flinch from admitting: "Your honor, the case you mention is indeed inconsistent with our theory. But we think that case was wrongly decided, for the following reasons." Honesty, straightforwardness, respect for truth—these are vital to effective lawyering.

Finally, the law should—over time—embody the accumulated wisdom of the people. Because lawyers are constantly being called upon to exercise judgment, it behooves the lawyer of faith to return continually to the wisdom literature of the Bible. When I received the fateful phone call in August 1994 indicating that I would be named Independent Counsel in the Whitewater investigation, I promptly went into a period of quiet reflection. I read in the Psalms, I scanned over familiar passages from Proverbs, and then prayed, fervently, for wisdom. I continue to do so.

Seeking wisdom is a way of re-expressing one's own limitations. That quest—a simple form of saying "I need help from higher authority"—is a useful antidote for the disease that ails many of us in our profession—the deadly disease of arrogance. That antidote is like a vitamin pill. It needs to be taken daily. My own sources continue to be found in the wisdom literature of the Old and New Testaments, as well as the teaching of the Apostle Paul in those extraordinary letters to the early churches and to young ministers of the gospel, Timothy and Titus. I discipline myself to repair to those humility pills on a daily basis.

Scriptural sources not only guide us in our imperfect ways toward loftier reaches, but they serve as sources of inner strength when, on the one hand, demands are high and, on the other hand, energy and courage levels may be low. Orel Hershiser, it has been reported, sings hymns to himself to stay calm when the going gets rough out on the pitcher's mound. Before court appearances, my sources of strength are Bible verses, committed to memory, that I repeat quietly to myself. My all-time favorite, always said silently several times before standing up in a courtroom, is: "I can do all things through [Christ] who strengthens me."[6] That simple verse brings a sense of calm, of peace, of perspective.

In the swirling demands of a demanding profession, we all can use a bit of calm and peace and perspective. To me, and to countless practitioners of an honorable and decent profession, the source of that calm is the never-ending fountain of faith.

Endnotes

1. Christian. Partner, Kirkland & Ellis, Washington, D.C. Currently Independent Counsel, Madison Guaranty Savings and Loan Case, popularly called the "Whitewater Investigation." 28 U.S.C. § 49 (1988). A.B. 1968, George Washington University; A.M. 1969, Brown University; J.D. 1973, Duke University.
2. Oliver Wendell Holmes, Jr., The Profession of the Law, Conclusion of a lecture delivered to undergraduates of Harvard University (Feb. 17, 1886), in Richard A. Posner, *The Essential Holmes* 219 (1992).
3. Micah 6:8 (New American).
4. Proverbs 16:18.
5. Philippa Strum, *Louis D. Brandeis: Justice for the People* 98, 253–54, 336–38, 347 (1984).
6. Philippians 4:13.

Part II.
WITNESSES

To Be a Professing Woman

Teresa Stanton Collett[1]

What does it mean to profess faith in the redeeming power of Jesus Christ while also professing a commitment to serving the system of justice in America? More particularly, what does it mean to be a Christian woman engaged in the practice of law? In first thinking about this essay, I asked myself what it means to be a faith-filled lawyer. I was dissatisfied with this formulation of the question because it reduced all life and experience to being "a lawyer." To describe myself so narrowly ignores the reality that I can also be described as a wife, a mother, a daughter, or even (by a few) as a pain-in-the-neck. More importantly, to identify myself as "a lawyer" suggests that being a lawyer dominates my concept of self over all of the other activities or relationships that comprise my life.

This is one of the dangers of contemporary society. Too easily we may come to identify ourselves primarily as what we do rather than what we are.[2] The danger of overstating the role of our professional activities in understanding ourselves is intense when practicing law in a firm that prides itself on the commitment each lawyer shows to serving clients. I realized I had lost the true sense of myself when I sat in a pediatrician's office with our sick son and measured time in terms of "billable hours wasted," not because pressing needs of my clients were being neglected, or some ogre-like partner would criticize my time records—but rather because I, myself, had come to believe that practicing law should be the exclusive activity of my "workday" and anything else was at best a distraction and at worst "a waste." I no longer understood myself to be a woman of God blessed with a family and a calling to serve God through helping my clients seek and do justice. Instead, I had come to understand myself as a lawyer, who "happened" to be religious and "happened" to have a family.

Such a false sense of self is not uncommon among lawyers. But ultimately, like all falsehoods, it proves to be enslaving or deadening.[3] It deadens relationships both inside and outside the office. Instead of encountering people who have legal needs as whole persons, such lawyers reduce clients to the elements of their legal claims. Often this means that the client becomes merely a bundle of legal rights or liabilities that can be operated upon in an isolated fashion independent of any needs or desires that appear unrelated. This vision frees the lawyer from any concern about whether the client's rights should be exercised or even whether the client will ultimately benefit from the assertion of his or her rights. Similarly, the lawyer comes to understand herself only as a source of technical knowledge—a sophisticated version of the Lexis machine. Just as a machine is properly evaluated solely on the basis of its efficiency and accuracy, the value of the lawyer is determined by immediate profitability and adversarial success.

This understanding of self and relationships with others is radically inconsistent with the way we are called to understand the world. As a Christian woman I have professed a belief in the God who calls me to care about myself and others—love your neighbors as yourself.[4] This duty is second only to my obligation to love God with all my heart, soul, and mind.[5]

Love cannot be measured in terms of profit, nor does it usually manifest itself through adversarial conflict. Rather, love born of faith causes us to love God and seek justice.[6] It calls us to relate to our clients in the fullness of their present pain or desire.

The wife probating her husband's estate receives both comfort and concern not only through the attention given to the details of the legal proceeding, but also by recognition of her fears and her loneliness. The son considering a will contest is provided both an accurate assessment of the legal issues present in the facts and a caution that such actions destroy family solidarity. The business partners seeking incorporation are given counsel concerning both the legal implications of creating such an entity and the manner in which such entities can contribute to or detract from building up the common good.

Practicing law as an expression of our love of God and pursuit of justice requires creativity and honest communication with clients. I had to be reminded of this when I first began practicing law. My first month at the firm, a senior partner called me into his office to give me an assignment. One of our corporate clients had asked a question about its ability to do something, and the partner was unsure about the law. He explained the facts of the situation, and the question he wanted researched. Then he told me to find the 'right answer." I asked him what answer the client wanted. He looked at me oddly, and began to describe the facts and the issue again. Not wanting to interrupt him, I waited until he was through, and said, "I understand the facts and the question, but I need to know what answer the client wants."

"Why?" asked the partner.

"Because the law almost never gives a 'right answer', and I need to know what the client wants to do, in order to construct an argument that it can do what it wants."

After a pause that seemed like it would never end, the partner said, "Teresa, our job is to find out if the law requires the client to act a particular way. If there is no clear answer under the law, then you must consider the issues the cases identify as important, as well as what your own sense of right and wrong tells you. That is how we decide what advice to give to our clients. This client has been with the firm for a long time, and it deserves the best judgment that we can give—not merely permission to do whatever it wants." I felt like an idiot, and an immoral one at that! But I never again thought my job was to give clients permission, instead of counsel.

A few years later I represented the administrator of a decedent's estate in a dispute over a creditor's claim. The decedent had practiced medicine in a small town all of his adult life. Unmarried and without children, he had devoted his efforts to caring for the local people. He had been the driving force behind establishing a hospital to serve the community and surrounding rural area. When he became elderly and infirm, the hospital authorities offered him free room and board in the hospital where he could be in daily contact with friends and colleagues, and all of his physical needs could be met. His residence in the hospital was not medically required, but rather was an expression of gratitude and concern by the community toward one who had shared his talents and energy so generously.

While there was some evidence that the doctor had talked about establishing a foundation for the benefit of the community, he died without establishing such a foundation, and without any testamentary documents. Having lived frugally, he left a sizable estate which passed through intestate succession to relatives. The hospital board, offended by this "windfall to laughing heirs," filed a creditor's claim for the value of the room and services provided to the doctor during the last months of his life. My client rejected the claim based upon the hospital records characterizing the goods and services as a "gift." The hospital sued claiming the rejection was not warranted.

In this case, the hospital was not legally entitled to payment. Pragmatically, however, arriving at the legally correct result was likely to be costly. The probate court hearing the controversy sat in the community in which the hospital was located, the hospital was struggling financially, and there was a sense throughout the town that, had the doctor been alive, he would have wanted his property used to continue his life's work. It is an understatement to say that there was some chance that the trial court would rule in favor of the hospital.

On my client's side was the positive law, as well as an argument that there is something repugnant about giving someone a gift and later demanding payment for it. In such a case, what does justice require?

After some preliminary discovery, I approached my client about settlement. I explained the costs that would be incurred if we lost at trial and had to appeal, and why the claim of the hospital had merit morally, even if not legally. I suggested that we offer a settlement, not by making an unrestricted payment to the hospital, but by making a conditional gift. The gift would be conditioned upon the hospital's use of the funds to make some needed improvement, or acquire some needed equipment, with the improvement or equipment publicly and permanently acknowledged as a gift from the decedent. In this way, we would honor the decedent's life, without validating the duplicity of the "creditor's claim." This proposal was approved by the administrator and all of the heirs, and ultimately accepted by the hospital. Recognizing the justice within the claims of others is one expression of our pursuit of justice while loving God and neighbor.

Not that justice is always easily recognized. In fact, recognizing what is just in particular circumstances often requires genuine humility—a trait lawyers are not noted for having in abundance. I learned this, in part, from a powerful and generous client, and the same senior partner who taught me to distinguish advice from permission. Our firm acted as local counsel for a large multi-national corporation. As it happened, the mother of the general counsel lived in Oklahoma. She was elderly and in poor health. During a visit, her son, the general counsel, observed that she had lost weight and stopped taking care of herself. He became convinced that she was not taking her medication and was not capable of living independently. He asked that our firm represent him individually, providing information about local long-term care facilities and initiating a guardianship proceeding. I had developed a recognized specialty in guardianship work, so one of the partners recommended that I handle the matter. The partner escorted the general counsel to my office and introduced him, both by name and status within the client corporation. At the end of the introduction, there was no doubt in my mind about how important it was that this man be happy with my legal work.

We discussed his mother's situation, and at the end of the interview the client invited my husband and I to have dinner with him that evening at the restaurant of my choice. He joked about how young lawyers rarely have the time to eat out, and noticing the picture of my young son, asked that I not pick what was probably our usual restaurant—Mcdonald's. He took us to a wonderful restaurant and charmed both my husband and I with stories of the challenges his company had to overcome when opening markets in Asia. During the last part of the dinner he asked about my professional aspirations and gave me advice about how to attain them. By the end of the meal, I would have championed this man's cause anywhere and any time.

The next day I prepared the guardianship petition and notice of the proceeding. It was my practice to personally deliver a copy to the prospective ward in order to observe the person. I took the notice and headed for the nursing home where my client had placed his mother after his last visit. Upon my arrival I was directed to the mother's room. I knocked on her door and she invited me in. As I entered the room, she lowered her copy of the "Wall Street Journal" and greeted me. As the mother of a young child, I had observed our three-year-old spend hours looking at books with no comprehension of the words they contained. The foolish hope flashed through my mind that my client's mother was doing something similar with her paper. She immediately destroyed that happy fantasy by folding her paper and commenting on the increased royalty payments being paid in Southeastern Oklahoma. I felt sick.

I handed her the guardianship petition and notice, telling her that I represented her son who was seeking court approval to make decisions for her. She indicated that she understood, and would have her lawyer look at the papers. She asked if I or any of my family owned land in Southeastern Oklahoma, obviously intending to continue the conversation about oil royalties. I mumbled something about my grandfather owning a small amount of property somewhere, and tried to return the conversation to the guardianship. I expressed her son's concern for her well-being, and told her that we would see each other again soon. Then I fled.

I did not return to the office. Instead I went home and cried until my husband returned from work. I told him how betrayed I felt—the client was trying to use me to do something fundamentally wrong, and he must have known it or he wouldn't have spent so much time charming us. I felt naive and stupid to be taken in by such an obvious ploy. I felt scared, because I could not continue with the representation—and I feared the reaction of the firm. My husband listened as I poured out the entire story. After talking the situation through, he asked what I intended to do. I told him the I was afraid I might be asked to resign if I refused to complete the guardianship. He said that resignation was preferable to doing something that I believed so clearly wrong.

I doubt I slept three hours that night. The next morning I was at the office before eight—a sufficiently rare event to evoke comment. My senior partner came in, saw me waiting at his door, and said "You look terrible." I replied, "We have to talk." "That's obvious. Wait for me in my office while I get a cup of coffee," he said.

I began by describing the previous day's interview with the client's mother. I said I could not go forward seeking a guardianship over a woman who was obviously competent. I acknowledged the possibility that the firm would disagree, and no longer wish to employ an associate that did not complete her assignments. Nonetheless I would not continue the representation. However, during the night, I had arrived at a compromise that might satisfy the firm's desire to provide personal representation to the general counsel, while allowing me to withdraw from the case. I would not personally represent the client, but I would review any pleadings prepared by other lawyers in the firm for technical accuracy. (In retrospect, I recognize the implicit message—I'm not sleazy, but I'm sure we have someone who is, and I'll help them. So much for great moral reasoning!)

My partner had been silent until this point. He asked me if that was what I wanted to do. I told him no, I wanted to tell the client that we were not that kind of firm. He asked why I was asking his permission. I explained that I recognized that my proposed conduct might harm the firm, and as an associate, I thought I should discuss the matter with him first. He then asked why he should approve the firm withdrawing from the representation. "I believe that I was hired with the expectation that eventually I will become a partner in this firm. Partners exercise judgment, including saying no to clients. This is a time that I would say no to the client. If I am to develop that judgment necessary to become a partner in this firm I must be allowed to make decisions. I think this is a good case to start with."

He asked what reaction I expected from the client. I told him that I did not know. I would do all that I could to explain why continuing the guardianship proceeding was not in the client's best interest, but possibly he would become very angry. The partner told me to call the client, and explain why the firm could not continue representation.

I was relieved, but nervous. I called the client's office. He was not in. He returned my call from the corporate jet. While irrelevant, this fact just reinforced all my fears—I was about to say no to a man who controlled millions of dollars of legal work and who probably would demand that the firm deliver my head on a silver platter.

I began the conversation by describing my encounter with his mother the previous day. I told him that she seemed remarkably lucid, and would succeed in persuading the court that she was capable of making her own decisions. I explained that, based on my interview with her, I was unwilling to go forward with the guardianship petition. After a pregnant pause, the client asked that I do two things: 1) talk with his mother's doctors, and 2) go see her again. When I had completed those tasks, I could dismiss or prosecute the petition as I saw fit. He left the ultimate decision to me.

I tried to talk to the doctor immediately, but he was with patients. His office would ask him to return my call. I was impatient to have the matter resolved, so I went to see the client's mother again. As I entered the nursing home, I asked one of the nurses about the mother's care. She replied that the mother was doing well because she took her medication everyday, but she had been in real trouble when she was admitted. I thought about this as I went to the woman's room. This time she was not reading, nor did she seem to recognize me. I identified myself as her son's lawyer and told her that we had met the day before. She told me that it was not possible that we had met because she had been out shopping the day before. I asked her if she remembered the papers I had given her, and she insisted that we had never met. I then asked about her family members, and she explained that she had no grandchildren (she had several), and her son was an airline pilot (he was general counsel).

Suddenly I remembered that I had read that many elderly clients have "windows of lucidity," or intermittent periods when they are rational and lucid. It was clear to me that this was what I was dealing with. The doctor confirmed this. When the client's mother received her medication regularly she experienced periods of lucidity, but even these were sporadic. Without her medication she was irrational and refused to eat or take care of the most fundamental tasks of personal hygiene.

I returned to the office and called the client immediately. I told him that he would have the order appointing him as guardian as soon as possible.

Approximately one month later I obtained the order, and forwarded it to the client. The firm sent a bill for my services. A few weeks later I received a letter and a check in the mail. The client wrote "I hire hundreds of lawyers throughout the country. All of them are smart. Most of them work hard. Few have courage. Thank you for what you did for my mother and me." The check included a substantial bonus.

This experience taught me many lessons—the most important being that clients are as often occasions of grace as of sin.[7] My client's generous response to my premature conclusions taught me to look more carefully at evidence before I reach a conclusion. His subsequent letter strengthened my belief that clients want and need lawyers who care about justice and compassion. My partner's advice and willingness to allow me to withdraw evidenced the reality that law firms can be moral communities.

In order for firms to be moral communities, we must act on our moral beliefs. For the Christian lawyer, we must express our love of God and neighbor in the way we act within the firm. We are called to build up a sense of Christian community. Daily tasks are undertaken with the prayerful sense that all we do should be offered to God.[8] There is no place for anything less than our best. In the practice of law our best compels us to envision what justice requires our society become, and to direct our efforts to promoting its creation. This requires more than contributing financially to charitable causes or occasionally providing pro bono legal services. It is much more personal. It means treating people in a manner consistent with their human dignity. Thus, the person working in the firm copy room is to be treated with as much respect as the managing partner. Secretaries, paralegals, and others subject to our review can expect fair and candid evaluations that are communicated to those with a need to know, and no others. Colleagues' achievements and successes are the legitimate subject of firm "shop talk," while their weaknesses and failures receive only private correction and attention.[9] When we, ourselves, are in need of correction, we receive it with joy.[10] In brief, we are called to treat those within the firm the same way we are called to treat all others—with love and justice.

Outside the firm, the requirements remain the same. But what does it mean to treat our families with love and justice? At a minimum, I believe it means recognizing their centrality in our lives. Pope John Paul II has described marriage as a communion of persons that leads to the creation of community.[11] Marriage is a sacrament—a special sign of God's grace in the world.[12] Through and with my husband, I come to see something of our preciousness to God and his plan for our lives. At our best, our marriage calls forth and affirms the life-giving nature of love—life-giving not only in the sense of bringing children into the world, but also in creating a place of hospitality for the stranger and renewal for the weary.

We have been blessed with three children. Each reflects the image of

God in a unique and special way. They have renewed our wonder at the world God has created, and inspired us to greater efforts in creating community. They are both our reward, and our challenge as we continue in our own efforts to become more of what God is calling us to be.

In my final year of law school an interviewer asked how I managed as a married woman with a small child. I explained that our son kept me sane. Unfortunately, it is too easy to marginalize and silence spouses when you are absorbed in the study of law. To any complaints of neglect or observations about increasing self-absorption, the ultimate answer is, "Leave me alone. I'm doing this for us!" Small children, however, live fully in the present. The implicit promise of "I'll consider you later" does not satisfy the three-year-old who needs you now. By caring for our child, ultimately my family was caring for me. I remained grounded in the present, and did not trade the love, joy and struggles of today for the false promise of comfort and abundance tomorrow.

This is the second challenge that practicing law poses. Not only must we resist the impulse to reduce our identity to that of "the lawyer," but also we must resist the siren call of future abundance through total consumption today. Many of us disregard the wisdom of scripture in managing our lives. We are like the rich man who ignored his duty to God and his neighbor in accumulating wealth for the future. When the man was at last satisfied that he had made adequate provision for the future, God appeared to him and said, " 'You fool, this night your life will be demanded of you; and the things you have prepared, to whom will they belong?' Thus will it be for the one who stores up treasure for himself but is not rich in what matters to God."[13]

Lawyers following Christ must constantly ask whether they are rich in what matters to God. Have we valued the relationships, talents, and wealth God has given us? I think it unlikely that God will be satisfied if I attempt to justify neglecting any of these gifts on the basis that "I had to be about my law firm's (or client's) business."[14]

Focusing on what matters to God is very difficult in the law firm culture. With few exceptions, every firm relies on associates' desire for wealth and prestige to motivate and shape the conduct of young lawyers. Yet the motivation of a Christian lawyer should be quite different. The stark contrast of these motivations is illustrated by an exchange I had with a partner one day.

Our firm had a number of hours that each associate was to bill annually. I assumed that this requirement represented the number of hours that had to be billed at the associate's average billing rate to obtain a reasonable profit for the firm, and recoup its investment in training and development. Assuming that clients' needs had been met, I thought that associates were free to devote any additional hours to legal matters that they believed most appropriate. For me, that meant providing pro bono legal services, and working for legislative reforms to protect the human dignity of the elderly.

One afternoon, as I was getting a book from a hallway bookshelf, a rain-making partner walked by. Instead of his usual greeting, he said "You make me crazy!" Uncertain what provoked this comment, I responded "What have I done?"

"We just finished deciding on associate compensation, and we never know what to do with you. There are several young lawyers who work very hard, do good work, bill lots of hours, and make a lot of money for the firm. They are easy; we give them big raises. And there are a few lawyers who don't work very hard, and we know what to do with them. And then there is you. Your work is good, and you work just as hard as almost anybody in the first group. If everything you did was billable, you would make a lot of money for the firm. But instead you have all this pro bono and teaching continuing legal education stuff, and we never know what to do with you! Why don't you just concentrate on billable hours?"

I tried to explain that I understood my job as a lawyer to encompass a lot more than providing legal services to clients who could afford to pay. I told him that I understood that my decisions about what was required of us differed from some of my classmates, and that these differences translated into more or less money for the firm. It didn't surprise or bother me that my more profitable classmates received larger raises.

My response seemed to confuse him. It appeared as if it had never occurred to him that I would take such a position. "You don't care that other people are making more money?" he asked. "No" I replied, "as long as we both agree that I am as good a lawyer, I don't care." He walked off, shaking his head, and probably feeling very relieved that he was not my supervising partner. Interestingly, this man urged me to reconsider when it was announced that I was leaving the firm to teach.

This exchange illustrates the reaction of many people when confronted with the very different priorities that Christians are called to have. Yet too often we are not consistent in our priorities. We want it both ways. We want to do pro bono work, and get big raises. We want to serve God and accumulate treasures in heaven, yet we also want treasures here on Earth. My experience teaches me that it doesn't work that way, at least not in the short-term. God does reward our faithfulness, but the rewards poured out by God are most often found in relationships, not bank accounts.

It seems that women often recognize this earlier than men. Perhaps it is because we are created to share our very bodies with those who will be heir to our lives. Our unique capacity to bear children is a great blessing, yet in the work place, it can be viewed as a disability or impediment. The tragedy of this view was forcefully revealed to me when I became pregnant with our third child. I had made an afternoon appointment with my supervising partner to tell him of my pregnancy. At lunch, I shared my good news with another woman lawyer. Yet, instead of congratulating me, her first response was a question, "Are you going to have an abortion?" Appalled, yet intrigued, I asked, " Why would I do that?" "Well, you'll never make partner with two maternity leaves," she said. "Do you really believe that would be required of me?" I asked. "That's the way it is," she responded. At this point my disgust got the better of me, and I asked, " And do you think that I am the sort of person that would give in to that sort of pressure?" The conversation and lunch ended quickly after that.

"That's the way it is"—an amazing statement about reality, and about acceptance of that reality. Yet, it was wrong on both counts. Our firm had elected women on maternity leave into the partnership, and one of the most powerful partners had taken two maternity leaves while working at the firm. That's the way it *really* was.

Even more frustrating than my friend's assumption about "reality" is my friend's apparent acceptance of, or perhaps resignation to, a reality that requires women to place their children upon the altar of professional success. Justice O'Connor evidenced a similar acceptance or resignation to the necessity of such a bargain when she wrote in defense of abortion, "The ability of women to participate equally in the economic and social life of the Nation has been facilitated by their ability to control their reproductive lives."[15] If the price of admission to the economic life of this country is aborting our children or even denying our childbearing capacity, we are bargaining with the Devil, and like the client of Daniel Webster, ultimately we stand to lose much more than we gain by the bargain.

Consideration for the whole person is the basis of the Christian under- standing of work. Pope John Paul II has written:

> There is no doubt that the equal dignity and responsibility of men and women fully justifies women's access to public functions. On the other hand the true advancement of women requires that clear recognition be given to the value of their maternal and family role, by comparison with all other public roles and all other professions. Furthermore, these roles and professions should be harmoniously combined if we wish the evolution of society and culture to be truly and fully human.[16]

In the New Testament, the Gospel of Luke tells us that Christ was accompanied by the twelve disciples, and several women "who provided for them out of their resources."[17] The description of the virtuous wife in the book of Proverbs contains praise for her acumen in business matters.[18] Christian women have never been called to remove themselves from the marketplace. Rather, we have been called to use our access to the market- place to serve God and care for our families.[19]

Staying focused on God and our families while practicing law is not easy. Certainly it cannot be done alone. To remain faithful and focused requires an active prayer life and the support of a community of believers in the work place. Friends at church can help, but faithful friends at work are irreplaceable. Finding those friends is both easier and more difficult than might be expected. Many Christians do not directly express their beliefs in everyday conversation, yet I found if I listened closely I could discern their faith. An example of this is a conversation I had with a partner about the legitimacy of drafting prenuptial agreements. His understanding of marriage as a lifetime commitment that involved more than consensual agreement to certain duties and rights signaled a religious belief system. The longer we worked together the more comfortable we became talking about how faith influences our conception and practice of law.

In casual conversation, another partner mentioned his work with a world-wide ministry dedicated to feeding the poor. Had I not known that the organization was Christian, the title would not have disclosed this fact. Yet, because of my familiarity with the organization, I found another lawyer who shared my commitment to Christ.

In my office, a crucifix stood on the credenza and a framed quotation from Pope Paul hung above my telephone stand. These symbols evidenced my faith, and indirectly encouraged others to speak of theirs. The symbols also reminded me of my accountability for my actions, and our obligation not to give scandal to others.

As I began the transition from lawyer to law professor I wondered if I could remain faithful in a secular law school. Media portrayals of higher education as hostile to religion were intimidating. Yet I have found that the same practices that helped form a community of faith in the law firm work in legal education. There are three colleagues that have substantially shaped my academic career. The first and most active is a man whose life evidences his belief in human dignity and freedom. His personal integrity shines through in his actions and his writing. He is Jewish and has been a great blessing to me. The second man refuses to speak of his religious beliefs. I am uncertain whether he even believes in God. Yet he knows that I do, and whenever I send him drafts of my writings he challenges me to consistency and depth. His insistence that I be better than I sometimes think I can has blessed me. The third man is a practicing Roman Catholic, and his writing explores the relationship of faith and the practice of law. We disagree on many things, but he has been faithful throughout his career, and his public profession of faith acts as an example. He too has read early drafts of my articles, and calls me back to the Christian understanding of the world when I stray.

The temptations in teaching law are different than those I experienced in practice. Time pressure remains, although billable hours disappear. The siren's call is not the promise of wealth, but rather prestige and academic reputation. Teaching and scholarship often seem a lonelier business than practicing law ever did. With the loneliness can come an overemphasis on self. My need for my family is even greater as an academic lawyer. When I think I'm too tired or too busy to pray, my husband prays for me and reminds me that I probably need prayer most at these times. When some failure or embarrassment looms larger than life, a child's voice will whisper, "You're the best mommy ever." And on the rare occasions when finally

I think that I'm in charge of my life, one of us gets a fabulous opportunity or has a compelling need that scrambles my schedule and reminds me that we are never really in charge. Often I feel that my family and I are ad-libbing our lives every day.

In those few quiet moments when I really focus on God, He reminds me that He is in charge. All He asks is that we love and trust him. At those times, I understand anew the wisdom of Mother Teresa when she said "God calls us to be faithful, not effective." If He wanted effective, there are more direct ways to achieve His will than relying upon human beings like me.

The Bible tells us that God delights in us.[20] May He grant us sufficient grace to delight in Him, and sufficient faith to believe that He will take care of the rest.

Endnotes

1. Roman Catholic. Professor of Law at South Texas College of Law. Visiting Scholar, Notre Dame Law School. B.A. 1977, J.D. 1986, University of Oklahoma.

2. See Pope John Paul II, *Evangelium Vitae* ¶ 23 (1995)("In the materialistic perspective described so far, *interpersonal relations are seriously impoverished*. The first to be harmed are women, children, the sick or suffering, and the elderly. The criterion of personal dignity—which demands respect, generosity and service—is replaced by the criterion of efficiency, functionality and usefulness: others are considered not for what they 'are,' but for what they 'have, do and produce.'").

3. John 8:32 (New American Bible) ("[Y]ou will know the truth, and the truth will set you free."). For a detailed discussion of the relationship between truth and freedom, see Pope John Paul II, *Veritatis Splendor*, ch. 3 (1993).

4. Matthew 22:39 ("The second [greatest commandment] is like it: You shall love your neighbor as yourself.").

5. Matthew 22:37–38 ("He [Jesus] said to him, 'You shall love the Lord, your God, with all your heart, with all your soul, and with all your mind. This is the greatest and the first commandment. . . .' ").

6. Micah 6:8 ("You have been told, O man, what is good, and what the Lord requires of you: Only to do the right and to love goodness, and to walk humbly with your God.").

7. Thomas L. Shaffer, "Legal Ethics and the Good Client," 36 *Cath.U.L.Rev.* 319, 320 (1987).

8. The point is explored in detail by Stefan Cardinal Wyszynski in his book, *All Ye Who Labor* (Sophia Institute Press 1995).

9. In this way we observe the admonition of Christ, himself, "go and tell him his fault between you and him alone. If he listens to you, you have won over your brother. If he does not listen, take one or two others along with you, so that 'every fact may be established on the testimony of two or three witnesses.' " Matthew 18:15–16.

10. "He who loves correction loves knowledge, but he who hates reproof is [a fool]." Proverbs 12:1. The reader should not confuse recognition of these

requirements with any assertion that my conduct consistently meets these standards, particularly this one!

11. See Pope John Paul II, *Familiaris Consortio*, ¶ 18 (1981).
12. Pope John Paul II, *Catechism of the Catholic Church*, ¶ 1617 (1994).
13. Luke 12:20–21.
14. Cf. Luke 2:49 (Christ explaining to Mary and Joseph why he remained behind in the Temple).
15. *Planned Parenthood v. Casey*, 505 U.S. 833, 856 (1992).
16. Pope John Paul II, *Familiaris Consortio*, ¶ 23 (1981).
17. Luke 8:1–3.
18. Like merchant ships, she secures her provisions from afar. She rises while it is still night, and distributes food to her household. She picks out a field to purchase; out of her earnings she plants a vineyard. She is girt about with strength, and sturdy are her arms. She enjoys the success of her dealings; at night her lamp is undimmed. She puts her hands to the distaff, and her fingers ply the spindle. She reaches out her hands to the poor, and extends her arms to the needy. She fears not the snow for her household; all her charges are doubly clothed. She makes her own coverlets; fine linen and purple are her clothing. Her husband is prominent at the city gate as he sits with the elders of the land. She makes garments and sells them, and stocks the merchants with belts. She is clothed with strength and dignity, and she laughs at the days to come. She opens her mouth in wisdom, and on her tongue is kindly counsel.
    Proverbs 31:14–26.
19. At the recent United Nations Conference on Women in Beijing, this responsibility was described:

    To affirm the dignity and rights of all women requires respect for the roles of women, whose quest for personal fulfillment and the construction of a stable society is inseparably linked to their commitments to God, family, neighbor, and especially to their children.
    Mary Ann Glendon, "Perspectives of the Vatican Delegation in Beijing," 25 *Origins* 203–4 (1995).

    The freer women are to share their gifts with society and to assume leadership in society, the better are the prospects for the entire human community to progress in wisdom, justice and dignified living.
    Id. at 206.
20. Isaiah 65:18 ("For I create Jerusalem to be a joy and its people to be a delight . . . .").

My Faith and My Law

Tom H. Matheny[1]

I am a country lawyer who came to religious involvement late in life. The timing of this probably helped me grasp the conflict between law and faith early on, and at the same time made me realize that the conflicts were fewer than I would have ordinarily anticipated, if I could rely on decisions made during that period in my life.

Robert Drake wrote about his father who loved three things: "the Methodist Church, the Democratic Party, and the St. Louis Cardinals."[2] I did something like that. I decided that if I was to be happy in my faith and happy in my profession, I had to make some choices and stick to them. I would have to modify them, hone them, adjust them—but stick to them.

And so in the beginning, I chose to try:

1. To never let my profession interfere with my religion.
2. To love people, love my clients, have faith in them. Or, at least try. This would include having faith in other lawyers and having faith in judges.
3. To have faith in the system, both the religious system and the legal system.
4. To have faith in myself.
5. To realize that none of these would work all of the time.

Later on, as I will comment, I had to add to these five things.

The decision not to let my profession interfere with my religion was at the same time easy and hard. For that means that I must take the opportunities as they come to do the right thing and seek the truth. The easy part of that was that I was trying to do that anyway.

I was only fooling myself into thinking that I was doing that on the basis of principle and not of faith. In thinking of this, I am struck by the word from Hebrews:

> Now faith is the substance of things hoped for, the evidence of things not seen.
> For by it the elders obtained a good report.[3]

> These all died in faith, not having received the promises but having seen them afar off, and were persuaded of *them*, and embraced *them*, and confessed that they were strangers and pilgrims on the earth.

For they that say such things declare plainly that they seek a country.

And truly, if they had been mindful of that *country* from whence they came out, they might have had opportunity to have returned.

But now they desire a better *country*, that is, an heavenly: wherefore God is not ashamed to be called their God: for he hath prepared for them a city.[4]

My friend, Don Benton, summed it up best in a sermon he preached on September 18, 1977, when he said:

> The author of our text says the more critical issue is, "Does it work?" "Are the results of its effectiveness verifiable in human experience?" And he answers with a long list of persons whose only life explanation was "yes, it does." He concludes his roll call by saying, "These all died in faith, not having received all that we promised but having seen it and greeted it from afar. They made it plain by the way they lived . . . . Therefore, God was not ashamed to be called their God."
>
> The explanation of their lives was that their confidence was not in what they knew but in whom they knew. They did not have to know in advance all that the future might hold, because of their relationship of faith with the One who they believed held the future. So they lived by faith, not fear, and God was not ashamed to be called their God. Indeed, He gave them all He had prepared for them.
>
> That is what real faith is about. It has substance. It is about an inner assurance of trust and a conviction of hope about things which may not be seen with our natural eyes but which are very real and reliable.[5]

I am from the deep South. But even in high school, I had some beliefs and practices that made me seem eccentric to my fellow students. I really didn't go to Church except for the social events. At the same time, I didn't believe in discrimination against anyone for any reason and said so, although I really didn't know anyone who was discriminated against. I was an integrationist, and said so, even though I really didn't know any black people. I liked Harry Truman and said so and ended up being one of two in my community for a long time.

Fortunately, I suppose, for the relationship with my friends they just passed all of this over as being eccentric and tolerated me and my views. My views didn't seem to interfere with my life. People in the South are like that as long as I was "their" eccentric friend.

My earliest memory of that conflict involved President Truman. My high school English teacher told the President of the local university, Dr. Jack Tinsley, that I was a fan of Harry Truman's. He was, too. As I recall it, he knew him rather well. At any rate, he sent word for me to drop by his office after school one day and I did. We talked about Harry Truman. He asked me to come to the local Rotary Club and give my view on Harry Truman and I agreed. I worked hard on that speech. I dropped by his office from time to time to go over what I was thinking about and writing about, and he encouraged me. And then came the week that I was to speak at the Rotary Club.

The day before or perhaps the day before that, President Truman fired General MacArthur. The next day the local papers were thundering that Truman should be impeached, and there were billboards put up instantaneously saying the same thing.

Dr. Tinsley called me at home that evening and said, "I know what you are thinking but you've got to go ahead and give that speech the way you wrote it." And so I did. And Dr. Tinsley was the only one who applauded. They didn't invite me back for years. But I was rather proud nevertheless, and Dr. Tinsley was my good friend until he died.

The transfer of principle to religious principle in the practice of law was harder. For if I continued that way some people said I would never get clients. But I kept on. I joined the Methodist Church, and continued to be involved in what was then and now is labeled religious expression in political life and activity. I became deeply involved in the Church and now serve two legal systems. I am the President of the Judicial Council of the United Methodist Church. This is the ecclesiastical court or Supreme Court of that denomination worldwide. Therefore, I look to the law in terms of my legal practice and I look to the law of the Church through what is called The Book of Discipline of the United Methodist Church.

The struggle for civil rights started developing when I was in school and continued to develop (and still does) in my early years of practicing law. I was involved in this. Although my community was not one in which there were demonstrations and a great deal of stridency, there was still tension. The schools were integrated without difficulty and the University was as well. Voting rights were established early on because of political pressures rather than the pressures of litigation or legislation. Nevertheless, I advised students in colleges and universities about sit-ins and served on a local biracial committee. Insofar as I know, I never lost a client over these activities.

Things became rather more severe when the movement for integration hit the organization of the Church. In that struggle, more than any where else, religious faith in the light of legal changes and in the light of the law of the Church, became more contentious. Integration of the Church seemed far more difficult than integrating society. For it was then that I had threats, crosses burned (32), and was even picketed on occasion.

And still I lost no clients, not that it would have mattered. Nor did I lose friends or allies. During this difficult time, I was under a lot of pressure but frankly I didn't really pay too much attention to the cross burnings or the threats. I had a friend who was in the Klan and he usually alerted me when they were coming. He contacted me one week and said that the next

Saturday night there was going to be a whole caravan and they were going to burn a cross in my back yard. I guess the thing that bothered me most was that they were burning the cross because of my position in the Church, which meant they may have been fellow Methodists.

So, I invited a few friends out who had never seen a cross burning. I thought they might enjoy it. We grilled some steaks and waited for them. They never showed. Bill contacted me the next week and said they had gotten lost on the way to my home in the country. The most grievous injury the Klan ever did to me was to ruin a major social event.

I was talking about writing about this to a friend of mine who was there that night. He said, "You had better hope that that book doesn't sell very well. Most people have forgotten about that and all of those things you did." I suppose so but I also suppose a lot of people never knew about it in the first place.

God is good.

In society, in the Church and in law, we must still give primacy to doing the right thing in seeking the truth. My choices were undergirded by the following verses:

> I must work the works of him that sent me, while it is day: the night cometh, when no man can work.[6]

> Whereupon, O king Agrippa, I was not disobedient unto the heavenly vision:
> But shewed first unto them of Damascus, and at Jerusalem, and throughout all the coasts of Judea, and *then* to the Gentiles, that they should repent and turn to God, and do works meet for repentance.
> For these causes the Jews caught me in the temple, and went about to kill *me*.
> Having therefore obtained help of God, I continue unto this day, witnessing both to small and great, saying none other things than those which the prophets and Moses did say should come:
> That Christ should suffer, *and* that he should be the first that should rise from the dead, and should shew light unto the people, and to the Gentiles.
> And as he thus spake for himself, Festus said with a loud voice, Paul, thou art beside thyself; much learning doth make thee mad.[7]

But then I found one of my other decisions was also more difficult than I had expected. That is, loving my clients and having faith in them and in other lawyers and in other judges can be hard to do. For this means that you must believe them and I do that, confessing that it has not always worked.

When I first started practicing law, practically all of the other lawyers in the area warned me about one particular man. They said he was one of the best lawyers in the State but that he was crafty, that he would not do the right thing, that he would lie, that he would take advantage of you. I didn't know him so I didn't worry about it. But I had been practicing law only a few days when my law partner of many years called in ill and said that I had to take a case that morning in the Court of Appeal. I had never heard of the file, I didn't know what it was about, I didn't know who the other lawyer was. I only had time to get the file, get in my car, and drive to the Court of Appeal. There, to my horror, I found that my opposing counsel was this lawyer that everyone had warned me about.

But I did the only thing I knew how to do. I went up and introduced myself, told him my predicament and confessed that I knew not the slightest thing about the case, other than its title. He took me over into a corner and outlined the case in a very succinct sort of way and then he said, "Son, if I were in your shoes, this is what I would do . . . ." and he told me the strategy that he would use. So, I did, and I beat him. And he has remained my friend across the years and is now one of my clients. Faith and belief in others sometimes pays off.

When I started practicing law, the legal profession was not held in high esteem. It is worse today. So, I don't take some kinds of cases. I don't take some clients. If I cannot enjoy the cases or enjoy the people, or have any fun, I'm not interested. But I still believe in my clients, in other lawyers and in judges, imperfect as all are.

This does not mean that I don't get angry, for I do, but I attempt to eventually see the humor in situations. I simply cannot practice in any other way. Here I am guided by the Psalmist, who said: "He that sitteth in the heavens shall laugh . . . ."[8] and by Proverbs where we are told, "A merry heart doeth good *like* a medicine . . . ."[9] I don't ordinarily do criminal cases but I enjoy helping students who get in trouble. I live in a university town and those are usually funny.

A not untypical situation was a call I received in the middle of night one hot August. A desk sergeant asked if I knew a certain person. I said, "No, I do not." The desk sergeant then named the young man's father and asked if I knew him, and I said, "Yes, he is a client of mine." The sergeant then wanted me to talk to the young man and I said that I would. He said, "Can you come get me out of jail?" So, I said "Yes." He then told me to bring a towel because he was naked. I said, "O.K." I was too groggy to do anything else. He then said, "Bring twelve more. There are thirteen of us."

I later learned that the air conditioning had failed in their dorm and they had decided to go skinny dipping in a city pool. And, so they did. They didn't realize that a fire station was right across the street and that the firemen slept upstairs. Somebody stole their clothes while they were in the pool. I think it was the firemen. I never found out.

But it was certainly a different kind of situation when I walked into the police station and saw thirteen naked college students. What was I to do to represent them? Well, I had to get the judge to see the humor of the situation.

Charles Stith has written a profound book, *Political Religion*.[10] He lists three issues that divide the people—the people of the Church, and the people of the country: prayer in school, abortion, and gay and lesbian rights.[11]

I would add race to that list, and of course, there are others. We see these issues debated with intensity in the body politic and in Church political systems. But as I mentioned before, I am now involved in the law of the body politic as well as the Church. I am not only involved, I can make decisions that affect the outcome. That is why I say race is still an issue.

When I started my activities in the Church, race was an issue and it still is. However, I believe as I did when I started out that our faith can draw people together and the law can be an instrument for doing that.

So, I would say that my religious beliefs teach me that I should place my religious beliefs first and this will help me to perform my profession of work. I find basically that my professional life is in harmony with my religious life and I find that my training in the law helps me to dissect the issues that confront the Church and sometimes helps to come to solutions.

For certainly in the South, the Church has taken the lead in resolving many of the social issues of the day in giving support and strength when the body politic could not deal with it in harmony. One can only have a little knowledge of Louisiana history to know that there was a long period of time in which the voices of the political leaders were in, many respects, voices of bigotry and stridency. Yet all the while in local communities, through Churches, people of good faith were attempting to resolve the issues of the day in a very quiet and purposeful way and it worked. And I am proud to say that lawyers have been involved in those struggles all through that history all through this State. And when we finish tilling the garden of issues that Charles Stith wrote about, there are more. There are issues in Louisiana such as gambling and the doing of political favors. In my State, we are in a crisis but I believe it will be the organized Church (of whatever nature) that carries us through and ultimately will give guidance to political leadership and legal leadership.

I was asked the question: "What advice do you have to someone faced with reconciling a legal career with his or her religious beliefs?" My advice is that there is no permanent conflict. It is but a temporary conflict. Faith will help one resolve it.

I said in the beginning that I had to add to the five choices that I listed in the beginning. One of the additions is that law is a living, constantly moving profession and life.

If I like my clients and communicate with them, through or in spite of fax machines and voice mail and E-mail, I recognize several things. Most people who come to a law office are afraid. People rarely come to a law office, and it makes them nervous. Most people only come in for the deed to purchase their house, or a will to settle their estate. We need to recognize that in the legal profession. And so we have to be concerned about our clients and we have to hurt with them when they are hurt and hurt with them if we lose in court.

Clients have frailties. They get sick. They have personal problems, and they die. And if you are to be a good lawyer, particularly a good country lawyer, you have to be involved in their lives. As I have been reading and thinking in writing this paper, I have received two calls informing me of the death of close friends, Brian & Grover. I had been thinking about them anyway as I was preparing this paper for their illustrations of the point that I made. I have had two close friends who were judges who were people of different but massive intellects. They were a joy to be with and they were a joy to represent.

One was named Ben and one was named Grover. Ben reminded me more of Atticus Finch in *To Kill a Mockingbird* than any other person I ever met. But they were frail. They had bad hearts, and it was a constant strain seeing them struggle to continue to live as they did and to continue to be active even until the day they died and they did.

And the third is named Brian, a little boy who contracted leukemia when he was a small child. In a sense, he licked leukemia but in a sense leukemia defeated him for in the process of the cure his body was basically destroyed. While he lived until he was twenty-one, he did not grow much beyond the time of the inception of his illness and still looked like a little boy.

It hurts to represent people like this and suffer with them. But if you are to be a good lawyer you have to suffer with them. Because none of them, Ben, Grover, or Brian, ever complained, why should I. They always had a smile, were always friendly, and were always kind.

Law is a mixture of belief in your faith, of belief in the law, and belief in involvement in the people you represent. Law and faith are inextricably linked with your relationship with the people you represent and to the world at large. And this is why I am content in what I have arrived at in my own relationship with my faith and with my law.

This, again, does not mean that I don't get angry. I get angry at clients and judges and secretaries. I have never been able to defeat a short temper. But I usually go back to those five choices I made and am comfortable with that.

Endnotes

1. United Methodist. Partner, Matheny and Pierson, Hammond, Louisiana; President, Judicial Council, United Methodist Church (Supreme Court of the Denomination). B.A. 1954, Southeastern Louisiana University; J.D. 1957, Tulane University.
2. Robert Drake, "The Methodist Church, the Democratic Party and the St. Louis Cardinals," *The Christian Century,* Aug. 1994, at 787.
3. Hebrews 11:1–2 (King James).
4. Hebrews 11:13–16.

5. Dr. Don Benton, A Collection of Sermons, in *Faith With Substance* 2–3 (published in commemoration of his pastorship, Lovers Lane United Methodist Church, Sept. 18, 1977–June 11, 1995).

6. John 9:4.

7. Acts 26:19–24.

8. Psalms 2:4.

9. Proverbs 17:22.

10. Charles Stith, *Political Religion: A Liberal Answers the Question, "Should Politics and Religion Mix?"* (1995).

11. *Id.* at 24.

Religion and Lifework in the Law

Ashley T. Wiltshire, Jr.[1]

Religion and Law: It's Not Just Happenstance

It was the summer of 1970 in Nashville, Tennessee. I had just finished my first year in law school and was employed as a clerk for the legal aid organization in town. It was Saturday afternoon and, rather than being at my employment, I was sitting with two of my colleagues and two private attorneys around a conference table at a law firm office in the Third National Bank Building. We were working on a case one of the lawyers had taken at the urging of the American Civil Liberties Union.

We must have stopped work, and one of us must have said something revealing about himself. I do not remember how the conversation started, but I do remember the remark that followed. A lawyer I had known ten years before in undergraduate school who often asked embarrassing questions, in the midst of our conversation looked up mischievously and with a sly grin and a sweep of his arm and a recognition of the work that had drawn us there, suggested, "Let's do this—let's go around the table and have each of us tell when he decided *not* to go into the ministry."

This is not to say that everyone who does civil rights or civil liberties or public interest or poverty law is just a closet preacher. Nor is the point that everyone doing those things would be comfortable talking about them or even thinking quietly about them in religious terms. Many, many would not. The group around that table was a small sample on a Saturday afternoon in the Bible Belt. The probing may never have occurred at another time or in another place or with another grouping of people. Nevertheless, for many of us who work for the poor or marginalized, the underlying motivation is there: religion made us do it. Truth to tell, the motivation is there whether we admit it or not.

Religion

At this point the skeptic will say "that depends on your definition of religion," and as is most always the case, the skeptic is right. There are many definitions of religion. Definitions of religion range from the precise and narrow to the far and wide. The Reverend Roger Thwackum in Henry Fielding's *Tom Jones* is one of the more precise among us: "When I mention religion, I mean the Christian religion; and not only the Christian religion, but the Protestant religion; and not only the Protestant religion but the

Church of England." The existentialist theologian Paul Tillich, on the other hand, concluded, "Religion . . . is ultimate concern."[2]

Somewhere in the middle, Winston King has fashioned a more workable definition of religion: "the attempt to order individual and societal life in terms of culturally perceived ultimate priorities."[3]

King's definition is contextual without being narrow. It is broad enough to exclude only the most idiosyncratic. It takes in most all of us, and it convinces me that most of us do what we do, practice what we practice, live our professional lives and pursue our careers as a reflection of and result of our religion. Some of us do it consciously and others do it unconsciously, but we are who we are, continue being who we are, and change who we are because of our religion.

One more definition of religion adds to this expansive claim. A Latin scholar close to me reminds me that our word "religion" means "being bound together." The Latin *ligo* is the root of the English word "ligament." Ligaments hold together our bones and enable us to move. Religion then is that which holds us together, corporately and/or individually, and enables us to move in some coordinated fashion.

Work

I decided not to be a minister lying on a hospital gurney in a Seventh Day Adventist hospital ward in Bangkok, Thailand, in 1968. I made two important decisions that day, one of which was to return to the States, go to law school, and become a legal aid lawyer. I had graduated from seminary; I had been the assistant school minister at a Presbyterian prep school and then the chaplain at a Unitarian prep school. I was in Thailand as a journeyman missionary, sent by the Foreign Mission Board of the Southern Baptist Convention. I was on the course that had guided me since early youth to be a minister.

Also in my experience, however, was my work in the summer of 1966 with the Student Interracial Ministry in Southwest Georgia. There, teaching in a Head Start program and working with local African-American farmers to try to get equitable peanut crop allotments from the Agricultural Stabilization and Conservation Service (ASCS) of the U.S. Department of Agriculture, I lived for the first time the call for justice voiced by the Hebrew prophets, reinforced by Abraham Heschel in *The Prophets*, and interpreted so vividly in seminary lectures by Samuel Terrien. The life on those sandy Georgia roads, in the segregated pre-school classes, under the suspicious, rejecting eyes of the local whites, brought together Terrien's interpretation and Heschel's poetry.

Heschel had written:

> Justice is not an ancient custom, a human convention, a value, but a transcendent demand, freighted with divine concern. It is not only a relationship between man and man, it is an *act* involving God, a

divine need. Justice is His line, righteousness His plummet. (Isa. 28:17). It is not one of His ways, but in all His ways. Its validity is not only universal, but also eternal, independent of will and experience.[4]

Regardless of the "will and experience" of a middle-class white southern male who had come of age in the Eisenhower 1950s, imbued with the Calvinist view that financial good fortune is the mark of God's good favor and that the converse is the mark of God's disfavor, the words of Heschel rang true. Working with those children in Head Start, working with those subsistence farmers taking the leftovers from the ASCS, the need for and "validity of justice" seemed to be "not only universal, but also eternal."

Heschel went on to explain:

> The prophets' preoccupation with justice and righteousness has its roots in a powerful awareness of injustice. . . . The distinction of the prophets was in their remorseless unveiling of injustice and oppression, in their comprehension of social, political, and religious evils.[5]

The teaching of the prophets was not limited to the personal piety and individual ethic with which I had grown up. The prophets demanded a discerning eye about what was happening to people, especially to the poor. Over and over the fatherless, the widow, the oppressed, the weak, the needy, the downtrodden, the afflicted, and always the poor, are identified as God's special concern.

That, however, is not the end of the message. There is the logical next step:

> [T]he calling of the prophet may be described as that of an advocate or champion, speaking for those who are too weak to plead their own cause. . . . The prophet is a person who is not tolerant of wrongs done to others, who resents other people's injuries. He even calls upon others to be champions of the poor . . .
> *Seek justice,*
> Undo oppression;
> Defend the fatherless,
> Plead for the widow.[6]

Heschel reinforces the breadth of the call: "It is to every member of Israel, not alone to the judges, that Isaiah directs his plea."[7]

Feeling the pull of these teachings, I also felt ill-equipped and unprepared to deal with the problems of race and poverty I saw in Southwest Georgia. Reading the ASCS rules and procedure in the Code of Federal Regulations was torture. I could not even find my way into the labyrinth, and when I managed to creep down one dark passage and make one simple turn, I could not find my way back out. I had never been confronted with the complexity of the law and its control over lives and economy. Surely, I thought, I must get the tools to unravel these mysteries.

In the same summer I was in Southwest Georgia as a seminary student, there were three law students on a separate project, clerking for the summer with the local civil rights attorney, C. B. King. I was impressed that they seemed better equipped to deal with problems faced by the people we served. They had tools to do specific tasks.

The other realization I had was that lawyers had levers for prying the white community out of its patterns of prejudice. I had told myself and others that real change would not come until there was change of heart, but that summer I came to understand that for some people change of heart only followed change of law. I further saw that in other cases change of heart may never come and one must seek to change the system of law regardless of those hearts. Law, it seemed to me in Southwest Georgia in 1966, was much more likely to change the systems of poverty and segregation than preaching or teaching.

I kept these observations with me but did not act on them when I returned in the fall to seminary. I did write for law school catalogs, but filed no applications. A year later I went to Thailand, still on course of the ministry, but still with Georgia on my mind.

While in Thailand I kept up with events in the States through the international edition of *Time* magazine, printed on tissue-thin paper and flown in from Europe, and from time to time there appeared in that periodical accounts of the work of legal aid lawyers, particularly with California Rural Legal Assistance, and I remembered Southwest Georgia and Amos and Isaiah.

It struck me that these legal aid lawyers, more than I, were doing the Lord's work, and in September 1968, in the Seventh Day Adventist Hospital, I resolved to change my course and to become a lawyer instead of a minister.

There are those who would argue, and I am among them, that by leaving the professional ministry I was not leaving ministry. There are many gifts of the spirit and many ministries. I believe there is a legitimate ministry through law. This belief is based on at least three tenets: 1) the priesthood of all believers; 2) the concern of God for the whole human being; and 3) the importance of law in society, which also is a concern of God.

As I look back on twenty-five years working in legal aid, as a clerk, a lawyer, and since 1976, as executive director of a local legal aid organization, I am as persuaded as I was in 1968 that it is, or can be, ministry. The mission statement of the organization I work for is this:

> The mission of Legal Aid Society of Middle Tennessee is to enforce, enhance, and defend the legal rights of low-income and elderly people.
>
> We provide legal advocacy and education to obtain necessities such as health care, housing, income, protection from family violence, and access to basic goods and services.
>
> We address those problems which have the greatest impact on

our clients because of either the nature of the problem or the number of persons affected.

I did not write the first draft of this statement. It was prepared by, of all things, a committee. The main drafter, as I recall, was a person who was a professed secularist. Yet I cannot read the statement without hearing in it strains of Biblical attention to the poor: "May he defend the cause of the poor of the people, [and] give deliverance to the needy. . . ."[8] "He judged the cause of the poor and needy; then it was well. . . ."[9] Reading the list of necessities in the second sentence of the mission statement, I am reminded of the list in Matthew: "for I was hungry and you gave me food, I was thirsty and you gave me drink, . . . I was sick and you visited me, I was in prison and you came to me."[10]

The third sentence, which speaks of impact, goes beyond individual instances of justice. It has a wider view and calls to mind the expansive language of Amos:

> Let justice roll down like waters,
> and righteousness like an everflowing stream.[11]

Heschel again is helpful. As he explains the significance of Amos's image, he suggests also why the sentence of the mission statement is important to our work: "A mighty stream, expressive of the vehemence of a never-ending, surging, fighting movement—as if obstacles had to be washed away for justice to be done."[12]

Here is how the words of the mission statement play out in actual cases. This list is a small sample from reports given to me recently by the staff of our organization:

—Helped client get a divorce and regain custody of her child who had been snatched by an abusive husband and hidden in another state for several years.

—Through a series of individual civil actions brought under various state and federal laws, stopped a collection agency from terrorizing debtors; the collection agency would have the city turn off the debtor's utilities even though the debt in question was to a retail store rather than the city.

—Brought suit against a landlord who had illegally evicted a young couple from their apartment by disconnecting the electricity. The landlord also illegally removed their personal belongings, destroyed some, and tossed others in a garbage dumpster. Obtained a $1000 judgment for the illegal eviction and additional compensation for the lost property.

—Concluded prison condition litigation begun in 1975. As results of the litigation, the Tennessee prison system changed from being one of the most violent in the country (according to U.S. Justice

Department statistics) to becoming the first in the country to gain complete accreditation from the national corrections body.

—Published *Financial Abuse of the Elderly: An Advocate's Guide.*

—Represented a seventy year-old woman whose two children had taken her home to use as collateral for their own debts; filed a lawsuit for the return of her home.

—Represented intact family with disabled father and two children. Mother had to leave her job to care for her husband, and as a result the family faced foreclosure on their home. We obtained medical coverage for the family and disability benefits for the father. The mother has been able to return to work and reports she has purchased new clothes for their children for the first time in their lives.

—Advocacy on behalf of our clients with the State of Tennessee in the design of its new medicaid managed care program that resulted in new coverage for 400,000 formerly uninsured people.

—Represented a two year-old girl born with one eye. Doctor proposed to insert a synthetic eye and reconstruct her head so it would develop symmetrically. The insurance company denied coverage on the grounds that the surgery was cosmetic. By letters and threats to the insurance company and State we persuaded the insurance company to relent; the surgery proceeded and the child is recovering beautifully.

Motivation

I do not remember any of the responses to the impertinent challenge about law and ministry in the Third National Bank Building in the summer of 1970. It may have provoked denials or dismissals. There probably were mixed responses, but the challenge itself was enough to suggest to me the thesis that (1) we are where we are and do what we do because of our religion, stated or unstated; (2) for many of us who do poverty law, being a legal aid lawyer is a religious act.

I have tested my thesis, albeit unscientifically, on colleagues. My sample is not random and may not be representative, but though the answers vary, they do have a substantial similarity about them. The question I asked most of the time was "Tell me what your religion has to do with your practice of law, the work you do. If that sounds like an inappropriate questions, for instance, if you choke on the phrase 'your religion', make up your own question and answer it, but tell me something about religion and what you do."

Karen is the director of a legal aid program in a mid-sized city and has worked in legal aid fifteen years. "I never was religious growing up. My parents were not religious; but I did have some sense of what are Christian values. I now am a 'studying Buddhist,' and I now feel more at home than I ever have, but what I do, my commitment to being a lawyer for the poor does spring in most part from my sense of those Christian values."

"For the most part?" I asked. "Were there, are there other values that influenced you? Political? Social?" Surely, I thought there must have been something else that motivated her since she admittedly had no religious instruction.

"Well," she replied, "they may be expressed in social or political terms, but at base they are core Christian values about helping the poor. I believe the teachings of Jesus are right about helping people."

Kevin is a younger lawyer who has worked for two legal aid organizations a total of five years after a brief stint with an insurance defense firm. He reminded me he had given me his answer several years ago in response to a simple, straightforward question in his job interview: "Why do you want to work here?" He had said then, and repeated now, that he never had been very religious but that he did go to Sunday School as a child and he was sure that the reason he wanted to do legal aid work had a lot to do with things he heard in Sunday School.

It gets more explicit. For Michele it is not merely that religion implicitly influenced her. It is a matter of vocation. Raised in a devout family, she took seriously the teaching of the Roman Catholic Church, "and even the Bible, if you can believe a Catholic reads the Bible. I kept reading in the Bible about helping 'the least of these . . .', and I felt I had to do it. I hoped I could satisfy my obligation by going for one month to a Jesuit work camp, and I did that when I was in college, but that was not enough; I had to do it all the time." She has been a legal aid lawyer for one year, with zeal and compassion for her clients, most of whom are disabled children, that causes her to push for and obtain results other lawyers would never request.

Michele came back to me several days after our initial conversation and said she wanted to give me a more precise answer to my question. She had thought about it and worked on a statement. I was impressed that she had given it a second thought. Here is her prepared statement: "Faith gives me the context to more clearly hear my calling and the courage to answer it every day."

Kitty thought initially she did not have much to say in response to my question. She allowed that there is a relationship between her religion and her practice of law: "Religion keeps me focused; it helps center me; it is a frequent reminder." Then she added a particular to the general: "A part of the Jewish liturgy is a series of things we thank God for; we thank God for raising the downtrodden, clothing the naked, giving sight to the blind, strengthening the weary. The effect of this recitation is to remind one of the partnership. This does not happen on its own."

I asked about her motivation for coming to work at Legal Aid eighteen years ago. After some disclaimer she remembered, "the first 'broader than me' experience I had was with civil rights in Chapel Hill in the Sixties. I got the sense of being responsible for making wrongs right. Actually, it was from my family. They were in a Presbyterian Church and the preacher was kicked out because of his stand on civil rights. Several families banded together around him and started a new congregation. So these ideas were associated with religion, but it didn't have that feeling, but they were associated. Then in 1964 I remember writing an essay in which I said, 'The problems have to do with poverty.' One set of problems (civil rights) led me to the other (poverty). There was still this sense of responsibility I had for making wrongs right."

I had talked to Steve many months earlier. He is the director of a large urban legal services organization. When I asked him why he did what he did, I warned him about my suspicions, but I cited no texts.

Steve said he did not consider himself religious. He proceeded, however, in everything he said next to give life to Winston King's definition of religion. First he observed: "Judaism is a religion which is also cultural. What I do does come from being raised as I was." Then he pointed out that an important part of that heritage is the idea of protecting the weak. "The treatment of people and people's rights are important. That's Jewish. It's not just happenstance."

"I wanted to be a part of a larger work. Maybe that is a religious notion, a moral notion of making a difference in an organized way, of being a part of something accomplishing something. There is a body of work that is doing something."

Neil's first answer was that the motivation for his work in a rural legal services organization is his personal philosophy. "It's not in a religious context. It's the kind of people it brings me in contact with, the satisfaction that comes from the people we work with and the people we serve. There is a real unity of what we believe in and what we do." He allows, however, that "when we talk about the obligation or the pleasure of service, if we explore where that comes from, there is often the question of how you think someone ought to live, how one ought to spend one's life, and that is a theological question."

Caveat and Disclaimer

Neil was the first to point out what should have been a caveat from the beginning of these discussions. "We need to avoid giving anyone the sense that just because we are in this work we are better people. Doing a work doesn't make you a better person. That is theological, too." How quickly we forget, and how important it is to remember. Neil went on with a caution about giving the wrong impression about people in our part of the profession. "There are people in public interest and poverty law who do it for attention and power, just like folks in other professions and other attorneys."

Neil and Gordon always see the other side. Gordon, whose prophetic words and far-reaching advocacy set the standards for us all, reacted to my question by saying it was "elitist." He began to list people who could not or would not ask this question about their work. They do not have the choices or opportunities we have. Then he pointed out how very fortunate we are to have work that seems to us to have a connection to faith.

Conclusion

We are indeed fortunate. Pat, who has been a legal aid attorney for twelve years, said right away, "It is impossible to separate religion from anything you do. When you believe something, you can't put it on a shelf and say 'I'll use it sometime.' It is a part of everything we do." Winston King would approve. Heschel probably would approve of what we do. Neil is right, too: As individuals we are no better than anyone else, and as a group we are no better than any other. As Kitty said for some of us though, religion keeps us focused. And as Steve said, "It's not just happenstance."

Endnotes

1. United Methodist. Executive Director, Legal Aid of Middle Tennessee, Nashville, Tennessee. B.A. 1963, Washington and Lee University; M.Div. 1967, Union Theological Seminary, New York; J.D. 1972, Vanderbilt University.
2. Paul Tillich, "Religion as a Dimension in Man's Spiritual Life," in *Theology of Culture* 7–8 (Robert C. Kimball ed., 1959).
3. Winston King, "Religion," in 12 *The Encyclopedia of Religion* 282–92, 285 (1968).
4. Abraham Heschel, 1 *The Prophets* 198 (1969).
5. *Id.* at 204.
6. Isaiah 1:17. *Id.* at 204–5.
7. *Id.* at 205.
8. Psalms 72:4 (Revised Standard). Unless otherwise indicated, all subsequent citations to the Bible are to the Revised Standard version.
9. Jeremiah 22:16.
10. Matthew 25:35–36.
11. Amos 5:24.
12. Heschel, *supra* note 4, at 212.

Lawyer, Lobbyist, and Latter-Day Saint

Marcus G. Faust[1]

In this time of widespread public dissatisfaction with government, Senators and Representatives have rushed to enact reforms requiring greater scrutiny of those who seek to influence the legislative process. The House of Representatives recently adopted internal rules implementing a total ban on gifts from lobbyists. A similar ban has also been adopted in the Senate. The 104th Congress also enacted a new, significantly enhanced lobby reform and disclosure law. The lawyer-lobbyist profession is perceived to be one governed by gifts, golf, graft, and greed. How is it then that a committed member of the Church of Jesus Christ of Latter-Day Saints has made a successful career as a legislative lawyer and registered lobbyist? How do my religious beliefs influence the practice of influencing others? How does a lobbyist who doesn't drink alcohol or smoke cigars in the back room compete in a profession that made the two martini-lunch famous? The truth is that I welcomed the new financial disclosure laws and gift rule changes. I self-imposed most of these reforms when I registered as a lobbyist in 1981. I believe that any professional success in large measure is *because* of strict adherence to my religious standards and beliefs, not in spite of them. How did a Utah Mormon become a Washington legislative counsel? It started with becoming a lawyer.

For as long as I can remember I always wanted to become a lawyer. This career choice was influenced greatly by my father and grandfather, both of whom had distinguished careers in the legal profession while simultaneously serving in various lay capacities in the Church. Both my brothers have also chosen to become lawyers. At the dinner table we were fed good food along with small portions of the law, as we would absorb the telling of father's latest case. When my father would have to work late or on Saturday, he would remark "the law is a jealous mistress." I often wonder what my mother thought of that quote.

I recall with fondness piling into the family car just before Christmas to deliver to father's clients both presents and goodwill. Most of those we visited were poor or disadvantaged, people who had turned to my father, their attorney, to resolve some personal crisis. I witnessed the trust, respect, admiration, and love these people had for their lawyer and I saw something noble in using one's knowledge of the law to help people through difficulties in their lives. For me, the work my father did as an attorney helping people solve their legal problems was another form of administering Christlike service.

My father practiced law while also serving as the lay Bishop of our congregation, then serving as a Stake President presiding over several congregations, and later he voluntarily abandoned his law practice to respond to a call by Church leaders to serve full-time as a General Authority of the Church.[2] I have seen how being a lawyer helped him become a better church leader and how being a church leader helped him become a better lawyer. From his example, I have never doubted that the legal profession was an honorable one which could be practiced in full harmony with Christ's teachings for the betterment of others.

I was shaped by these early experiences with a firm resolve to become a lawyer. This resolve was reinforced within me in a spiritual way at the age of fourteen. Within our Church, every member is entitled to receive once in his or her lifetime a blessing at the hands of a Patriarch who is called of God for the purpose of bestowing an inspired blessing from our Father in Heaven. This "Patriarchal Blessing" is viewed as sacred and contains guidance, information, and advice, both specific and general about one's future life. The blessings promised are predicated upon obedience to laws and ordinances of the Gospel of Jesus Christ. Because a Patriarchal Blessing is usually received early in life, it is recorded and transcribed so that it can be read and reread throughout the remainder of one's lifetime.

Because individual blessings are sacred and are not generally shared outside of family members and loved ones, I shall not discuss details of my own blessing. However, it does contain specific counsel concerning my chosen vocation and it has foreshadowed my career which began as a Congressional staff attorney, and later my life as a lawyer and legislative counsel. While I did not fully perceive all of the guidance given when I received my blessing twenty-eight years ago, I have since come to a greater understanding of its content and I have gained a fuller appreciation of its passages. I keep a copy of my Patriarchal Blessing in my office credenza where it remains a constant reminder of the importance of honesty, personal integrity, loyalty, and being trustworthy. These virtues, which I strive to emulate, have become my real stock in trade, while my legislative skills and legal expertise have become secondary. My Patriarchal Blessing provides me with a spiritual confirmation of the correctness of the professional choices I have made in my life.

I guess I have always been interested in government. I was the only student in the eighth grade who could name every Cabinet member in the Johnson Administration. I celebrated my sixteenth birthday in 1969 by attending a political dinner where the featured speaker was a young Senator Ted Kennedy from Massachusetts, who I recall coincidentally was also celebrating his birthday. In high school I was chosen the "Sterling Scholar" in Social Studies. For my undergraduate education, I attended the University of Utah graduating cum laude in History in 1974. I obtained

my Juris Doctor degree cum laude from the J. Reuben Clark Law School
at Brigham Young University.

During the first week of law school in the fall of 1974, I attended a
mini-course on Constitutional Law taught by the Law School Dean Rex E.
Lee.[3] Dean Lee's classes spurred my interest in the law and its governance
of the conduct of individuals. Shortly thereafter, Dean Lee took a leave of
absence to serve as Assistant Attorney General in the Ford Administration
and later he served as Solicitor General of the United States in the Reagan
Administration. My own desire to work in government and politics grew.

It was during law school that I obtained my first political job working
on the state staff of Utah Senator Frank E. Moss. It was my hope that after
graduation from law school, I could be transferred to the Senator's legislative staff in Washington, D.C. Six weeks before graduation, these plans
suffered a setback when Senator Moss was defeated in the November 1976
election. My disappointment was short-lived, however, because within a
few weeks I was offered a position as legislative counsel to U.S. Congressman Gunn McKay, who represented the First District of Utah. In February
1977, the day after I finished taking the Utah State Bar Exam, my family
and I departed Utah for Washington, D.C. pulling all our worldly possessions behind us in a U-Haul trailer. I believed then—and remain so
convinced—that our move to Washington, D.C. was a part of God's plan for
me and for my family.

In 1977, Congress as an institution was at an all-time low in public
opinion polls. People asked why I wanted to go to work at a place that was
suffering from sex scandals involving two powerful House Members and
was the subject of an unfolding Abscam sting operation in which several
House members were videotaped accepting bribes from an F.B.I agent
posing as an Arab Sheik. I was told by family and friends to go back there
and "clean that place up."

The L.D.S. religion teaches patriotic duty and encourages its members
to actively participate in government at all levels. The late L.D.S. Church
Apostle Bruce R. McConkie said:

> In view of the troubled times which the nations of the earth are
> experiencing at present, it is well for us as members of the Lord's
> kingdom to understand clearly our responsibilities and obligations
> respecting governments and laws as declared in the Twelfth Article
> of Faith: "We believe in being subject to kings, presidents, rulers,
> and magistrates, in obeying, honoring, and sustaining the law."[4]

Mormon doctrine and scripture also teach that we should revere our
government and its institutions. We believe that this nation was established with a divine mission. Quoting from L.D.S. scripture in the Book of
Mormon and the Doctrine and Covenants, Elder McConkie stated further:

> America was to be a land of liberty upon which no kings should

rule. (2 Nephi 10:11–14.) The nation to possess it was to "be free from bondage, and from captivity, and from all other nations." (Ether 2:12.) The Gentiles were to "be established in this land, and be set up as a free people by the power of the Father," so that . . . the covenants made with ancient Israel be fulfilled. (3 Nephi 21:4.) "And for this purpose have I established the Constitution of this land, by the hands of wise men whom I raised up unto this very purpose, and redeemed the land by the shedding of blood."[5]

Working in the U.S. House of Representatives as a Legislative Counsel provided an exciting opportunity to blend the use of one's legal training with political skill and judgment. The responsibilities of that position vary from office to office. I received good training because I worked for a Congressman who relied heavily upon his staff for legislative research on bills and votes and who more generally sought our judgment and advice.

Each morning, I would review the bills scheduled for debate on the House floor and then I would prepare a list of recommendations of how the Congressman should cast his vote on both amendments and final passage. It is simply impossible for any Senator or Representative to know all there is to know—or all they need to know—about each issue brought to the floor for a vote. My recommendations were based upon a knowledge of the Congressman's previous voting record and his political philosophy, which was an interesting mixture of Roosevelt New Deal democrat with conservative Utah Mormon. I would inform the Congressman during our briefings if we had received constituent mail or phone calls from the district on a particular vote. Ultimately, of course, the Congressman would decide how to vote. Sometimes he would vote contrary to my recommendation because of other factors such as floor lobbying from colleagues, party leadership, and outside lobbyists. I learned this was also part of the process.

I am often asked about whether individual Senators and Representatives can always vote their consciences or whether they are pressured by lobbyists and party politics to vote a different way. I reply that members of Congress usually do vote for what they believe in their conscience is right for their constituency. Congress, however, by its nature is a political institution which is controlled by political parties. Each party has a platform and a legislative agenda. One of the most difficult things for a member to do is resist party leaders when one more vote is needed for an important measure. I have worked with members who have strived to maintain complete independence from the party leadership. They usually find themselves isolated from their natural allies and disadvantaged in Committee assignments. It is difficult for them to obtain support from other members for legislation they are sponsoring on behalf of their own district. Total independence usually ends up hurting that member's overall effectiveness and ability to represent his constituency in the institution to which he was elected.

The legislative system, as established in the Constitution, is predicated upon compromise and accommodation. There must be a reconciliation of differing political opinions for both houses of Congress to pass a bill using precisely identical language. I do not view this process of negotiation and compromise as unseemly or improper. "Making a deal" involves seeing someone else's point of view and making an accommodation of that person's perspective in such a way so it can coexist with your own. This may not always be possible on all issues. Then it is time to respectfully disagree. Even husbands and wives have honest disagreements!

In my experience, what is important is the manner in which a legislator conducts himself throughout this give-and-take process. A Congressman must be as good as his word when it is given. One must be able to disagree without being disagreeable and one has to learn how to be a good loser on occasion and not hold a grudge. The most effective legislators play the game by these rules. One anonymous Senator is found of observing about the Senate, "Here there are no permanent friends or permanent enemies, only permanent interests." One day, two senators can be fighting like cats and dogs on one matter while, the very next day, they will join together as an effective team on an issue on which they agree. In the reception area of Senator Orrin Hatch's office is a painting of the Kennedy compound at Kennebunkport which was painted by Senator Ted Kennedy. Inscribed in the corner are the words: "We will leave a light on for you." Kennedy and Hatch are on opposite ends of the political spectrum but they have become the Senate's odd couple.

Ultimately, an elected official will be held accountable for his conduct by both the electorate and by God. The doctrine of the L.D.S. Church teaches that those who make our laws, as well as those who administer them, are not only responsible to the public but also to God for this public stewardship.

The Book of Doctrine and Covenants, which is a compilation of revelations and scriptures received principally by the Church's first Prophet Joseph Smith, teaches: "We believe that governments were instituted of God for the benefit of man; and that he holds men accountable for their acts in relation to them, both in making laws and administering them, for the good and safety of society."[6]

When I am to be judged in heaven for my work for Representative McKay, the repeal of the Edmunds-Tucker Act will be on the plus side of the ledger. This Act was passed by Congress in 1887 to punish the Mormon Church for its religious practice of plural marriage. Wilford Woodruff who served as L.D.S. Church President at that time wrote: "The Edmunds-Tucker Act, the high water mark of anti-Mormon legislation, was enacted by the U.S. Congress in 1887, dissolving the Church and its corporate life and confiscating its property; an action which the Supreme Court of the United States upheld May 19, 1890."[7]

The Edmunds-Tucker Act required that any property owned by a church located in a territory[8] of the United States with a value in excess of $50,000 would automatically escheat to the United States Government. It was under this statute that the federal government briefly occupied Temple Square in Salt Lake City, the Vatican of our faith.

The Edmunds-Tucker Act was passed despite the fact that less than two percent of the Church's members actually practiced plural marriage. Although the Church abandoned the practice of polygamy altogether in 1890, this offensive statute remained on the books. Its existence came to light in 1979 when the Church sought to construct a Temple in the Territory of American Samoa for use by its members throughout Polynesia. Because of the Edmunds-Tucker Act, however, if the Temple was constructed it automatically would become the property of the United States! The American Samoan Temple project was abandoned and another was constructed in the independent nation of Western Samoa. Nevertheless, Representative McKay set about the legislative process to repeal the Act. Ultimately, we were successful in enacting a statute to repeal the Edmunds-Tucker Act.[9]

Another highlight of my tenure on the Hill involved advising and managing the judicial appointment process for Congressman McKay. The period from 1977 to 1980 was a unique time in Utah politics because both the White House and the Congress were controlled by the Democrats. Since Congressman McKay was the only Democrat in Utah's congressional delegation, he was able to nominate to the President for appointment several prominent L.D.S. attorneys to serve on the federal bench in Utah and in the U.S. Court of Appeals for the Tenth Circuit.[10] I believe I was blessed in the work I performed in helping to repeal the Edmunds-Tucker Act and in helping to secure the appointment of L.D.S. judges.

Approaching the election of 1980, I anticipated that Congressman McKay would be reelected, as he had been five times previously. He was defeated, however, in the Reagan landslide, despite the fact that he had led in every poll taken before the election. Suddenly, I was unemployed with a wife and four children to provide for. Nevertheless, while attending Church the following Sunday, rather than feeling anger and despair, I felt overwhelming gratitude to my Father in Heaven for the precious blessings which life had given me: my family and my faith.

Indeed, I was blessed and, within two weeks of the election defeat, I was hired as Counsel to the House Interior Committee to work for the Mines and Mining Subcommittee. This was a period of great professional satisfaction because it enabled me to focus on the specific legislative jurisdiction of the Committee, rather than follow every bill and amendment which was brought to the floor. I drafted legislation and Committee reports, prepared testimony and floor colloquies, wrote legislative histories, and staffed Committee hearings. I planned and staffed a Congressional delegation tour of the strategic mineral deposits in South America and I authored a report for the Subcommittee on our nation's dependence upon imported minerals from abroad. My tenure on the Committee staff followed the national energy crisis which heightened public awareness to the importance of developing our own nation's natural resource base. I worked to develop an expertise in the field of natural resources involving water, energy, mining, public lands, and environmental legislation.

This gained expertise eventually became the basis of my law practice, which I opened at the end of 1982. My first clients were mining, oil and electric utilities, with whom I had become acquainted during my time on the Hill. Today, my clientele still reflects this expertise and I perform many of the same functions, such as drafting legislation, preparing floor statements, and writing testimony for Committee hearings. It is important for others to understand that a lobbyist functions for his clients in a manner very similar to the way a congressional staffer serves a Member of Congress. We track legislation of importance to our clients and we work with elected representatives from the states where our client is a constituent to make the legislation more favorable. In many ways, a good lobbyist can become an important resource of information and assistance to a Member of Congress and his staff.

There are many lobbyists, perhaps most, who sell their services based upon some political connection to a Member of Congress, usually a former employer. Both my former Member-employers were defeated at the polls. Other lobbyists offer close relationships based upon service performed for the party such as fundraising and campaign management. My practice, in contrast, was not built upon any political connection or party affiliation. I believe it was built primarily upon my knowledge of how Capitol Hill works, my legal expertise, and my reputation for always being truthful, always keeping a confidence, and always putting the client's interest first. This has led to success in the legislative endeavors I have undertaken. These successes have produced referrals of additional clients and consequently my practice has grown and prospered.

I have adopted an approach to client management which I call the "long distance runner." My goal has been to develop a long-term relationship with a number of core clients by delivering results for a fee, a fee which is affordable and which my clients are happy to pay. One of my father's sayings is that you don't want a client who doesn't want you to be his lawyer. Many of my long-term clients originally hired me only to solve one specific legislative or administrative problem. After that goal was accomplished, they felt good enough about the experience that they were interested in working on a second problem, then a third, and so on. Because the federal government touches so many aspects of our lives, most clients quickly become convinced that having a Washington, D.C. representative is an ongoing advantage in their dealings with the government. Because I have represented most of my clients for a number of years, I have developed choice friendships with all of them. Although my clients are different from the individual widow or the injured worker my father represented, I still find great satisfaction in helping them solve their problems with government.

I believe a major reason for my success is striving to achieve a reputation for being nonpartisan. It is important to be able to talk to both sides of the aisle. A lobbyist who is limited to contacts in one political party is handicapped. The principle of political neutrality is one also adhered to by the leadership of my church.

It is sometimes incorrectly believed by political analysts that the Church of Jesus Christ of Latter-Day Saints supports Republicans. This is simply incorrect. The Church maintains strict political neutrality on elections and nonmoral issues. Even before statehood was granted in 1896, the leaders in the Church in Utah preached political neutrality. In 1892, the Church issued the following statement:

> Each party should have the same rights, privileges and opportunities as the other. If any man claims that it is the wish of the First Presidency that a Democrat shall vote the Republican ticket, or a Republican the Democratic ticket, let all people know that he is endeavoring to deceive the public and has no authority of that kind from us. We have no disposition to direct in these matters, but proclaim that, as far as we are concerned, the members of this Church are entirely and perfectly free in all political affairs. But they should not indulge in ill-feeling or personalities.[11]

Each election year the First Presidency of the L.D.S. Church issues the following statement:

> In this election year we reaffirm the policy of strict political neutrality for the Church.
> • The Church does not endorse political candidates or parties in elections.
> • The Church does not advise its members how to vote.
> • Church facilities are not used for political purposes.
> Church members should study the issues and candidates carefully and prayerfully and then vote for those who they believe will act with integrity and will most nearly carry out their ideas of good government. Members are encouraged to participate as responsible citizens in supporting measures that strengthen society morally, economically, and culturally. They are urged to be actively engaged in worthy causes to improve their communities and make them more wholesome places in which to live and rear families.
> Political candidates should not imply that their candidacy is endorsed by the Church or its leaders. Church directories or mailing lists should not be used for political purposes.[12]

Excessive partisanship was preached against by L.D.S. Church President Heber J. Grant who said:

> I regret exceedingly that in political controversies men seem to lack
> the courtesy and that respect for their opponents that I believe all
> Latter-Day Saints ought to have. I have never yet heard a Democrat
> make a political speech that I felt was fair to the Republicans. Being
> a Democrat, I shall not say anything about what I think of the
> speeches of Republicans regarding Democrats. . . . From my own
> personal contact with dear and near friends, Republicans and
> Democrats, I have not been able to discover the exercise of what
> you might call charity, if you like, for the opinions of others who
> oppose them politically; at least not as much charity as should exist
> among our people.[13]

In retrospect of my tenure working as a staffer for the Congress, if there
is anything I regret it would be those occasions when I allowed the
partisanship of being in the majority party to overrule charity and courtesy
to the minority.

There are fourteen L.D.S. Members of Congress from both political
parties. They include Senator Harry Reid, a moderate Democrat from
Nevada and Chairman of the Senate Democratic Policy Committee as well
as Representative Ernest Istook, who is a conservative Republican from
Oklahoma.

One of the toughest legislative battles I have ever been involved in
culminated in 1992 when Congress enacted legislation authorizing completion of the $2 billion Central Utah Water Project. That bill could not
have become law but for the bipartisan support of the entire Congressional
delegation from Utah, which then included a liberal Democrat in the
majority and four conservative Republicans. Overcoming strong philosophical disagreements among the delegation concerning environmental
issues, through gentle persuasion, longsuffering, shuttle diplomacy, and
the ability to find common ground, a consensus bill was forged which was
ultimately enacted.

It is my goal to accomplish this type of bipartisan cooperation on every
measure I set out to get enacted. Frequently, I have served as a communications bridge to bring together members who previously were not even
speaking to one another. I have at times threatened to withhold my
assistance in passing a bill to stop a Senator who wanted to "go it alone"
and steal the headlines on the introduction of a bill which I knew required
bipartisan support to be enacted. I have observed that Congress itself has
become increasingly partisan over the eighteen years I have been in
Washington. Both parties seem to adopt legislative strategies that are
calculated solely on how it will injure their opponents and benefit themselves in the polls. There are many issues for which the right decision is
not necessarily the popular decision. For instance, both parties know that
the federal budget must be balanced and that future Medicare spending
will become unmanageable unless it is curtailed somehow. Rather than

cooperate to solve these problems, they try to score debating points off the others' position, to the overall detriment of the nation.

Since becoming a legislative lawyer and a registered lobbyist, the most important legislation I have been involved with was the passage of the Religious Freedom Restoration Act (RFRA).[14] I did so on behalf of the L.D.S. Church on a *pro bono publico* basis. The Church participated with many other denominations and political organizations to lobby Congress to reverse the Supreme Court's burdensome decision in *Employment Division v. Smith*.[15] In the *Smith* case, Justice Scalia, writing for a majority of the Court but writing for a plurality on the legal issue, said that application of the "compelling state interest/least intrusive means" test in protecting the exercise of religious activity was a luxury we "cannot afford . . . ."[16] The decision announced a new standard which permitted government regulation of religious activity where the state could show the regulation was generally applicable and was not targeted at a specific religion.

The *Smith* decision was immediately denounced by churches and numerous political organizations, both liberal and conservative. A significant number of the nation's denominations joined with civil liberty organizations to form the Coalition For Religious Freedom. Legislation was drafted with the assistance of prominent First Amendment scholars from law schools around the country to create a federal statutory cause of action that reinstated the compelling interest test in First Amendment free exercise cases in state and federal courts.[17] Participation by the L.D.S. Church in the Coalition was a unique occurrence.

Most mainline churches develop a legislative agenda which is advanced by full-time registered lobbyists. The L.D.S. Church, however, does not maintain a legislative agenda and does not retain a paid lobbyist. This policy to avoid political involvement is grounded in the Church's early history of unfair treatment at the hands of government and its strong belief in the Constitutional doctrine of separation of Church and State. The Doctrine and Covenants states: "We do not believe it just to mingle religious influence with civil government, whereby one religious society is fostered and another proscribed in its spiritual privileges, and the individual rights of its members, as citizens, denied."[18] However, the *Smith* decision, which weakened religious freedom protections provided by the First Amendment contradicted the Church's eleventh Article of Faith written by Church founder Joseph Smith: "We claim the privilege of worshiping Almighty God according to the dictates of our own conscience and allow all men the same privilege, let them worship how, where or what they may."[19]

Therefore, despite a general policy of political noninvolvement, The First Presidency of the L.D.S. Church joined by the Quorum of the Twelve Apostles unitedly decided that this judicial attack on the constitutional standard of protection previously afforded by the First Amendment must be rectified. In this decision to support federal legislation, the Church leaders were guided by the Doctrine and Covenants which provides:

> We believe that rulers, states, and governments have a right, and are bound to enact laws for the protection of all citizens in the free exercise of their religious belief; but we do not believe that they have a right in justice to deprive citizens of this privilege, or proscribe them in their opinions, so long as a regard and reverence are shown to the laws and such religious opinions do not justify sedition nor conspiracy.[20]

The Church's support for the bill and its involvement in the Coalition For Religious Freedom ultimately was critically important to the bill's passage. Mormon legislators were in key positions to help move the legislation. Senator Hatch, who was the ranking Republican on the Senate Judiciary Committee, became the bill's principal sponsor and strategist in the Senate. Senator Hatch persuaded Senator Kennedy to join him as a sponsor of the bill, which provided strong bipartisan leadership to the effort.

When hearings were held before the House Judiciary Committee on the bill, the Coalition requested that L.D.S. Apostle Dallin H. Oaks be included as one of its expert witnesses in support of the bill's enactment. Before becoming a full-time Church Apostle in 1986, Elder Oaks had enjoyed a distinguished career as a jurist,[21] President of Brigham Young University, law school professor, author and legal scholar. It was my personal privilege to work with Elder Oaks as he prepared and presented his eloquent testimony.

Although the RFRA legislation had the strong support of almost all of the nation's religions, concern was expressed by the United States Catholic Conference of Bishops that the bill as introduced could be construed by the federal courts to protect the claim of a woman who sought to obtain an abortion as a matter of her religious belief. This position was not inconsequential because many pro-life members of Congress responded to the lobbying effort of the National Right to Life Organization and refused to cosponsor the Coalition's bill. During this legislative process, legal representatives of the Catholic Bishops sought a dialogue with the L.D.S. Church relative to this abortion concern. There were many contacts and conversations which occurred at various levels of both churches. These discussions were important in ultimately securing the Catholic Bishops' support of a slightly amended version of the bill, which support was essential to its enactment.

Throughout the RFRA legislative process, I felt Divine assistance that is not present during the conduct of my normal lobbying activities. I believe that God blessed the efforts of all those who were working to protect the free exercise of religious expression in this nation. I developed great respect for the good men and women from the various churches and organizations involved in that effort. I remain in awe of the judgment and skill that several of the key lawyers provided. I continue to enjoy association with many of them. They are examples to me how one can be a good lawyer-lobbyist and a good Christian. I am grateful for the experience which brought us together in a common cause on behalf of religious freedom.[22]

In conclusion, I hope that this essay will help the reader to understand that the lobbying profession is just like any other legal career or discipline. There will always be those who cut corners, find loopholes, and who give the practice a bad reputation. It is not necessary, however, to practice political lobbying in this way to become successful. One can follow the teachings of Christ and adhere to the doctrines of one's religion and succeed as a lawyer-lobbyist. I believe that I have been blessed in my professional pursuits because of my religious beliefs and standards. I acknowledge the hand of the Lord in my life. I am grateful to be a legislative lawyer, a registered lobbyist and a Latter-Day Saint.

Endnotes

1. Church of Jesus Christ of Latter-Day Saints. Lobbyist, Washington, D.C. B.A. 1974, University of Utah; J.D. 1976, Brigham Young University.
2. The author's father presently serves as a member of the First Presidency of the L.D.S. Church and was awarded the Distinguished Lawyer Emeritus Award for 1995 by the Utah State Bar Association.
3. Rex E. Lee served as President of Brigham Young University before being forced to resign due to a long-term battle with cancer. After an heroic fight, Rex E. Lee died March 11, 1996.
4. Bruce R. McConkie, *Mormon Doctrine* 160 (2d ed. 1966) (quoting *The Pearl of Great Price* at 60 [1983]).
5. Bruce R. McConkie, *Mormon Doctrine* 160 (2d ed. 11th prtg. 1990) (quoting *The Book of Mormon* (1983) and *Doctrine and Covenants* 101:80 and 109:54 [1983]).
6. *Doctrine and Covenants* 134:1 (1983).
7. *The Discourses of Wilford Woodruff* 331 n. 1 (G. Homer Durham ed., 1946).
8. Utah was a Territory until 1896 when statehood was granted. See generally *Reynolds v. United States*, 98 U.S. 145 (1878) (George Reynolds, Secretary to Brigham Young, lost his challenge to a federal law in the Territory and went to prison for acting on his sincere religious belief in plural marriage).
9. Act of Nov. 2, 1978, Pub. L. No. 95-584, 92 Stat. 2483. The statute which repealed the Edmunds-Tucker Act contained a provision granting the Territory of American Samoa a nonvoting seat in the U.S. House of Representatives. This seat is now held by Democratic Congressman Eni Faleomaveaga who is a Mormon.
10. One such appointment was Rep. McKay's brother, Monroe G. McKay, to serve on the Tenth Circuit. Judge McKay had been unanimously recommended for appointment by the judicial nominating and screening committee, but ironically was handicapped because of his relationship to the

Congressman. This political difficulty was overcome by strong support from the Utah State Bar Association and the instrumental political assistance of House Speaker Thomas P. O'Neill. Judge McKay recently took Senior Judge status after serving as Chief Judge of the Tenth Circuit.

11. *The Discourses of Wilford Woodruff, supra* note 6, at 203–4.

12. Letter from the First Presidency of the Church of Jesus Christ of Latter-Day Saints to Church Leadership (Apr. 2, 1992) (on file with author).

13. Heber J. Grant, *Gospel Standards* 133 (G. Homer Durham ed., Deseret Books, 1976).

14. 42 U.S.C. §§ 2000bb-2000bb-4 (1988 & Supp. V 1993).

15. 494 U.S. 872 (1990).

16. See *id.* at 888.

17. See generally "James R. Browning Symposium," 56 *Mont. L. Rev.* 5–306 (1995).

18. *Doctrine and Covenants* 134:9 (1983).

19. Letter from Joseph Smith to John Wentworth (Mar. 1, 1842), in *The Pearl of Great Price* at 60–61 (1983).

20. *Doctrine and Covenants* 134:7 (1983).

21. Dallin H. Oaks served as a Judge on the Utah Supreme Court from 1981–1984.

22. After this essay was written, however, the Supreme Court voided RFRA. *City of Boerne v. Flores*, 65 U.S.L.W. 4612 (1997).

The Deliberations of Mortals and the Grace of God

Joanne Gross, OSU1

This is a far different essay than the one I expected to write. Most of my years of legal practice have been spent as general counsel to a Roman Catholic religious congregation of which I am a member—the Ursulines of Cleveland—and Ursuline College, which the congregation sponsors. Almost four years ago, I joined a law firm which staffs the in-house office at Case Western Reserve University where, for the past three years, I have served as an Assistant University Attorney. Originally, I had intended to offer a fairly thoughtful reflection on my experience as a religious woman practicing law at a secular university.

In the spring of 1995, however, one of my Ursuline sisters, Joanne Marie Mascha, was raped and murdered in a wooded area of our congregation's property in a suburb of Cleveland. A young man with a history of mental health problems was arrested and "confessed" to the police within hours. In the following days, as the lone attorney in a congregation of 300 women, I found myself fielding numerous questions from my sisters—many of whom assumed that a "confession" meant the young man would go to prison without a trial and never be heard from again.

Because of my legal training, I have now spent a good portion of the past year immersed in the criminal justice system, explaining to my sisters in religion the political and procedural nuances of a capital murder prosecution and translating for my peers in the bar the enigmatic details of convent life in the Twentieth Century.

Many aspects of this experience can only be understood if you believe in God—an ironic God—and one who is both just and merciful. For having been thrust by personal circumstances into the unfamiliar arena of the criminal justice system, I found myself profoundly affected. That is why I have chosen to write an essay different from the one originally intended.

Within days of Joanne Marie's death, as it became clear that someone needed to act as a liaison between the police and the prosecutors and my congregation, I offered to do just that. I went to the arraignment, disappointed that it was held by closed-circuit television, because I wanted to see, in person, this man who had actually taken the life of another human being. I sat with other Ursulines as they were questioned by the police and prosecutors, hoping that my presence was a small reassurance that they need not do this alone. I read autopsy and trace evidence reports, competency and sanity evaluations, true bills and criminal discovery motions, aware that I read with both dispassion and disbelief.

Because the state was looking for some connection between the defendant and the victim, I spent Holy Week going through her possessions. On Good Friday, I found it, a paper written almost a year and a half earlier, after a day of prayer in the woods. Noting that the day commemorated the French Ursuline Martyrs, Joanne Marie wrote of feeling united with these women whose lives had been sacrificed hundreds of years before. I remember being shaken as I read, trying not to cry, wondering if she had ever imagined how prophetic her reflections would sound such a short time later.

In this paper, she recorded her encounter with a troubled young man searching for peace in the quiet of our forest, ending with the hope that he could hear the words she sang as she walked out of the woods that day: "May the blessing of God be upon you. May God's peace be with you. May God's presence illuminate your heart, now and forevermore." I tried to pray for him too, convinced that he needed God's peace now more than ever.

From the start, the prosecutors sought the death penalty. And from the start, my congregation opposed the death penalty. Pope John Paul II had issued "The Gospel of Life," the Catholic Church's most recent proclamation on capital punishment and other life issues, on the very day our congregational leadership made our opposition known to the media. The prosecutors told me they thought the timing of the Pope's statement was a bit unfair.

Meanwhile, the defense attorneys were searching for an expert to declare their client insane. In what I suppose was an attempt to prove just how insane he was, they released his written "confession" to the media. The defendant's story of how and why he killed and raped was sad and bizarre. Unfortunately, for him, it also revealed that he knew what he was doing and understood the consequences.

As the months dragged on, the defense and the prosecution were decades apart on a plea bargain. Believing that a twenty-one year-old man with a borderline IQ, no prior felony record and a sordid childhood of abuse did not deserve to be treated like a drug-dealing killer, the defense asked for twenty years. Concluding that the kidnapping, robbery, rape and murder of a nun deserved the electric chair, the state was willing to plead him for fifty years certain. As far as I know, the two sides never got much closer than that.

The trial date loomed and a plea seemed improbable. I arranged a meeting between the prosecutors and my congregation's General Superior, Maureen McCarthy, and our Social Justice Coordinator, Beverly LoGrasso. Because they wanted to more personally and firmly express our position on the death penalty, Maureen and Beverly talked about Joanne Marie's life, her commitment to nonviolence, and how the killing of this man would be against everything she ever stood for. They also spoke about how minorities and the poor are disproportionately sentenced to death in this country; and how every other supposedly enlightened nation in the world has done away with state-sponsored killing. The prosecutors were polite and sympathetic but ultimately, unmoved.

We gave them a copy of *Dead Man Walking*,[2] Sister Helen Prejean's account of her ministry to death row inmates; they gave us an article about death penalty politics and how prosecutors across the country are being elected and rejected based on their stance on capital punishment. We were not comforted by comments that this defendant would be safer on death row than in the general prison population because he had raped and killed a nun. Even among criminals, it seems, some crimes are worse than others.

The final pretrial was scheduled for August 28, 1995—the Feast of St. Augustine. I suggested to the prosecutors and defense attorneys that it was a good day for a conversion experience. Neither side budged, and no deal was made. I was angry that day, angry that all of us, Joanne Marie's family and her congregation, would have to go through this trial. As I prayed that evening, it occurred to me that many people with far less personal support and fewer resources live with violence and suffering and death on a daily basis. Certainly Joanne Marie herself was not spared; and perhaps God's message to my congregation, in our comfortable suburban setting, was that we could not hide from the chaos and the heartache of the world.

On the first day of jury selection, I waited in the courtroom while the judge "death-qualified" jurors in her chambers. When a young man sitting in the courtroom asked me if this was the "nun-killer" trial, I said yes and asked him why he was there. He was to be sentenced for "a minor drug problem." He had come with his girlfriend and their baby and they had been waiting for two days. This judge, he said, had given him one chance to get his act together. He had gone back to school, was working at night, had been "clean" for months and now he was waiting to be sentenced. I remember wishing him luck and telling him that I'd pray for him.

Once they moved the general voir dire to the courtroom, supposedly only death-qualified jurors remained in the pool. But when asked by the judge if there was any reason she should not serve on this particular jury, one little elderly woman said clearly and unashamedly, "Yes, because I don't believe in taking a life for a life." I wanted to applaud.

A few days before the trial began, Maureen had written to remind the prosecutors that our opposition to the death penalty would be public. And once the jury was seated, religious congregations from around the world flooded the prosecutors' offices and the judge's chambers with phone calls, and letters and faxes, all decrying the state's intention to seek this man's death. The judge, of course, could say nothing. But the prosecutor would comment daily on his letters, amazed, for example, that a nun in Peru would know about and take the time to write about a murder trial in Cleveland. He also received a number of voice mail messages, about which he was only partially amused.

The trial itself went rather quickly. After the usual coroner and police testimony, the prosecution called others. Joanne Marie had told a few people about this troubled young man and how he needed someone to talk to. She knew his name; he knew hers. He would look for her, stopping a friend to ask where she was. As each witness testified, especially the other Ursulines and Joanne Marie's family, I prayed that God would give them strength and peace.

On the third day, the prosecution rested. Earlier, the defense had withdrawn the insanity plea and we recessed for lunch, unsure of what the defense would do. Returning from lunch to find the courtroom filled with reporters and camera crews, we knew.

The defendant took the stand and told his story. He claimed to have met her only once before, walking in the woods. On the day of the murder, he wanted to tell her something. She screamed because he startled her; he stuck the scarf in her mouth because she was screaming. He pulled the scarf out when she turned blue. He thought she would wake up and tell someone, so he moved her where she couldn't be found. He went home and ate dinner. Then he came back and raped her but he thought she might have been dead when he did that.

It's a fundamental principle—when criminal defendants testify, they do so of their own choice, in their own defense. After this defendant's testimony, I was certain he had talked himself into the electric chair.

On a Sunday morning, after deliberating some thirteen hours over two days, the jury returned its verdict. They looked exhausted and oddly bonded somehow. Two weeks ago, these twelve ordinary people did not know each other; then they had been chosen by lot and had decided a man's fate.

Not surprisingly, they acquitted him on the first aggravated murder count, essentially deciding that he had not killed with prior calculation and design. On that same count, they found him guilty of murder, a noncapital offense. Then came verdicts of guilty of aggravated robbery, guilty of kidnapping, and guilty of rape. All that was left was the capital count of aggravated murder with felony-murder specifications. Logic would dictate a finding of guilt and the jury so found.

The judge released the jury for the day. Approaching the bench to read the verdict forms, one of the prosecutors reacted, and pointed to the papers. The bailiff left the courtroom quickly and within minutes, the jury was ushered back into their seats.

The judge advised the jury that they had not properly attached the felony-murder specification form to their aggravated murder verdict. The jury's failure to do so meant that the defendant could not be sentenced to death. They were free to go and she would sentence the defendant the next day.

We learned later that the jurors had misunderstood the form. Apparently, they believed that they had to find the defendant was the principal offender *and* had killed with prior calculation and design to check the felony-murder specifications form. Many also believed that the aggravated murder conviction alone would get them to the death penalty phase.

The prosecutor sat, stunned and dejected. After the courtroom cleared, he turned to me and said: "Beware of what you pray for."

On the Sunday those verdicts were returned, the first reading from the liturgy of the day came from the Book of Wisdom:

> For who can know God's counsel, or who can conceive what our Lord intends? For the deliberations of mortals are timid. . . . And scarce do we guess the things on earth, and what is within our grasp we find with difficulty . . . . [3]

The jurors "misconstrued" or "misread" or "misinterpreted" the verdict form—this man would not face the death penalty. I believe that the unexpected, always merciful but just God, intended it to happen this way. Those who do not believe in God need "rational" explanations for everything. To this day, there is a rumor going around the courthouse that a lawyer got to the jury, advising them how they could ensure convictions without dealing with the death penalty. Those of us blessed with faith know better.

We returned the next day for sentencing. The young man's adoptive father spoke, describing the desperate attempts he and his wife had long ago made to restore some normalcy to the life of a five year old traumatized by abuse. The prosecutor read a letter from Joanne Marie's family, expressing their grief and desire for justice. Maureen spoke for the congregation and while noting our gratitude that he would not face death, she asked for a lengthy sentence. The judge then imposed a sentence of fifty years to life, the maximum on each count, to be served consecutively.

The media accurately reported the prosecutor's disappointment with the verdicts, the adoptive father's poignant words, the judge's swift and maximum sentence. The media did not report that the leaders of my congregation and Joanne Marie's family embraced the distraught father of a convicted killer as he tried to express his sorrow. They did not report that many of the jurors returned for the sentencing and offered their sympathy and their prayers to us all.

After sentencing, the judge asked our congregations's leaders to meet her in chambers. I knew this was her first capital case and one she would not easily forget. She seemed genuinely moved by what had happened and told us that we had "prayed this man out of the electric chair." It was, she said, the only possible explanation for what happened. During their deliberations, the jurors had asked for many clarifications on her instructions and their consideration of the evidence. They never indicated confusion about the felony-murder specifications or the forms.

My congregation had had an experience with tragic death before.

Dorothy Kazel, one of the four churchwomen killed in El Salvador in December 1980, was a Cleveland Ursuline. Several years later, random death had claimed one of our sisters when she was struck and killed by a car as she walked down a street. But Joanne Marie's death was different—far more intrusive, far more jarring, far more palpable, if you will.

Once the trial was over and the crime scene released, we held a prayer service to "reclaim" the woods. We prayed in memory of all those whose lives have been scarred by violence, including the man who took Joanne Marie's life. The service was calming and peaceful, and it reminded me that tragedy can bring people together as well as drive them apart.

I returned to my university office after the trial, counseling on the finer points of dismissing students and terminating employees, and crafting policies that do not run afoul of academic freedom. I realized then that I was practicing a "clean" kind of law, one that rarely brought me into contact with poverty, illness, hunger, or violence. I was more keenly aware than ever that I did so in an atmosphere of prestige, if not privilege. In the days and weeks following the trial, much of what I did on a daily basis seemed trivial and even absurd.

Instinctively I knew that the violence wrought against my Congregation by the murder of Joanne Marie could never be avenged by the state's execution of the man who took her life. Merely glancing at the newspaper or television, however, heightened my awareness of the horrors we humans are capable of inflicting upon each other. And I thought that vengeance must feel so good—at first.

I struggled with how and to whom to respond. Within a month of the trial, I decided to leave the law firm and my CWRU position. With no idea where I would go or what I would do, I knew it was time to move on. I gave my boss plenty of notice and spent the next several months pondering my next move. (While religious are less secure than in other ages, it remains a peculiar benefit of the vow of poverty that I could "afford" to give notice without another position waiting in the wings.) I kept looking for signs.

On the anniversary of Joanne Marie's death, a group organized by sisters in my Congregation held a prayer service on Cleveland's Public Square. We recalled again the victims of violence and read aloud the names and ages of all the woman and children who had been murdered in the Cleveland area that year. There were children as young as a few months old; women in their eighties; they lived in the suburbs and in the city. For a while, I wondered if God was leading me away from college and university law to a practice that would bring me closer to these people—and the poor, the hungry or the homeless.

I found myself reading more about the death penalty. On what would have been my maternal Irish grandmother's 95th birthday, a very short article appeared in our local paper quoting the public defender for the first Ohio death row inmate expected to be executed. The attorney shared the same name, first and last, of my grandmother! (Ohio's Attorney General has decided to push for execution of death row inmates. Our current Governor, a devout Catholic and a man educated by Cleveland Ursulines, has said he will not stop the executions.) I wondered whether God was calling me to an even more radical role defending those who had been condemned to death.

My personal struggles to reconcile the meaning of Joanne Marie's murder and the curious verdicts at the subsequent trial of her killer mirrored those of my Congregation as a whole. In fewer than fifteen years, this relatively small group of religious women has seen two of its own murdered. Joanne Marie's death, and Dorothy Kazel's before her, have been mythic events for my Congregation, hinting at mystical truths that we cannot quite grasp. We spent a good part of our congregational meetings this past year questioning aloud God's message in these events and the actions demanded in response. I suspect we will continue to do so for a long time.

As for me, for many good and practical (and hopefully, spiritual) reasons, I finally decided not to give up my college and university practice. As I write, I am back at Ursuline College, serving as legal counsel there and at John Carroll University, the local Jesuit institution. I find myself drawn to this kind of law, here in the sustained anarchy of a higher education environment. Here, I am part of something bigger than who wins or who loses. And I get plenty of opportunities to practice the admonition of my labor law professor — "an attorney should be a peacemaker." As one who considers herself an educator trained as a lawyer, these things are important.

Dealing with Joanne Marie's murder and its aftermath was a difficult experience but one for which I am strangely grateful. I continue to reflect on the experience, unsure of its ultimate meaning, but secure in my belief in a God who can use the timid deliberations of mortals to save one life at a time.

Endnotes

1. Roman Catholic. Member Ursuline Sisters of Cleveland; Legal Counsel, Ursuline College and John Carroll University; formerly Associate Attorney, Kelley, McCann & Livingstone, Cleveland, Ohio and Assistant University Attorney, Case Western Reserve University. B.A. 1978, Ursuline College; J.D. 1986, Cleveland-Marshall College of Law, Cleveland State University.
2. Helen Prejean, *Dead Man Walking* (1993).
3. Wisdom 9:13–14, 16 (New American Bible).

My Faith and My Work

Thomas M. Reavley[1]

On so serious an undertaking, I must strive to be honest. That means, from the beginning, that I cannot boast about my faith. The truth is that I am beset by doubts and unbelief; I am sometimes fearful of what is in store for me; I am not sure that the Creator will preserve my miserable being beyond this life. At times I do better, but I falter and fail in my spiritual journey too often for me to try to pretend that I am a paragon of faith.

I do have my own beliefs about creation and destiny. Conceding all the mysteries of earth, heaven and hell, unknown and unknowable to me, I decided long ago what my assumptions would be for the answers to some of those mysteries. By those answers I decided, and have tried, to live.

I believe that all of us were created by one Creator. We were created for a purpose. We are not here by accident, and an overarching design is violated by the waste and destruction of our lives. What we see and feel is but a small island in a sea of unseen, upon which spiritual forces move. The dominant force calls to us to be true and to do our duty to each other.

This belief requires no effort on my part, because it would be beyond all possibility for me not to believe so much. I see so much grandeur and beauty, especially of the human spirit, and can imagine no way to reduce it all to accident or the elements of nature. I respond to scenes of human goodness and nobility with a surge within my mind and breast, sometimes leaving me breathless and in tears. There, says my very being, is what the Creator gave us and to what we are called.

I do believe in an after-life. As I cannot believe that the nobility and yearnings of human mind and heart are merely the product of chance and cellular development of the flesh, I believe that far greater virtue is behind our existence. There must be purpose in our creation. If so, no fair purpose could be served if this time of mortality is all there is. What absurdity, what cruelty, if sacrifice and virtuous service should end in the same trashcan with evil and immorality. That reasoning affirms the spiritual life, and I am led to accept the authority of Christ in his promise of the life beyond.

Malcolm Muggeridge, that fascinating spokesman for Christianity, wrote in the first volume of his autobiography, *Chronicles of Wasted Time*, of a discussion with his former teacher on the subject of what human life is about. She took the view that mankind had their destiny in their own hands and would ultimately be masters of their own universe. Muggeridge writes:

I stayed awake a long time thinking of the chasm which divides
those who believe in a mortal destiny, however glorious, and those
who cannot find the heart to live at all, to go on from day to day,
except on the basis of an immortal one. Belonging, as I do, so
strongly to the latter category, the former seem to me fated, either
to suppose themselves to be gods and, like Icarus, fly into the sun,
there to perish, or to fall back upon their animal nature, and the
Sisyphus task of maintaining a condition of permanent rut.[2]

Whether or not my individual being is immortal, it is related somehow
to beings and a Being who are immortal. Of that I am very sure. And I hold
to the truth of that prophecy from the first chapter of Ephesians: in the
fullness of time all things in heaven and earth shall be united in Christ.[3]
In Christ, because his gospel reveals the very best within us all and, it
seems to me, offers the only hope that history and religious thought have
given us. I need not accept every rule and report that mortals have pasted
on the life and witness of Christ, but at the center lies the supreme
revelation about human existence. If that revelation be anything less, if it
be untrue, all other visions breaking through from the unseen lack coher-
ence.

If there is where I live and where I stand, certain values and conduct
follow. Human life is sacred. It must be protected and enhanced. No
cheating or lying is acceptable. We care for each other because of our
Creator and kinship and common destiny. We do not insult or harm
helpless or "different" people, because we are together in the eternal
scheme and because our physical differences are only cosmetic. We are one
people to be united indeed in the fullness of time.

We work with what we think, with how we feel, and with who we are.
Without faith in the Creator and creation, we are in bad trouble. The
remnants of ill-tempered disputes at home, or the feelings of despair during
sleepless night hours, cannot be entirely dismissed though we are ever so
busy studying the law or deposing a witness—not even when we are young
and healthy. And as the flesh weakens with age and infirmity, the burdens
of rejection and meaninglessness overcome us whatever our pursuit.

It is necessary that there be others with whom we share respect and
caring. None of us can endure the life of the one and only. The universe at
which I am the center is a very flimsy, make-believe place.

The rootless mind is bound to be upset by exposure to the morning
newspaper. It consists largely of fuss and failure. Without some purpose
and good that will last a lifetime and beyond, how can we justify and
sustain this scrambling to succeed? What is success, anyway? These
questions may be ignored during the rash lustihood of youthful powers.
But they are there, sure to emerge sooner or later.

Anchoring roots grow for different reasons and causes. It helps to
recognize that we are needed and are able, in some measure, to meet those

needs. By bolstering the virtues of others, we nurture our own virtues. By loving, we learn how to receive love; by recognizing the love we receive, we learn to love. The contemplation of the divine grace and gifts and call will lift us and open us for the intended response.

Ego, self at the center of it all, self exposed to praise and censure: that is the most common threat to our happiness and satisfaction. It bars good relations with others, anchors our abuses of ambition, and eats at our feelings. Only by getting outside and beyond self, only by caring for people and causes, only by catching the gleam of a distant horizon and responding to a stirring song, only above sordid selfishness can we find it all worthwhile. We were made for a better life. And no one violates life for which we were made with impunity.

Ah, ego. There is the snare, our misdirection and betrayer. No matter what our work or station, it bestrides us to make fools of us and undo our good works. It is the wonder of human weakness that we can always and everywhere find some excuse for elevating ourselves to rule over others. And if we cannot control them, we fancy ourselves as better and wiser and thereby entitled to do so. Give ego a robe and perch it upon a bench, and it can run rampant. The judge who puts self at the center or atop his universe will fail to observe the limits of his knowledge of the facts and the law, and he will abuse his authority. He will exceed and misuse that authority. He will show-off when he should be listening. He will complicate the rules to display his intellectual superiority when he should be simplifying them for the benefit of those who must obey them.

All of us, and judges especially, need to pray. We need, desperately need, to bow before the God who gave us all that we are and in whose presence our ego evaporates. Facing our Creator, do we not cry out for forgiveness and grace? Then, tomorrow in our robes, will awareness of our limitations not replace our arrogance?

When you are sitting in judgment of another, civil or criminal, the rank you give yourself in creation matters greatly.

Suppose another judge, or a student law review editor for that matter, dislikes what you have written. Your supervisor, as the other sees himself, rewrites as he demeans your ideas as well as your expression. Or suppose that the court is attending its conference on an opinion that you have written after exhaustive study; and while you are giving your oral explanation to the conference and answering questions, one of the judges goes over to the table, picks up the court papers and begins his own research to be satisfied that things are regular. He is thinking that the judgment may not have been appealable, or the notice of appeal may not have been timely. Judges, like everyone, suffer put-downs all the time.

I will not tell you that this treatment does not annoy me. It does. But I can shrug it off without letting it fester, because the other person is probably only thoughtless, as I am too often thoughtless myself. If perchance, the other is unaware of his imperfection, that is his problem. He needs my help, if he will accept it, not my hatred.

Few people are needed so much as lawyers are. Angry men and women suffer from what they perceive to be the neglect and violation of their rights. "Rights" have so obsessed us that mutual obligations and community have been eroded. People need representation, advice, and healing. Controversies cry out for thoughtful and fair compromise. All over this world, as surely as in America, people must learn to appreciate the necessity of social order and community. Until the fullness of time, humans must work for both. Chaos awaits this persistent trumping of positive law by the claims of conscience and natural rights. Likewise, no society can persist on a battlefield; we need common ground, devices to bring us together and notions to bond us. It is a world of need to quicken the heart and resolve of every member of this profession.

I submit that my conduct has been fairly consistent with my faith. From my boyhood I objected, privately and publicly, to the mistreatment of black people. I was outraged to see the neglect and abuse of the children in the black schools in Nacogdoches when I went there to look after World War II. When I was Secretary of State of Texas in 1956, I said that we were wasting our most valuable resource by denying opportunity to minorities. In 1967 I asked the council and organizations of Austin to declare our readiness for open housing.

My position on racial issues was used against me in my campaign for Attorney General in 1962, but I would have lost anyway. It was used against me again in my successful campaign for the Texas Supreme Court in 1968, and the effort then probably boomeranged in my favor. I know that minority support assured my election as Travis County District Judge in 1964. Except for the temporary alienation of a few friends during those early days, I lost nothing. And I gained a host of dear friends by my efforts.

Having decided that trust and honesty are part of our joint heritage and destiny, I did not need the rules of professional responsibility to tell me I should be honest. Indeed, I must be. This is not intended to be boastful. How could I choose to be dishonest? Dishonesty is so foolish, so self-defeating. I am constantly mystified by the deliberate, or perhaps careless, harm people cause, to themselves as well as to others, by violations of trust and promise. Theft to avoid starvation is understandable. And I can see how some gangs or groups might see an advantage to its members in excluding nonmembers from those to whom trust is owed. I cannot, however, perceive any reason or justification for dishonest conduct by a person living in most sectors of our society. To write "cheater" or "liar" on one's forehead, to violate the trust of a spouse or child, to steal from a partner, to default on commitment to a profession or legal system—this simply makes no sense.

In our time we are partitioned into many parts, distinguishing ourselves by looks or location or mere happenstance. We compete and condemn, we claim and clamor, all the while winning only paltry prizes without perceiving how great is our losing. On that scene we need mediators, farsighted people who understand where we can go when we go together, and leaders whom we can trust. Trust, that is what we so desperately need: in our families, in our cities, in our profession, and in all public affairs.

Honesty works in practice, and in the practice of law. It is true that some clients aim for ends regardless of means, and want lawyers who will serve the same ends at the cost of ethics and honesty. Sometimes those clients can be shown that their ultimate ends are best served by honesty. I have had clients who would have violated rules or orders, and who would have distorted the truth, but they were willing to accept my explanation of how that conduct would eventually defeat their purposes. Whether the client realizes it to be true for him, the lawyer should know that her reputation for honesty and dependability is essential to her success in obtaining the clients she wants and in winning their causes with judges and jurors.

I am now a judge, and that position makes it easier to treat others with respect and with honesty. In any work, however, we are more likely to fail in meeting moral and ethical standards by marginal slippage rather than by sudden collapse. The public official loses her integrity bit by bit as she favors her supporters on more and more issues. The judge gives more attention to the briefs of one side, or is driven by a personal agenda, without realizing her breaches. On a multi-judge court in this time of deeply infecting partisanship, a group of judges may agree to protect capitalism or the social welfare by coordinating views and by voting together to control the court. Those judges may never recognize how this conduct eats at their integrity and cheapens the court. It undermines public respect for the law and its administration. To be sure, judges are entitled to their own values and philosophy of the law, and they are entitled to discuss the cases with each other individually, but they must study the views and contentions of all parties without always pursuing a preordained and fixed agenda. They have to look at the particular facts of each case; they must allow the possibility that they just might learn something more. And they should present their views to all other judges on the court on the strength of those views and not by force of a prearranged majority vote. Nor should they default on their responsibility by abdicating their decisions to staff or law clerks.

Manipulation and flattery, surrender to party preference or indolent default—these are the paths by which judges violate their obligations to their office and to the common good. Eventually these are losing ways, because they lead to the loss of respect from others as well as the loss of self-respect. The choice of paths should begin at the beginning, not by balancing immediate gains, but by deciding *who* we are and by what values and commitments we will live.

The reader may challenge my refusal to vote to stay the execution of capital punishment as the violation of my precept of the sacredness of life. Some judges have great difficulty with this. But the application of our faith and values to the decisions of life usually requires the exercise of judgment. The consequences of most decisions may serve some good while harming another. How often we see protest demonstrations intended to persuade the public on behalf of a meritorious cause but which do nothing more than alienate the public for that cause. As for my allowing the state to put a man to death, I must consider my authority and its limits. My office does not endow me with the decision on capital punishment; it only authorizes me to ensure compliance with the United States Constitution. If the state has satisfied the requirements of the Constitution, I have no legal authority to grant the stay of execution. I abuse my office and the law if I use them to impose my moral beliefs. And even if the punishment decision were properly mine, the consequences of allowing a person so fatally bent on mischief as to be a constant danger to fellow prisoners, would inform my moral judgment on capital punishment.

How consistent have I been with what I say is the foundation of my life? Have I failed to act accordingly? Of course, I have failed. I have pretended to know more than I know and to be more than I am. I have pretended to be better, smarter, and more righteous than others. Rising to my defense, however, I insist that faithfulness has outweighed pretensions. My regrets look back upon silly error and mistaken judgment more than upon serious violation. For the flesh of my make-up, I have done pretty well. Yes, just pretty well.

Has my belief helped or hurt my career? Well, I am a federal judge with my bills paid and a wonderful family. I have long ago gone beyond what the Peter Principle would allow me. I would have had none of this if people had not believed me. I could not have prevailed in my important lawsuits if I had not spoken with and from integrity. Had I not believed in the sacredness of human beings, I would have been deprived of the friendship and support of people in many walks of life. My ground has been firm enough to stand upon. My faith has served me well. I recommend it for others, without reservation.

Some may ask whether my faith interferes with my judicial application of the First Amendment guarantees of free exercise and against the establishment of religion. As I understand those guarantees and my judicial responsibility, I see no problem. Not only can I follow the law that allows every individual the freedom to believe and worship as she chooses, I strongly approve of that law. It is a law indispensable to a society of such diversity. From the beginning of this nation, and throughout the centuries since, most of the draftsmen and enforcers of that law have believed in it even though they, personally, were Christian.

Furthermore, I return to what I said about my judicial role in capital punishment cases. I act as a judge only under and within the law. I dare not go beyond the law when coming to a judicial judgment. All identities and alignments and beliefs of the participants, and all facts irrelevant to the issues that the law makes dispositive to the individual case, all of that must be disregarded. No one is entitled to sit as a judge if she is unable to restrict herself to the area wherein she is entitled to judge.

More than that, whether in my robes or not, I do not judge the eternal destiny of others. They have their beliefs and I have mine. I am not relativist, however. I am entitled to attempt to persuade others to adopt my faith, but I proceed with respect for them. I know where I stand, but there is a universe, seen and unseen, beyond my understanding. I shall struggle with my limitations to see the light more clearly, but for many of the answers I must wonder and wait.

Endnotes

1. United Methodist. Senior Judge, U.S. Court of Appeals for the Fifth Circuit. B.A. 1942, University of Texas; J.D. 1948, Harvard University; LL.M. 1982, University of Virginia.
2. Malcolm Muggeridge, *Chronicles of Wasted Time* 65 (1973).
3. Ephesians 1:10.

Javert or Bebb

Alan W. Perry[1]

> God knows, it's easy to be kind; the hard thing is to be just. If you
> had turned out to be what I suspected, Monsieur le maire, I should
> have shown you no kindness! I must treat myself as I would treat
> any other man.
> —Inspector Javert, in *Les Miserables*.[2]

> We all got secrets. I got them same as everybody else—things we
> feel bad about and wish hadn't ever happened. Hurtful things. Long
> ago things. We're all scared and lonesome, but most of the time we
> keep it hid. It's like every one of us has lost his way so bad we don't
> even know which way is home any more only we're ashamed to ask.
> You know what would happen if we would own up we're lost and
> ask? Why, what would happen is we'd find out home is each other.
> We'd find out home is Jesus that loves us lost or found or any
> whichway.
> —Leo Bebb, in *Love Feast*.[3]

A Preliminary Disclaimer

The invitation to contribute this essay suggested that I describe "how I
have reconciled my faith life with my professional life as a lawyer."

The only honest answer that I can give to that question is "Not very
well." While that truth is only too obvious to those who know me, still it is
embarrassing to admit, even to myself much less in a published essay, how
far my life, both professional and personal, falls short of the aspirations of
my faith.

On the other hand, if only those people who actually live up to their
vision of faith wrote these essays, there would be far fewer essays in this
volume. And those few that were written would probably discourage more
than inspire, since the words that have had an impact on my life have
invariably come from fellow strugglers. Sharing the stories of the "dangers,
toils and snares"[4] which we have encountered in our lives is what is
important, notwithstanding that we have far to go.

My Practice

Since the assignment calls for me to delineate how my faith makes a
difference in my professional life, which is for me the practice of law, some
brief description of my professional life is required.

Since leaving law school I have clerked for a federal judge, become a partner in a large law firm, helped start a small law firm that is beginning to become a big firm as measured by small town standards, gained some general idea of how to try at least some types of commercial litigation cases, learned to recognize when a case shouldn't be tried, cross-examined enough witnesses to gain some sense of which questions to ask and which questions not to ask, learned how to make a client reach an agreement on a business deal and when to advise a client not to make a deal, acquired a moderate degree of local reputation and respect, and honed my judgment, and had it honed by others, on the rough stone of experience. In the course of my practice I have won and lost cases, done some good work, and made some mistakes. In sum, the course of my law practice has been interesting, challenging, reasonably successful, and largely unexceptional.

In my practice I have tried to follow the law, the ethical rules governing professional conduct, and the informal rules of civility that still exist to some extent in our profession. But since obedience to those rules is required of all lawyers, regardless of their faith or lack thereof, I preclude discussion of those conventional and accepted standards. Instead, I have tried to identify what, if anything, in my practice of law arises distinctively out of my faith.

My Faith Perspective

The question posed by the invitation necessarily calls for me to speak from the perspective of my personal faith. Since I was brought up as a Christian and, more importantly, since I count myself a follower of Jesus Christ, the language that I use to describe my faith comes largely from that tradition. This does not mean that I believe the Christian tradition is the only valid way to experience God or to speak of faith; however, it provides the only language in which I can speak of faith more than abstractly.

My faith, at least the part that really makes a difference, cannot be described by merely enumerating the theological propositions in which I believe, though I once would have thought that affirming those propositions was the very essence of faith. Indeed, this essay would have presented a far different view of faith had it been written when I graduated from Harvard Law School in 1972. Then, I was sure that I had the right view of God, Jesus, doctrine, faith, and salvation, and I was also fairly confident that I knew how to apply them in my life. I fully expected that the same effort and talent that had produced academic success would produce spiritual success. Indeed, when I was younger and naively believed I knew much more about God and faith and myself than I do now, I considered whether God wanted me to use my legal training to write a book, which I imagined would be organized with the precision of a well-crafted examination answer or brief and would set out and elucidate the irrefutable axioms of the true faith of a logical Christianity. So little did I know about faith that I seriously thought such a book could somehow create faith by the sheer force of logical argument.[5]

Since then the journey of life has carried me, by a meandering course I only partly understand, to a much different understanding of faith. While I still count myself a serious, albeit self-taught, student of religion, scripture, and theology, I no longer understand faith as something that can be acquired by force of intellect, study, or will, though all of those are involved. Although I still accept some, but not all, of the established and traditional propositions of my religious tradition, I no longer see my beliefs *about* God as synonymous with my faith *in* God. And while I am now much more conscious of my doubts and uncertainties than I would ever have dared admit even to myself in 1972, paradoxically[6] I now have far more faith—of the real faith upon which I can rely in the dark—than I ever dared to hope.

As I have progressed through life with all of the concerns, anxieties, and terrors that are common to those of my profession, age, and family status, I have found that the faith that comforts me in the middle of dark nights has not come as doctrine or in the form of black letter law. It has come in hints, signs, and intuitions that just as easily could have been ignored or discounted, and it has come from the oddest sorts of places and persons and at the most unlikely times.

Since the faith that has made a difference in my life has come, not through acceptance of creed or dogma, but through the story that has made up my life, and through the stories that others have shared with me on the shared journey of faith, any truthful effort to describe my faith must come from telling my story.[7] I am encouraged to such a vanity as to believe that my own story might have some interest to someone else by Frederick Buechner, who has told his own story so truthfully and with so much courage that I list him as one of my personal saints.[8] Buechner states: "[I]t seems to me that no matter who you are, and no matter how eloquent or otherwise, if you tell your own story with sufficient candor and concreteness, it will be an interesting and in some sense a universal story."[9]

Thus, even though the writing of this essay has become so personal as to create embarrassment and second thoughts about its publication in so public and secular a forum, I submit it with the hope that Buechner is correct and that there may be some meaning in my story for others.

Where My Faith Started

Marcus Borg[10] restates an obvious point. We all know it, but by very definition we are all blind to the phenomena he describes: *all of us look at faith through the lens that our faith history has provided to us.*

Borg suggests that one way to begin to understand and to correct for any distortion created by those lenses of our past is to examine our faith journey by remembering our earliest childhood memories. That is where I begin.

I grew up in the county seat First Baptist Church in Philadelphia, Mississippi. Events associated with that church[11] make up a large part of my childhood memories, which is not surprising since regular attendance at church services on Sunday morning and Sunday night, Sunday School, Baptist Training Union, and Wednesday night prayer meeting took up a lot of time. That church, though it disapproved of formal written creeds, had its own beliefs, traditions, customs, and assumptions that were as strict, rigid, and unchangeable as the creeds, dogmas, and hierarchies of other ecclesiastical bodies. Like other churches, some of that church's theology and practice was good and nurtured the congregation. Other parts of its tradition continued, not because of any real benefit to the adherents, but because both congregation and clergy were reluctant to question established familiar frameworks. That church had its share of saints, who were mostly unrecognized by me at the time. And, as I now know, it had its share of scandals of the type that still attract notice in the church, though at the time they went virtually unrecognized by me because of a general tacit understanding that such things simply were better not discussed, and certainly not with children. In sum, I acquired my first views of God in a church that was "typical"—no worse than most and perhaps better than many places where people worshipped.

Borg suggests that many and maybe most of us who grew up in such places—irrespective of differences between the Christian denominations or churches of our childhoods—have a common view, that is the lenses through which we view faith are more similar than we might at first suppose. He suggests that our lenses cause us to view faith through an overlay of two different, related, and somewhat contradictory, images of Jesus and salvation—the images of faith as being an issue of (1) right belief and/or (2) right action.

Though my childhood was separated from Borg's by a few years and the Mason-Dixon Line, and though our childhood churches were separated by centuries of differences in culture and tradition, Marcus Borg's description of his experiences growing up in a Lutheran church in Minnesota rings true to my experience. As Borg suggests, I too viewed faith through a lens shaped by the same images:

1. The first image that I was given by my childhood church was that salvation is dependent on believing the right thing. Borg calls that the *fideistic* image of Jesus, where faith is understood to be believing certain propositions *about* Jesus.[12] At least as I then perceived it, the church of my childhood was dominated by this view. That religious tradition saw and in large part still sees the goal of faith as achieving salvation by believing the right things about God, Jesus, and scripture. The acceptance of this saving belief is marked by a public profession of belief in Jesus Christ, followed by adult baptism.[13] The goal of the church was to reach those who were "lost" because they either did not know or refused to believe the theological propositions requisite to being "saved." Most sermons, even those on Sunday nights when most of those in attendance were long time active church members and presumably had been "saved" for years, were not

directed at ministering to the already "saved"; rather the typical sermon was a "conversion" sermon designed to encourage the "lost" to "accept Jesus as Savior."[14] This model of faith—that salvation (understood primarily as "going to Heaven") was dependent on intellectual acceptance of certain propositions about Jesus—dominated my view of faith until I was well into adulthood.

2. The second image of faith that absorbed as I grew up in the church was what Borg calls *moralistic*—the image that salvation is accomplished by doing the right thing. Although Baptists are, in theory at least, strongly supportive of Luther's declaration that we are saved by faith alone—*sola fide*—we also had a real and sometimes overtly expressed sense that "real" faith would necessarily produce good works. Works were understood to include the avoidance of sin—at least those sins on which the church and the community had fixed its attention. These were chiefly the sexual sins and the other "sins of the flesh." It was generally understood that those who regularly engaged in such actions probably were "lost."[15] While I was exposed to enough theology to intellectually recognize the fallacy of accepting a doctrine of salvation by works, my claim to "salvation by grace" had at least a subtle emotional underpinning that, to my own eyes and in the eyes of the community, I was not the worst of sinners.

I suspect that Borg is right in suggesting that these two views of faith—that faith means believing right and acting right—cut across most Christian denominational lines in varying permutations. But in any event some mixture of these two images provided my perspective of faith from childhood, through college, law school, and young adulthood. While I understood that salvation was by grace, at some level I also believed that grace was the reward for right belief and right action.

How My Faith Has Changed

Change in matters of faith occurs both slowly and in dramatic events.

I can only suggest, for lack of space, the nature of the gradual growth that started when I entered adulthood and began to acknowledge the doubt and ambiguity that I had long resisted and denied. Suffice it to say that I had the good fortune (providence) to find myself in a church with John Claypool, one of the best preachers ever produced by the Baptists.[16] John Claypool shared the story of his own struggle with faith in a way that caused me to listen rather than to argue, and that found me open rather than closed to understand how God spoke to people in ways that were different than what I had always believed them to be. I began to discover that God was bigger, more complex, and more clouded in mystery than the propositions about God that I had believed. I began to realize that logic would carry me only so far in proving God, and that the actual experience of God is far more credible in times of crisis than in the study of abstract doctrines drawn from supposedly inerrant scriptures. In short, I began, hesitantly and in fits and starts, to experience the God of scripture—rather than to believe in God because of scripture.

This process of gradual growth was already well along—the lens I was using had developed cracks—when an event occurred that caused a complete shattering of the lens through which I viewed faith. The easiest way to tell my own story of conversion to a different view of faith is to begin by quickly recalling the familiar parable of the Prodigal Son. Of course, the story[17] is so well known that I need only summarize.

It is a classic drama with three main characters, a father and two sons. It begins with the demand of the younger son that his father anticipate his own death by delivering to the younger son a share of the father's wealth. The son promptly wasted it all, on high living and loose women, in a far-off country. These actions, coupled with taking care of religiously unclean pigs for a gentile, made him an outcast from the community of his family. Finally the younger brother came to himself. He carefully rehearsed his confession and plea—"treat me as one of your hired servants"—and started home. As the parable presents it, the son never figured on a full pardon; he hoped merely for a grudging acceptance of his return as a hired hand.

But even as the prodigal approached, the father came running and threw his arms around his son's neck. Before the son could get halfway through the opening statement he had been practicing all the way home, the father told the servants that the prodigal would be treated as a son, furnishing him a robe, a ring, and sandals as symbols of his status. Then the father said: "Let's have a party; kill the fatted calf, because this son of mine was dead and has come back to life; he was lost and now is found." And they began to celebrate.

The older brother heard the party going on, but "he was angry and he refused to go in." When the father went out and entreated the older son to come in, the older brother retorted: "All these years I have slaved for you. I never disobeyed any of your orders; yet you never once provided me with a kid goat so I could celebrate with my friends. But when this son of yours shows up, the one who has squandered your estate with prostitutes—for him you slaughter the fat calf."

But the father said to him, "My child, you are always at my side. But we just had to celebrate and rejoice, because this brother of yours was dead, and has come back to life; he was lost, and now is found."

The parable ends there. We don't know what the older son did, or whether he ever joined the party.[18]

I suspect that this omission of the older brother's decision by Jesus, the master storyteller, was not accidental and was intended to raise questions and thus prompt some response from the hearer.[19] But if so, I was deaf and blind for years to the question raised by this silence. I filtered this parable through my moralistic lens, and saw it as a lesson for right living—as a condemnation of filial disrespect, loose living, and waste. If I thought about the older brother at all, it was wholly without seeing in him any reflection of myself.

I now realize that parts of me were and still are like the older brother. Not completely and not obviously, since decent manners and an adequate degree of that gracious indifference masquerading as tolerance usually enabled me to avoid the overt condemnation of others. But I was like the older brother in large part, by believing that, even if I wasn't perfect, I was still "better than most." Like Victor Hugo's Inspector Javert, I expected myself and others to do what was right, and I neither gave nor expected forgiveness for failure to follow the conventional righteousness of my tradition. And like Javert, my condemnation of the failures of others led to and supported my inability to see or acknowledge my own mistakes.

My view of faith changed when I was forced by circumstances to lose the illusion that I was one who believed the right things and did the right things. To use a religious word that makes me cringe because it sounds so old-fashioned and out of place in a legal essay, I realized that I too had sinned.[20]

Like everyone else, I had of course sinned before, many, many times. But I always had managed somehow, through the alchemy of denial, to persuade myself that I was really not that bad, that everyone messes up, and that it wasn't really that big a deal. All of these self-justifying explanations enabled me to hide from the real truth behind the facade that I was somehow better than "real" sinners. After all, I was a pillar of the church, a successful lawyer, and generally a "good guy."

But finally events created a situation where I could not deny, rationalize, or ignore what I knew was wrong. I finally had to accept the fact that I was not nearly as righteous as I had always believed. In losing the illusion of my own near-sanctity, I came to understand the truth that I was not merely an honorary sinner. I realized that I was no better, and maybe in some respects worse, than many of the people I had always looked down on as being beneath me. In sum, my self-created and self-deceptive facade of being a successful, righteous person was totally destroyed.

After this self-made image of myself had been shattered, I had to pick up the pieces and try to discern who I really was. Putting the pieces back together didn't mean just putting them back where they had been; that would have been pretending nothing had ever happened. Either I would remain shattered or be transformed into something new.[21] I felt very far from God.

But, in that peculiar type of reversal that is characteristic of things of the spirit where evil can and often does lead to good,[22] this experience in my life presented the opportunity for real faith.

First, in trying to find some kind of light in the darkness that surrounded me, I experienced real prayer. I had always said "prayers" of a more or less petitionary nature. But in this time of openness I learned something I had never learned when I had felt more self-sufficient. I learned that prayer involves more listening than talking.

The other gift that I found in this experience was that I started living, at least some of the time, by grace rather than in reliance on my own self-perceived merit. Out of the dark silence that at first seemed to be spiritual death and the total absence of God, I heard for the first time—in the way that one hears the things of God, in the heart—the Good News of unconditional love.

My Faith and My Practice

Thus, my faith is the product of my own life experience that grace precedes, rather than follows, right belief or right action. I have come to believe, with Borg, that the message of the story of Jesus is that compassion, not right action or right belief, is the defining quality of the Kingdom of God.[23] The Good News of this gospel is that, by grace, we do not get what we deserve.

Of course, the primacy of grace over belief or works was no stranger to the best expressions of the faith community of my childhood.[24] But I had failed to make this truly part of my own faith, since grace, at least in my mind, had been overlaid with the conventional emphasis on correct belief and actions. Thus, the marvel of my journey of faith is not how far I have gone, but rather that I found my true self so close to where I began and then discovering that place to appear so different viewed through an altered lens. But after all, this is the human experience:

> *We shall not cease from exploration*
> *And the end of all our exploring*
> *Will be to arrive where we started*
> *And know the place for the first time.*[25]

There is more Good News, however, that frightens and angers some of the people (including me) most of the time, and most of the people at least some of the time.[26] The Good News that scares us is that the people we justifiably are afraid of, are angry with, or that we hate don't get what they deserve either. God's love is not limited to the righteous or even the near-righteous.

Thus, the Good News carries with it the implication that (speaking not altogether figuratively) scares the Devil out of me, which is that I am also called to love the people that God loves, and not just some of them. And this view of faith is difficult to reconcile with the life, including the professional life, that I actually live.

Does God really love all of the people that we justifiably fear and hate—even the advocate of ethnic cleansing, the murderer, the rogue cop, the lazy or crooked judge, the witness who lied, the lawyer who broke his agreement or helped conceal evidence? I am persuaded, not so much by logic as by experience, that God does love all of them, just like Jesus loved the sinners and harlots.[27]

Where does God draw the line? When does He give up on people? I don't know. But if He does draw lines, I am sure He doesn't give up on people until long after I have written them off, that He uses insights and knowledge that are far beyond my capacity, that He forgives far more than seventy-seven or even seven times seventy times, and that, if He finally judges, He judges with a love and mercy that those of this world never have and never will fully understand. And that probably means that I have no business attempting to make such decisions in the first place.

Where then are the limits of our own love toward those we hate and fear? I don't know. How are we to live out such a vision of love in our lives? I don't know. I wouldn't be telling the truth if I claimed I easily forgive people who have hurt or wronged me. For example, I certainly don't know how or even if I could forgive somebody who hurt one of my children.

But I find a suggestion about how I should act in two recent news stories reporting the different reactions of two mothers who had lost children to senseless acts of criminal violence. One of the mothers reacted by seeking vengeance, screaming at the sentencing of the killer that she hoped he burned in Hell. The other mother reacted by beginning a prison ministry of reconciliation and redemption.

I don't honestly know how I would react in such circumstances. I am afraid I would be seeking vengeance. But it seems to me, at least when I am most in touch with the best that God inspires in me, that the mother who sought to redeem, not to destroy, is doing the work of the Kingdom. And at the same time she is doing the work that is most likely to preserve and to redeem her from the corrosive effect of deep-seated hate.

While I have never faced such a personal test, I regularly fail many other, and far easier, challenges almost on a daily basis. My family, my partners and those with whom I work are only too aware of my anger, impatience, and self-centeredness. They know that I am only too quick to judge and condemn those who break laws, those who ignore court rules, and even those who do nothing wrong except disagree with me or interfere with what I want. Those who know me well would not be convinced by any argument that my professional or personal life mirrors or even greatly resembles the spiritual vision that I have described for myself.

So I come to the reluctant but unavoidable conclusion that my professional and personal life only occasionally and dimly reflects the spiritual light that I sometimes see. But I am not without hope.

Because some of the time I can remember that the lawyer on the other side is also a hurting person who gets angry and makes mistakes, just like me. And while I may be obliged to take the action necessary to make the legal system work in such circumstances, I at least occasionally am able to do so thoughtfully and deliberately, tempering what I at one time would have considered an entitled and righteous anger.[28]

Though I still find myself judging and condemning, sometimes I come to my true self and remember the grace I have experienced. Then I can remember that the person who has embezzled from my client has not been written off by God, and I find myself able to pray for that man and his family, as I hope they pray for me.

Sometimes, by remembering that litigated disputes involve not only issues of fact and law but also frightened, hurting and fallible people, I can see beyond the technical law—which tends to focus on finding one side right and the other wrong and evaluating only legally recognized rights, duties, and obligations—and recognize that the real truth of the matter may lie somewhere in between and beyond the letter of the law.[29]

In sum, I am beginning to learn to forgive others and myself. What little I have learned about forgiveness has for the most part come from other people, and not from doctrine or theory. I have learned forgiveness from watching other people forgive others when forgiveness was neither easy nor cheap. My family and those who work with me have made forgiveness a living reality by forgiving me on more occasions than I can or would enumerate.

I also learned about forgiveness while representing a client who happened to be a lawyer. All of the parties were trying to find a way out of a disappointing business deal which involved very substantial sums of money. My lawyer/client gave me clear instructions that his sincere concern for another co-venturer would not end merely because that person was acting selfishly and unfairly. That client taught me that, for those of real faith, it actually is possible to turn the other cheek, even in circumstances where our profession teaches us that "hardball" is the rule.

Hopefully, though I admit that signs of progress are slow to appear, I will be given enough grace to respond with at least some measure of such compassion and forgiveness in similar circumstances.

I have found that forgiveness of this type—forgiveness when it is not easy—grows out of a living faith that I have to rediscover and live from day to day, rather than from faith that is stored up or saved.[30] When I am most aware of the presence of God in my life, I can give up the need to be perfect and realize that I had far rather live with many mistakes and the gifts of compassion and forgiveness, like Bebb—felon, fraud, and sinner that he was—than be as righteous and honorable, and as unforgiving of myself and others, as was Inspector Javert.

I wish I could say that I always, or even most always, practiced law as if my faith were a reality. I wish I could always, or even mostly, find compassion instead of anger. But faith and compassion intervene in my life often enough for me to say that God remains at work within me, though I remain very much a work in progress.

So, in spite of my many and almost constant failures, my experience of grace makes me able to join in the old slaves' prayer with which Martin Luther King, Jr. used to end many of his talks:

> *O God, I ain't what I ought to be,*
> *and I ain't what I'm gonna be,*
> *but by your grace,*
> *I ain't what I used to be.*[31]

And I know that, even though I fall far short of reconciling and living my faith in my law practice, Jesus is still home for all of us, "lost or found or any whichway."

Endnotes

1. Episcopalian and Southern Baptist. Member, Foreman, Perry, Watkins & Krutz PLLC, Jackson, Mississippi. B.B.A. 1969, University of Mississippi; J.D. 1972, Harvard University.
2. Inspector Javert speaking in Victor Hugo, *Les Miserables* 200 (Norman Denny trans., Penguin Books 1982).
3. Words of The Reverend Leo Bebb, convicted flasher, operator of a mail order ordination mill, and spiritual leader of the Church of Holy Love, Inc., from Frederick Buechner's novel, *Love Feast*, one of four books making up *The Book of Bebb* 306–7 (Atheneum 1979).
4. From the hymn Amazing Grace, written by John Newton, a former slave trader.
5. I have since realized that, so far as we can tell, Jesus was singularly uninterested in challenges to debate the legal talent of the day on theoretical terms.

    An example is the discussion leading up to the parable of the Good Samaritan, which itself begins with a question from a lawyer: "What must I do to inherit eternal life?" Jesus responded, not with an answer but with another question and a story. Luke 10:25–35.

    Why didn't Jesus answer with the clarity of a brief? Perhaps he didn't trust the lawyer. Or perhaps he was acting out of the truth that most of us have learned over the years, that people are resistant to hearing anything that contradicts their long-held conventional wisdom and that a story that invites them to see things from a different perspective may be the only way that they can hear.
6. Now I realize that everything really important about faith is paradoxical.
7. The editors apparently anticipated such a personal response to the invitation, since they advised that the essays "are expected to be personal narratives, exercises in story-telling."
8. Frederick Buechner, The Sacred Journey (1982); *Now and Then* (1983); and *Telling Secrets* (1991).

    In addition to Buechner, I would also list among my personal saints John Claypool and Marcus Borg, some of whose books are cited in this essay, as well as Roger Paynter, Pastor of Northminster Baptist Church in Jackson, Mississippi, and Vester Hughes, a lawyer in Dallas, Texas.

    I have talked with Frederick Buechner and Marcus Borg only briefly at conferences; their ministry has come to me largely through their books.

John Claypool, Roger Paynter, and Vester Hughes are my friends, and their ministry has come in many ways. I am sure that all of these will understand the sense in which I use the word saint. (For what it is worth, I think Leo Bebb is a saint too.).

I trust that they will accept my apology if I have so much—if not so well—assimilated their work that any part of what they have so eloquently said has inadvertently found its way into this essay without proper attribution. But, as John Claypool has said somewhere—or for all I know quoted from somebody else—only God is original.

9. Buechner, *Now and Then, supra* note 8, at 2–3.
10. Borg's works have immeasurably enriched my life of faith since I discovered them last year. He is the author of several books, including *Meeting Jesus Again for the First Time* (1994).

Borg is also a member of the Jesus Seminar, a collection of scholars from a wide array of religious traditions and academic institutions. The Seminar is best known for its color coded rendition of the sayings of Jesus, with various colors representing the collective judgment of the scholars making up the Seminar as to the degree of historical accuracy of the sayings recorded in the Gospels. Robert W. Funk et al., *The Five Gospels* (1993).

At one time my faith would have been shocked by Borg's suggestions that sayings attributed to Jesus in the Bible may actually have been the statements of the early church. See Borg, *supra* note 10, at 20–21. And out of fear of destruction of my belief system which was grounded on the "factual" veracity of the Bible, I would have found Borg's work anti-faith. Now, with a different ground for my faith, I have found Borg's works a great spiritual gift helping me to focus more clearly on Jesus' concern for the outcast.

11. I became an Episcopalian in 1992. The story of the events that led to that change of church membership is not part of this essay. But because some may see my recollections of the church I grew up in some forty years ago as a criticism of my birth denomination, I add the following notes:

First, the Baptist denomination is composed of autonomous congregations with an extremely wide range of theology, liturgy, and practice, which have historically been bound together in large part by their loyalty to the principle of exercising that autonomy. Nothing annoys me more than criticism of "Baptists" by persons who assume that their stereotypes are typical of all Baptists.

Second, Baptists, like other religious groups, have changed a great deal since I was a child in the First Baptist Church of Philadelphia. Even if my memories of that church of that day are accurate and fairly stated, they certainly are not intended to describe that or any other Baptist church of today.

Third, churches of any denomination are not now, and have never been, perfect. Moving from denomination to denomination has at least one advantage—the lens through which you see church is altered enough that you can see more clearly that all churches are man-made and very imperfect.

Fourth, many Baptist ideas, such as separation of church and state, the soul competency of all believers to interpret scripture, and the importance of the laity have influenced the church as a whole and, in my view, have enriched us all. Most of the faith that I have today was created while I was a Baptist, particularly at Northminster Baptist Church in Jackson, Mississippi. Much of what nurtures me today came from the Baptists. I will always consider myself at least still part Baptist.

12. Textual Biblical support for such a belief-based "faith" is not hard to find. "Believe in the Lord Jesus, and you will be saved." Acts 16:31.

13. The more accurate term is "believer's baptism," as contrasted to baptism of infants incapable of making the required personal intellectual assent to Jesus. The line is fuzzy. I was baptized at the age of five. My parents tell me I went forward to join the church much to their surprise and that I was able to articulate what I was doing. I do not recall.

14. Baptist emphasis on a one-time conversion experience derives in large part from the traditional Baptist theological doctrine of "once saved, always saved."

15. While my memory may be at fault, I recall little or no attention focused on the sins such as pride, greed, and anger.

    As might be expected, there was no condemnation or even discussion of the racial attitudes of the day, which is a chilling reminder for those of us who grew up in that culture that institutional and social evil often is deemed acceptable by the church.

16. John Claypool, then Pastor of Northminster Baptist Church in Jackson, Mississippi, is now rector of St. Luke's Episcopal Church, in Birmingham, Alabama.

17. Luke 15:11–32.

18. Madeleine L'Engle, in *The Rock That Is Higher* 87–88 (1993), suggests that one possible ending to the parable would have the older brother leaving home in anger and thereafter making his fortune in the city by skill and hard work, only to realize that his material success had left him lonely and empty. When the older son returned home he would find his father, though old and tired, still there waiting to welcome him home, just as the father had welcomed home the prodigal son.

19. The view that the omission is intended to provoke a response is supported by the definition of parable offered by C. H. Dodd:

    At its simplest the parable is a metaphor or simile drawn from nature or common life, arresting the hearer by its vividness or strangeness, *and leaving the mind in sufficient doubt about its precise application to tease it into active thought*.
    John R. Donahue, *The Gospel in Parable* 5 (1988) (citing C. H. Dodd, *The Parables of the Kingdom* 5 (1961)) (emphasis added).

20. Precisely what happened in my life is really not important. If, as Buechner suggests, there is indeed a universality to our stories, your own experiences will cause you to recognize any truth in what I am trying to say.

21. Victor Hugo's Javert, unable to reconcile his own humanity with his code of righteousness, "was not so much transformed as a victim" of this intrusion of God into his soul. Hugo, *supra* note 1, at 1107.

22. Goethe suggests the inherent possibility of such a reversal in evil when Mephistopheles describe himself as "[a] portion of that power which always works for Evil and effects the Good." Johann Wolfgang von Goethe, *Faust* (Peter Salm trans., Bantam Books 1962).

23. Borg, *supra* note 10, at 136.

24. Most faith communities include some members who have struggled to make the faith their own and others who assume the faith is simply a set of beliefs to which a dose of "common sense" should be added. No community stands up well if judged by the conventional wisdom expressed by those in the latter category. It is a tragedy that the views ascribed by many Christians to those who differ with them in the particulars of faith or religious polity usually are derived from such expressions and often are mere caricatures even of them.

25. T. S. Eliot, "Little Gidding," in *Four Quartets* 29 (1968).

26. Lee Smith captures our intractable fear that this expansive reading of grace is far too good to be true in the words of her eponymous Grace in the novel *Saving Grace*:

> Travis Word was the first preacher I ever ran into that placed works above grace in order of importance. As a person even then searching for hard ground in a world of shifting sands, I liked this. I was real glad to hear it. For privately I had always questioned Daddy's belief that a person could just go out and do whatsoever they damn well pleased, and then repent and get forgiven for it, over and over again. In my own mind this made God out to be too easy, a pushover. . . . Travis Word's idea of the true nature of God came closer to my own image of Him as a great rock, eternal and unchanging. Even though I did not believe I was saved at that time, I did believe in Him, and I also felt that if He was worth His salt, He'd have no place prepared in Heaven for the likes of me.

Lee Smith, *Saving Grace* 164–65 (1995).

27. The scriptural basis for this understanding of the centrality of compassion in the message of Jesus is insightfully presented by Borg in *Meeting Jesus, supra* note 10, at 46.

28. By hindsight I know that in many circumstances my anger has been far from righteous, and by experience I have learned that a desire to punish is often neither helpful to my clients nor conducive to maintaining the integrity of the judicial system.

29. When I can have compassion enough to see the case from the emotional perspective of the adversary and am able to help my client see it from that perspective, it has usually resulted in a better resolution for my client and all others concerned. Among other things, this type of view will often help avoid the unpleasant surprise that can be created when a court or jury decides to do justice, even if it means stretching the letter of the law.

30. When I am caught up in my own professional self-sufficiency, little progress is made and more often I regress. But I have found by experience that God can accomplish at least a little in me and through me when I take the time to pray and meditate on a daily basis.

31. Quoted by John Claypool in *Stories Jesus Still Tells: The Parables* 164 (1993).

Part III.
REFLECTIONS

Reflections on the Contents of the Lawyer's Work: Three Models of Spirituality—and Our Struggle with Them

Charles R. DiSalvo[1] and William L. Droel[2]

Growing up Catholic in the fifties and sixties, as we both did, meant growing up with an easy-to-read road map to holiness, handed to us by our Church. The map routed us through familiar spiritual pieties and disciplines ranging from daily prayer to the sacraments. The map took us deep into the interior life and away from the world. At its core the map was based on a monastic model—that is, it assumed its user had unlimited time, no spouse, no children, and no job. It was only natural, therefore, that the prevailing orthodoxy was that, to be truly holy, one ought to seek the life of religious orders and become either a celibate priest, brother, or nun.

American Catholics of our age took the route outlined in the map, joining seminaries and convents in great numbers. We both personally accepted the official church recommendation and entered the seminary in 1962. But by 1971, in the wake of the Second Vatican Council, we, as well as all eighty-eight of our seminary classmates and thousands of other young Catholic men, had left the seminary and gone our separate ways.

Our departure left us at the side of the road. If we were to find salvation, we would have to do it without a map, for there were no maps to help lay people find holiness while they worked in the world. We would have to forge our own way. Bill served as a community organizer before becoming a free lance writer, a lay campus minister, and a philosophy instructor. Charlie worked as a poverty lawyer in Appalachia before entering his current employment as a law professor. While each of us took great satisfaction from our work, we lacked the sure sense of wholeness and completion we had when we were in the seminary. We *believed* we were on paths to holiness, but we lacked a clear and precise understanding of how work in the world related to our identity as Catholic Christians. What did our faith have to do with our work?

We quickly learned that this was a question that plagued many of our fellow Catholics. Indeed, we were soon swept up into a Chicago-based organization, the National Center for the Laity, whose sole purpose is to promote and explore the idea that all lay Christians have vocations in and to the world. We became active members of the Center's Board of Directors, with Bill editing its newsletter and Charlie serving as its counsel. Eventually Bill wrote and edited *The Spirituality of Work*, a series of booklet-length essays under the Center's auspices, on the "lay vocations" held by nurses, teachers, homemakers, business people, and others. When it came time to tackle the subject of lawyers, Bill asked Charlie to collaborate with him.

As we volleyed drafts back and forth, we realized that the two of us had two very different ideas about how to encourage lawyers to connect their faith and their work. Bill's goal was to open a dialogue among lawyers, bringing as many lawyers as possible into the debate about what makes a lawyer's work holy. Charlie had his own specific idea of lawyerly spirituality and wanted to argue for it in the booklet. Eventually we agreed that the booklet would offer the reader three different models of lawyer spirituality without proselytizing for one over the others. The booklet was published and soon thereafter was given a favorable review in *The New York Times*, to our pleasant surprise.[3] A deluge of requests for the booklet poured in to the National Center for the Laity.

We continue to debate the wisdom of our different paths. This essay permits us to grapple with our differences in the hope that doing so will provoke others to give some hard thought to the spiritual nature of the lawyer's work. We welcome the opportunity here to present our on-going argument.

But, first, allow us to review the models we have devised for understanding how a lawyer's life might be a spiritual life.

Three Models of Lawyer Spirituality

We have interviewed scores of lawyers about their understanding of the relationship between their work and their faith.[4] Based on what we learned from them and based upon our own theorizing, we propose three different ways to understand the spiritual content of the lawyer's work. We put forth these understandings as answers to the question *"Who is your employer?"*

We do not advance the typical answers to the question—"the firm," "the attorney general," "my company." Being interested in the spirituality of the lawyer's work, we ask this question from an entirely different angle, as evidenced by these alternative answers:

"The client is my employer."

"God is my employer."

"I am my employer."

Model One: "The client is my employer"

Lawyers who give this answer mean that they play a small part in a larger system—an imperfect system certainly, but one to which there is no better alternative and thus one that, on the whole, they judge to be good.

"The lawyer's relationship to justice resembles the piano tuner's relationship to a concert," explains criminal defense attorney William Raleigh. "The tuner neither composes the music nor interprets it. The tuner merely keeps the machine running. As a lawyer, I am paid to defend people. It is not for me to decide if the person is guilty or innocent. The judge or the jury must make that decision. The jury can best make that decision if I give my client the best legal advice and representation possible. The other attorney best helps the jury and serves justice by trying to prove that my client is guilty. This is the way the system is set up. I am moral by trying to do the best possible job that I can. The system will take care of justice in the long run."

This explanation, which many lawyers apply with equal force to civil as well as criminal practice, is sometimes lost on the general public. How can lawyers represent people with whom they don't agree? Much worse, how can they defend someone who they know is criminally guilty or civilly liable?

"Some people wonder how lawyers can defend the rights of a neo-Nazi or a Mafioso," says Donna Krier Ioppolo of the College of Law at DePaul University. "Yet the protection of one person's rights strengthens the rights of all of us." This same understanding of the lawyer's role can be applied to the civil lawyer who represents anyone who seeks his or her services: justice is an objective good that can be realized when all parties are given their day in court. One of the most elegant expositions of this proposition occurs in Robert Bolt's play about Thomas More's resistance to the demands of King Henry VIII to renounce Rome in favor of Henry's new Church of England. In *A Man for All Seasons*, More, a lawyer who would later be canonized, takes up this argument with Roper, his son-in-law, who would have More cast aside his allegiance to the law in favor of More's self-interest:

> Roper: So you'd give the devil the benefit of the law!
> More: Yes. What would you do? Cut a great road through the law to get after the devil?
> Roper: I'd cut down every law in England to do that!
> More: Oh? And when the last law was down, and the devil turned round on you—where would you hide, Roper, the laws all being flat? This country's planted thick with laws from coast to coast—man's laws, not God's—and if you cut them down—and you're just the man to do it—do you really think you could stand upright in the winds that would blow then? Yes, I'd give the devil the benefit of the law, for my own safety's sake.[5]

As Robert Bolt's More implies, many lawyers believe that the legal system is a complex, finely tuned, deliberately designed machine that produces justice by applying objectively fair rules to all parties. As a consequence of this theory, individual lawyers understand that they serve the greater good by staying within their respective roles. It is not a breach of their morality to represent civil or criminal clients whose positions or actions, in other settings, would violate their Christian beliefs.

"As a Christian and a lawyer I try to ensure that my clients get the respect they deserve as full human persons," says attorney and nun Sr. Catherine Ryan. "Young people sometimes run afoul of the law. Crime is wrong. Yet criminals still need protection. My job is to be there for that person, even if the person is guilty. This is my ministry."

"I would represent someone who is guilty," says another respondent. "Our Constitutional rights are maintained only through the vigorous representation of criminal defendants by lawyers. That is how we keep the system honest."

"I am being asked to represent a person and force the system to fulfill its motto: Innocent until proven guilty," says lawyer Lawrence Suffredin. "My oath of office is to uphold the Constitution, which says that everyone with certain limits has a right to a vigorous defense. The limit is not to perjure testimony."

Lawyers who say, "the client is my employer," do not see themselves as amoral "hired guns," catering to the whims of each client. They understand that illegal, uncivil, or immoral tactics do not serve the cause of justice, nor the client's best long-term interest. "I've been known to fire clients," says Gwendolyn Moreland, who became an attorney after a long career as a social worker. "I reach a point where the client is making certain demands and I know that we cannot operate in that fashion."

"There is a fundamental tension in the profession," explains William Raleigh. "It is zealously protecting your client while acknowledging your duty to the judicial system. The ability to tolerate and balance this tension differentiates the average lawyer from the exceptional lawyer. An exceptional lawyer has the fortitude and self-confidence to convince a client not to misuse the system."

Still, the lawyer who answers, "the client is my employer," has made a positive moral judgment about the system. The spirituality of work thus requires a lawyer with this perspective to do the best job possible through the competencies expected of a lawyer: thorough research and mastery of the law, thorough investigation of the facts, careful and persuasive writing, meticulous preparation for court appearances, etc. This lawyer's normal, day-to-day work does not have to somehow be "additionally spiritualized." His or her competency within the legal system is the basic element of the lawyer's spirituality of work.

Model Two: "God is my employer"

A small number of lawyers seek a closer identity between the causes and people they represent and their religious beliefs. For example, such lawyers might work for a legal aid society, believing that helping the poor obtain food stamps or housing is a way of fulfilling the Christian corporal works of mercy. Similarly, other lawyers might work in projects to improve prison conditions on the theory that this is the direct legal equivalent of a Christian work of mercy. Other lawyers might do nothing but civil rights work for racial minorities or for women, believing that Christian social teaching demands that they defend the dignity of each person. Still others might focus entirely on process and might try to mediate every dispute, for example, because they believe alternatives to litigation are more harmonious with the message of the Gospel.

While increasingly greater numbers of lawyers, regardless of their areas of practice, perform some pro bono work, lawyers who answer "God is my employer," do this type of work exclusively and think of their work as nearly a literal response to the gospel. Because they do not tolerate much moral ambiguity between the causes they represent and their personal beliefs, these lawyers usually have serious reservations about the legal system itself and the assumptions upon which the system rests. One of those assumptions is fairness—that the parties to a dispute will be able to marshall equal resources and talent on their behalf. "In fact, this assumption is seriously flawed," says one lawyer who practices in Appalachia. "For a variety of reasons, not the least of which is the uneven distribution of wealth in this country, the system produces lousy results."

"There might generally be equal representation in areas of family law or in mergers," says Thomas Geoghegan, a noted labor lawyer and the author of *Which Side Are You On?*[6] "But there are vast areas of the law where rich people use the system to protect themselves. Thus the rules are really stacked against certain kinds of outcomes. For example, when I represent participants in pension fund suits against corporations I encounter enormous legal hurdles. There are big, powerful law firms who use those hurdles to achieve ends that are not right, not good. Morally, I could not be representing the other side in such cases. The system is quite often unfair to the poor and to working people."

Or take the example of a landlord-tenant contest between a small shopkeeper renting space in a large complex owned by a corporate agency. The shopkeeper probably will be represented by a solo practitioner of limited resources who is hired for the occasion. The corporation, by contrast, will have in-house counsel or be represented on retainer by a large law firm with all the resources and prestige of a large firm. Does the tenant, represented by an over-worked attorney with a small support staff, get the same quality of representation as the landlord who is represented by a well-paid, well-supported staff of attorneys, paralegals, and investigators? The answer usually—though certainly not always—is no. There are always solo practitioners who can out-hustle any large law firm. But such people are exceptional.

On the criminal side, many lawyers live in jurisdictions where the government fails to adequately fund appointed counsel for indigent defendants. Even where funding is available, it often comes so slowly and in such small amounts as to guarantee that only novice lawyers, trying to build their practices, will put their names on the list for court appointments. These lawyers are then faced by career prosecutors with staff and investigative resources that easily out-match those of the novice. In addition, the appointed counsel in many jurisdictions usually have little or no government money to secure capable expert witnesses. The prosecution, meanwhile, usually has a stable of highly skilled expert witnesses of every sort and description.

"Those who can afford an expensive trial attorney will probably get better quality representation," says one criminal defense attorney. "This is a generalization, of course. But it is also wrong. Sometimes those who need representation the most are the poor or the middle class."

"The question is whether in real life the advocacy system fosters responsibility to justice or only to certain individual clients," says Martin Burns, who has practiced labor law for over thirty-five years. "I myself have a problem separating myself as a Christian from myself as a lawyer and so I have to wonder if I should accept a system in which the end results depend so much on the particular qualities of the lawyer."

Lawyers who believe that God is their employer say that this serious imbalance in the system has undermined their belief in the system itself. They reject the notion that the system will produce justice if each lawyer simply plays his or her appointed role. Such lawyers also reject the adversary system for more personal reasons. They believe that playing by the rules of the system damages their moral sensitivities. What effect does it have on a man or a woman to articulate positions day after day to which that person has no real allegiance, they ask? Can I really do or say things for clients that I would never do or say for myself? Can I really divorce my professional self and my personal self?

The lawyer who answers, "God is my employer," more often than not is skeptical about the legal system. The spirituality of work for such a lawyer will mean vigorously seeking out those clients who are short-changed by the system. It will still mean that aspiring towards greater competency is a basic element of the lawyer's spirituality of work. At the core, however, these lawyers have a very personal regard for integrity and for taking personal responsibility for the consequences of their work.

Model Three: "I am my employer"

This answer does not mean that the lawyer is in solo practice. It means that the lawyer appreciates the multi-colored and complex character of his or her work. Such a lawyer believes God's hand is hidden in the practical details of his or her work—in the deeds and wills drafted, in the contracts reviewed, in the real estate closing performed, in the accused person defended, in the people and institutions represented in a thousand contexts.

Such lawyers think of God as a creator with whom they are in partnership. They believe that lawyers can reach the goal of communion with God by acting as God acts. "It strikes me that lawyers try to put order into a situation," says one older attorney. "This is what the Lord does to his universe and I see the law as a way of sharing in that creative activity. I try to keep this in mind when I am working on the details of a case."

Lawyers who share this rather open approach reject the absolutes of the previous two positions. They reject the view that says the only route to salvation is in performing pure work full-time, yet they also do not believe in representing everyone who walks in the door based on the idea that the system will sort the just from the unjust. Instead, they make regular and frequent judgments about the content of their practice, based on their belief in the holiness of ordinary work.

Such lawyers see everyday responsibilities not as weights dragging them down, but as opportunities to do God's work in the world. These lawyers believe that almost any job can make a contribution to the kingdom of God. For example, a bond counsel must decide whether the projects being underwritten are worthy of respect and, therefore, his or her talent and efforts. Does this water treatment facility, housing project or road contribute to the well-being of humanity and thus to the kingdom of God? Or is it a project that is nothing but a political boondoggle, with no practical justification, from which the lawyer would be better to walk away?

Similarly, a solo practitioner makes judgments every day about the appropriateness of bringing suit on behalf of injured parties. In one instance, a suit against a drug company or a manufacturer will promote better corporate behavior in the future and compensate an injured person. In another case, the lawyer might refuse to represent someone whom the lawyer suspects of being a malingerer, someone only pretending to be hurt or someone whose own behavior was the chief cause of the accident.

"There is a limit to how I can fit the law to a particular set of facts," explains one veteran attorney. "I once represented a union that wanted to file suit for severance pay at the time a company was sold. In this instance I could not think of a justifiable theory to file the suit. The union would have been satisfied if the court turned us down. They could tell the members that they tried. But I cannot tie up the court's time without a theory. This is a somewhat rare situation but it is a moral issue for me and my business suffers if I tell clients things they don't want to hear."

The lawyer who answers, "I am my employer," is, above all, realistic when it comes to the legal system. The spirituality of work for such a lawyer will mean competency and integrity. It will also mean, however, helping the client to see more than the personal dimension of the situation as the lawyer sorts out the just claim or defense from the unjust. Lawyers who see themselves as participating in God's on-going creation do not seek dramatic changes in people or in the system. Rather, they believe in incremental progress, in the notion that ordinary work gradually builds the kingdom.

Reflecting on a Larger Debate: The Prophetic versus the Complex

The question of the lawyer's spirituality has at least two dimensions to it. On the one hand, the way the lawyer chooses to practice law will have an enormous impact on the state of the lawyer's own soul and, presumably, on the lawyer's ultimate fate as an individual, spiritual being. In other words, the lawyer has an enormous personal stake in the way he or she chooses to practice. At the same time that the lawyer is concerned about personal salvation, however, the lawyer also has to be worried about the social impact of his or her lawyering. A lawyer, let us remember, is a professional whose advocacy affects the commonweal. What the lawyer does in representing a client has an effect on other people, government, businesses, and the public, not just in the raw terms of civil and criminal law—a financial settlement here, a transaction there, a plea bargain here—but in much broader terms as well: the lawyer's conduct helps shape the culture. A legal profession, for example, that puts the substantive justice of claims ahead of procedural defenses will have an influence not simply on how people view lawyers but on how people view their obligations in society.

A lawyer must, of course, be concerned with both of these dimensions. Do the models we have offered here provide guide posts to both personal salvation and community redemption? Each of us takes a different route. Our reader needs to hear from us separately.

Charlie's View

Charlie's view is that only the second model, in which God is considered the lawyer's employer, is defensible in the light of the Gospel and the twin goals each Christian lawyer should have. Here is how he summarizes his point of view:

> I take as my starting point the proposition that Christianity is a call to a radically different way of life. Jesus Christ did not come to live an ordinary life. Rather he came to get beyond ritual, formalism, class, and structure and on to love, compassion, equality, and sacrifice. Indeed, he expected his followers to suffer because they had chosen a path different from that of the prevailing culture. Thus Christ does not call us to an easy complacency with the status quo in which the poor remain poor and the powerful remain powerful. In fact, challenging the status quo is an inevitable consequence of heeding the Gospel call to feed the hungry, clothe the naked, and perform the other corporal and spiritual works Christ prescribes.
>
> Given this clear challenge, it seems irresponsible to be lackadaisical, as an attorney, about the social dimensions of one's work. As an advocate, the lawyer is always taking a position. Each position the lawyer takes has to be understood as being in the service of *some* social philosophy. Even no social philosophy is a social philosophy—

it is a concession to the status quo. If the lawyer's work is inevitably in service to some social philosophy, the lawyer has an obligation to decide what philosophy his or her work will serve. In this there can be little choice for a committed Christian. The lawyer's work must have as its primary and overriding purpose to serve substantive Christian goals. What are those goals? About that there can be great debate, but one thing is certain: unconscious lawyering is not in service of Christian goals. Yet, this is the essence of the first and third models. They accept the lawyer's position—with a firm, with government, with any employer whatsoever—and then they try to find some good in it. This is law for the dead. A Christian lawyer must be conscious, alive to the choices life offers. A Christian lawyer must take the initiative and make a deliberate choice about his or her life and profession. Whom shall we serve?

Apart from the question of what impact the lawyer's work has on society is the question of the impact the lawyer's work has on the individual lawyer's soul. The sharpest threat to the lawyer's soul is the pernicious notion among lawyers that the profession's ethics permit conduct that would be blocked in private life by the lawyer's personal morality. This notion is especially appealing to lawyers who are by nature a competitive lot, a characteristic that is reinforced and encouraged by clients who expect their lawyers to make any move necessary to win. This notion of doing whatever is necessary to prevail is complemented by the further notion that the lawyer's soul bears no personal responsibility for actions taken in the profession. Work is considered work and life is considered life. Work actions are considered somehow separate from all else. This artificial division, this false dichotomy, this concession to the world, however, has the inevitable consequence of damaging the lawyer's moral sensibilities and eventually the lawyer's soul.

My position does not mean every firm and government lawyer must quit and go to work for legal aid, the public defender, or some other public interest organization, although I believe those are the clearest choices for the good. No, a lawyer at work in some less clear setting has choices, too. The central choice is the choice of clients. Who is it that the firm is serving? What are the ends of one's clients? Are those ends consistent with the lawyer's Christianity? Is the lawyer's work for these clients simply in service to the status quo? If it is in service to the status quo, how can the lawyer justify doing nothing for the poor, for God's air and water, for those who are discriminated against because they are the wrong color, gender or religion? How can the lawyer justify work that keeps the poor, poor? Should the firm aim for a different clientele? This discussion should call to mind, as an extreme example, the lawyers for Charles Keating's financial empire who not only failed to blow the whistle on a thief, but actually helped advance his cause. How many of these lawyers were Christian? How many consciously took personal responsibility for the consequences of their work upon their individual souls and upon society? My thesis is that there should be no separation in roles between the lawyer as lawyer and the lawyer as a moral agent whose actions affect the lawyer's soul and society.

Throughout the New Testament, we find the expectation that Christians are to be *palpably different* from non-Christians. If lawyers do not treat their professional lives as integral to their entire spiritual lives such that they take responsibility for being faithful to a radical gospel in their personal *and* professional lives, how then can they call themselves followers of Christ?

Bill's View

Bill takes what he believes is a more balanced approach:

> I believe each of the three models has its rewards and its risks.
>
> The lawyer who believes that the client is his or her employer can take satisfaction in his or her faithful service to people in need, regardless of status or cause. But such a lawyer must worry about a schizoid-like division between who she or he is as a lawyer and who she or he is as a critical, moral human being possessed of a free will.
>
> The lawyer who believes that God is his or her employer works with confidence and a clarity of purpose perhaps unequaled by others. But such a lawyer is subject to burnout, prone to self-righteousness, susceptible to a single-mindedness that excludes other priorities like personal health and family obligations, and too often gives in to a certain intolerance of others who follow a different path to holiness.
>
> The lawyer who believes that she or he is ultimately her or his own employer has an integrated and realistic set of responsibilities. But this lawyer too runs great risks, the chief of which is complacency. It is too easy for this approach to result in a *pro forma* view of the Christian obligation—a view that equates the unreflective performance of a job with the discharge of spiritual obligations, a view that fails to distinguish the Christian lawyer from other humanists who do not have a spirituality of work rooted in the Gospel.
>
> The question of which of these models is best is not the issue with which we ought to be concerned. There is no one best answer. To say that one model is universally the best is to espouse a narrow-minded fundamentalism that takes no account of individual personalities, histories, limitations and circumstances. What might be proper for one, might be wholly improper for another.
>
> Even apart from individual circumstances, the choosing of a specific model is ill-advised. For these reasons, I believe that none of the answers to the question "Who is my employer?" offers a perfect model for every lawyer in search of a spirituality of work. Each offers advantages and disadvantages. Indeed, there are not many lawyers on this earth whose practices fit perfectly into any one of the three answers suggested. I am reminded here of Reinhold Niebuhr's experience in the world and his principal message: people

and their societies are imperfect.[7] Niebuhr came to understand that human nature is so limited as to make any idealized and over arching philosophy (such as pacifism which he came to reject) simply unattainable and thus wholly unacceptable. Thus he rejected the path that identified idealism with salvation, choosing instead to argue that one's salvation is worked out in a real world characterized by sin and failure. He saw man as an entity struggling to make smaller journeys in life, from the imperfection of here to a somewhat less imperfect condition there. That is how I view our struggle for spirituality. We live in a very, very complex and imperfect world that makes many conflicting demands upon us. How we resolve these conflicts should not be a matter of dogmatically following some universal principle, but should be, instead, a matter of experimentation in faith and work, guided by the virtue of prudence. We begin in the world as it is; we work toward the world as it should be. By the necessity of human nature, this will mean an experiment flawed by sin, imperfection, and at least some failures.

I do not mean to argue that this condition of imperfection relieves the Christian lawyer from choosing his or her path and from reflecting on the nature and direction of the lawyer's practice. Lawyers who care about developing a spirituality of work will carefully analyze these approaches, squaring them against their capabilities, limitations, and experiences. The question, "Who is my employer?," I believe, forces lawyers to think about the spiritual dimensions of their work and the moral quality of the untidy legal system in which it takes place. If lawyers will simply do this, I would be quite happy.

A Postscript

Just as we cannot resolve this debate between ourselves, we cannot resolve it for you, our reader. By examining and debating it, however, even in this most cursory manner, we hope that we have provoked you to take responsibility for the state of your practice, your community, and your soul.

Endnotes

1. Roman Catholic. Woodrow A. Potesta Professor of Law, West Virginia University College of Law. B.A. 1970, St. John Fisher College; M.A. 1971, Claremont Graduate School; J.D. 1974, University of Southern California.
2. Roman Catholic. Acting Director of Campus Ministry, Archdiocese of Chicago. B.A. 1970, St. John Fisher College; M.A. 1980, Mundelein College.
3. David Margolick, "At the Bar: Searching for Godliness in a Profession With a Tarnished Reputation," *N.Y. Times*, Nov. 17, 1989, at B9.
4. Quotations here are from those interviews and we thank our colleagues for their permission to attribute their insights and comments.
5. Robert Bolt, *A Man for All Seasons* 66 (1962).

6. Thomas Geoghegan, *Which Side Are You On? Trying to Be for Labor When It's Flat on Its Back* (1991).
7. See generally *Reinhold Niebuhr, Moral Man and Immoral Society* (1932); Reinhold Niebuhr, *Christianity and Power Politics* (1940).

Reflections on Vocation, Calling, Spirituality and Justice

by John L. Cromartie, Jr.[1]

In 1990, after five years in private practice, a federal clerkship, and twenty years as a legal services attorney for Georgia Legal Services Program, I left the full time practice of law and began working as an Associate Minister at a large urban church—Peachtree Road United Methodist Church in Atlanta, Georgia. It was neither through dissatisfaction with the practice of law nor dissatisfaction with my work as Executive Director of Georgia Legal Services Program that I decided to leave my legal work, but my denomination required that I work full time within a local church in order to be ordained as an elder in the United Methodist Church. During a conversation in 1989 with a United Methodist Bishop, I posed the question: "In order to be ordained, why is it necessary for me to leave an active, most meaningful ministry among the poor and work full time within a local church? In essence, isn't the Church asking me to leave ministry in order to become a minster?" Far from being removed from spirituality and faith, I felt that my legal aid work put me more in touch with my spiritual life and drew me deeper into the faith. As I look back over my school and professional life, I realize that my work as a legal aid lawyer was deeply influential in the development and deepening of my faith and has great implications for the ways in which I look at the legal profession today.

Over the past several years, I have considered the ways in which the practice of law has both challenged and helped me grow in my faith. My query to the Bishop reflected my view that the vocation of legal services worker was, for me, a deeply spiritual calling, and I have grown to understand that it was likewise true for so many of the wonderful people with which I have worked in my years in legal services. In my legal aid work, I was increasingly aware of and fascinated by the persistence and dominance of the themes of spirituality, faith commitment and vocation within the people who work within the legal services community—even among people who had seemingly rejected their religious roots and even among people who professed little or no interest in or downright hostility to organized religion. In fact as I entered legal aid work, I was myself very cynical about organized religion, was not active in the Church, and was disappointed in the ways in which the Church had handled issues of justice and fairness. In legal aid work, I got in touch with my deeper feelings about justice issues and met and worked with people deeply committed to working for justice. As I gained renewed confidence in the legal system, I also began a pilgrimage back to the Church.

In writing this essay, I have been asked to reflect upon such pilgrimages or faith journeys, especially as those journeys relate to, are informed by and are shaped by the practice of law. My seminary experience called for a great deal of writing and reflection on the connections between one's life experience and the growth of faith. For me, the most meaningful of these papers was required in a course taught by Dr. James Fowler, who at that time was the Director of the Center for Faith Development at Candler School of Theology. He asked us to write a paper on *Reflections on The Unfolding Tapestry of My Life—Movements and Chapters of My Life*. We were asked to write this paper correlating the chapters and events and movements of our lives with the people, events, influences of our lives and then discuss these matters with the writings of developmental thinkers such as Daniel Levinson, Erik Erikson, Evelyn Whitehead and James Whitehead. The powerful insights gained from this experience have caused me to return time and time again to this productive method and to recommend the method to others. An excellent model of how this can be done is found in two of Frederick Buechner's books: *The Sacred Journey*[2] and *Now and Then*.[3] In the introduction to *The Sacred Journey*, Buechner outlines the connections between autobiography and theology:

> [A]ll theology . . . is at its heart autobiography, and . . . what a theologian is doing essentially is examining as honestly as he (she) can the rough-and-tumble of his (her) own experience with all its ups and downs, its mysteries and loose ends . . . . It seemed to me then, and seems to me still, that if God speaks to us at all in this world, if God speaks anywhere, it is into our personal lives that he speaks. . . . To try to express in even the most insightful and theologically sophisticated terms the meaning of what God speaks through the events of our lives is as precarious a business as to try to express the meaning of the sound of rain on the roof or the spectacle of the setting sun. But I choose to believe that he speaks nonetheless, and the reason that his words are impossible to capture in human language is of course that they are ultimately always incarnate words. They are words fleshed out in the every-dayness no less than in the cries of our own experience . . . . We must learn to listen to the cock-crows and hammering and tick-tock of our lives for the holy and elusive word that is spoken to us out of the depths. It is the function of all great preaching, I think, and of all great art, to sharpen our hearing to precisely that end . . . . [Y]ou may in the privacy of the heart take out the album of your own life and search it for the people and places you have loved and learned from yourself, and for those moments in the past—many of them half forgotten—through which you glimpsed, however dimly and fleetingly, the sacredness of your own journey . . . .[4]

I grew up in Gainesville, Georgia, had a happy childhood, was active in sports, spent a great deal of time in the outdoors, and participated in Boy Scouting. Much of my summer was taken up with baseball or as a counselor at Scout camp. During high school I did a great deal of public speaking through the debate program, served as Governor of the Georgia Key Clubs and literally made hundreds of public speeches throughout Georgia and the southeastern states. Subsequently, I attended Emory University—confident that I would either end up in theology school or law school with some thought that I might even end up in politics. The early 1960s, when I attended Emory, were tumultuous years in our nation—the Civil Rights movement raised fundamental questions about the justice of our institutions, the Vietnam War raised fundamental questions about our national psyche and national priorities, and the cultural changes taking place were striking. It was a time of great unrest, that forced reexamination of virtually everything. To an idealist kid out of a small Georgia town, the ideas presented at Emory were mind-boggling. Dr. Tom Altizer taught me a basic Bible course, right in the midst of his "God is Dead" writings. I had no clue what he was talking about then (and still haven't figured him out) but the results for me were disorienting and confusing. I quickly realized that the ministry was not a realistic option as I was not solidly grounded in my own faith and I was certainly not about to inflict my uncertainties on others. So, law school was the choice. In the summer between my graduation from college and starting law school, I worked in Washington, D.C. on Capital Hill. During that time, I witnessed large gatherings on the stairs in front of the U.S. Senate that celebrated the passage of the Economic Opportunity Act of 1964 and the Civil Rights Act of 1964, both of which would figure prominently in my professional life in the decade that followed. After law school, I spent two years clerking for U.S. District Judge Sidney O. Smith at a time when a number of civil rights and poverty law issues were making their way through the courts. Again, I did not foresee that these issues would someday play a much larger role in my future work. My plans were to engage in a typical small town practice with an emphasis on tort litigation. The firm that I went to work for had a heavy insurance defense practice. Occasionally I got involved in a few legal aid cases and even started several volunteer legal aid operations, but initially there was little to indicate that my career path would soon change. Gradually, the legal aid clients and cases began to command more of my attention and interest. My wife and I became active in some local civil rights issues. Then, in an unsolicited and unexpected turn of events, I was offered a position as Director of Litigation with the newly created statewide legal aid program. My decision involved many different and some difficult considerations, but when I got in touch with my deepest longings, I knew that it was the right decision and indeed it was. During my eighteen years with legal aid, I never had to worry when I got up in the morning whether

I was doing the right thing in terms of my vocational choices and the use of my gifts and graces.

The deepening of my vocation as a legal aid worker also gave rise to a greater understanding that I was indeed involved in ministry. Ironically, what I thought had been a journey away from the Church became in reality a journey back into the Church. It became a journey deeper into faith.

I recall that in July of 1987 in Pawling, New York, at a training conference for experienced project directors, some of my thinking about spirituality and legal aid work, which had been in process for some time, began to be much more specific and cohesive. During the conference, I noticed that a common and persistent theme that kept emerging during so much of our informal discussions—among persons who called themselves Christians, among persons from the Jewish heritage and even persons whose religious heritage was more ambiguous—had to do with the spiritual journeys of those attending and the frequency with which people were re-establishing and re-exploring some of the faith traditions from which they had come. While some of the return to our various religious backgrounds was a product of our stages in life, I was led to see and appreciate the underlying spirituality in the legal aid movement. As I began to talk about these impressions with others, it came as a surprise to many people within the legal aid movement because on the surface there was a widespread impression of an almost total rejection of organized religion among the attorneys working within individual legal aid programs. On a superficial level there was some reason for this perception, but as religion and faith were explored in a less sectarian sense and as the Biblical connections with the Hebrew prophets and the Biblical message of liberation to the poor and the oppressed were considered, suddenly the legal services network becomes a rich environment for exploring the issues of the connectedness to spirituality and faith development.

I have long been fascinated by the correlations between the passions of the legal aid community and the passions of the Old Testament prophets. Prophets such as Isaiah and Amos looked at the economic and political abuses of their country,[5] the neglect of the poor,[6] the accumulation of wealth by the few,[7] the arrogance of the rich and pride of the religious insiders,[8] the neglect of the disadvantaged,[9] the ignoring of the fundamental issues of justice.[10] Isaiah and other Old Testament prophets had no problem identifying the cause of these conditions: the people had neglected justice—economic, social, political justice. The more I read the Hebrew prophets, the more relationships I saw between the passions that drew so many people to legal aid work and the passions of the Old Testament prophets.

But legal aid lawyers do not have a corner on justice issues. As I worked more closely with attorneys in private practice or in other areas of public law, I realized that there were often common concerns for justice issues and common concerns about the need for correlation between day to day work and an individual's particular gifts and talents and sense of calling. And that caused me to think more intentionally about the meaning of work, especially my work in the legal profession and the work of others I have known in this profession. As my faith has been nurtured, developed, and evolved through the years, I have appreciated more keenly the need I have always had for a sense of satisfaction in and from my work. I felt a particular calling into legal aid work and it was very satisfying to me. Now my calling into ordained ministry is most compelling. I now know some of the wisdom of the Bishop's wanting me to work full time in the local church. It has been a rich and powerful experience and I'm not sure that I would have ever understood or appreciated the gifts and opportunities for ministry within the church itself had I not worked on a full time basis within a local church. But along with this appreciation of the importance of my work in various settings also comes a more intentional desire to develop and articulate a theology of work that has applicability to and connects with my calling as a minister, as a legal aid lawyer, and as a lawyer in private practice. I would not claim that all lawyers would agree with my conclusions, but I suspect that many lawyers would not only agree but would contribute much to this discussion.

In addition to tiresome and unimaginative lawyer jokes I constantly hear (although most people now concentrate on minister jokes when I'm around), I also hear variations on the comment that the legal profession does not have a soul, and by implication that those within the profession are involved in work that kills the spirit and the soul. I do not believe this. It has not been my experience with the legal profession or with most lawyers. Yes, there are pressures in the profession that present enormous challenges and yes the changes in the profession from economic and societal pressures have to be reckoned with. In fact, the overall level of cynicism in our culture has grown to frightening extremes to where it is very difficult for most professions or groups of individuals to feel very positive about anything. And while I think that self analysis and the willingness to grow and change are vital, I also feel the need to speak up for our profession—to proclaim and celebrate the ways in which it continues to represent some of the best of our culture. The professionalism movement has grown in recent years and has fostered a healthy dialogue about the deeper values represented by and manifested by the legal profession. I personally find that much of what the professionalism movement is really attempting to explore is tied into what some have called a sense of vocation. The reclaiming and recapturing of this sense of vocation in the practice of law is critical to the success of the professionalism movement.

Hence, it is important to look a bit more closely at the meaning of this term. James Fowler in his book *Becoming Adult, Becoming Christian— Adult Development and Christian Faith* gives this definition of vocation: "Vocation is the response a person makes with his or her total self to the address of God and to the calling to partnership."[11] Thus, the sense of vocation involves an interplay of all aspects of our lives but certainly for professionals who spend much of their waking hours in work related activities, the time and energy spent in our work is very important in defining and fulfilling our vocational needs and aspirations. But this sense of vocation is much more than just a job. Vocation suggests much more of a sense of calling; a deeper sense of connectedness to others; a deeper sense of connectedness to our God given gifts and graces; a deeper sense of doing work that matters to us and to others; and a deeper sense of passion for justice, fairness, and the healing of brokenness. Walter Brueggeman has said: "Vocation . . . is finding 'purpose for being in the world which is related to the purposes of God.'"[12] Vocation has to do with "[t]he centers of value and power that have god value for us . . . that confer meaning and worth on us and promise to sustain us."[13]

Barbara Brown Taylor's book, *The Preaching Life*, looks like it would be just for preachers and those called to ordination in the Church, but is really for the priesthood of all believers. Her chapter on "Vocation" is especially helpful for purposes of our discussion:

> What many Christians are missing in their lives is a sense of vocation. The word itself means a call or summons, so that having a vocation means more than having a job. It means answering a specific call; it means doing what one is meant to do. In religious language, it means participating in the work of God, something that few lay people believe they do. . . . Somewhere along the way we have misplaced the ancient vision of the church as a priestly people—set apart for ministry in baptism, confirmed and strengthened in worship, made manifest in service to the world.[14]

Barbara Taylor argues quite convincingly that we share a common vocation of being God's person in the world, called to different roles (or offices) but as long as our work and our activities accord with the gifts and calling given to us by God, then we all are involved in vocation. When we can understand our work in this way, whatever that work may be, we are equipped and empowered to see the sacramental[15] aspects of whatever we do. Another creative and imaginative resource for looking at the sacramental and vocational aspects of work is Matthew Fox's *The Reinvention of Work—A New Vision of Livelihood for Our Time*.[16]

I do think that many people are attracted to and remain attracted to the practice of law because it is a helping profession and our gifts and our needs call upon us to be involved in helping others. I recall back in the 1970s being involved in one of the constant life and death struggles over the funding for legal aid. At that time we received funding from the Georgia Legislature and most of the opponents of legal aid were having a field day complaining about all of the unfair things we had done—like making them comply with the laws of Georgia when they dealt with poor people. It took a lot of time and energy in the political struggles to protect our funding and the State Bar of Georgia was very helpful in assisting our program in making a case for our survival. Stell Huie was at that time President of the State Bar and spent an enormous amount of time helping me persuade opponents and explain our position to the general public. In an apologetic tone, I conveyed to Stell my appreciation for the Bar's efforts and all of his time and also conveyed my regrets that he was having to take all of this time from the practice of law to help solve our problems. I'll never forget his answer. He said: "John, as lawyers, we are basically in the profession of helping people prevent problems or solve their problems. Anyone who doesn't like to work with problems should probably find another field of work. I'm simply doing what any good lawyer does, I'm helping you solve a problem." That made quite an impression on me. Yes, solving problems or helping people prevent problems represents a great deal of what many lawyers do and those who see the challenge of and like to solve problems would tend to enjoy the practice of law.

To carry this problem into more spiritual language, I turn to some writing done in *Weavings*.[17] Vocation, in part, has to do with locating our God given gifts and graces and satisfying the deep longings that we have to use our talents to help others and thereby find fulfillment for ourselves:

> The place God calls you to is the place where your gladness and the world's hunger meet. . . . [D]iscovering our deep gladness is not a luxury; it is a necessity. It is a necessity precisely because it helps us perceive where God is calling us to be and in so doing, shepherds us all toward healing. Our deep gladness is a gift of the Spirit that draws us more fully and freely into life. . . . Our daily work can lead us toward both—the discovery of our own deep gladness and the filling of the world's deep hunger.[18]

I now know that at this particular stage of my life the work of ministry in the local church is where my deepest longings and God's call have converged. I strongly felt that the same was true during my years with legal aid. To me a part of what drew me to the practice of law was the need to have my work reflect the intellectual challenges I need, to reflect opportunities for helping other people and to engage my people helping skills. Many have remained in the practice of law whose lists of inner longings would contain these same qualities and find that the practice of law is not a time away from their spiritual life, but is the very place where they enflesh that which God has called them and continues to call them to be.

Endnotes

1. United Methodist. Associate Minister, Peachtree Road United Methodist

Church, Atlanta, Georgia. B.A. 1964, Emory University; J.D. 1967, University of Georgia; M.Div. 1988, Candler School of Theology, Emory University.

2. Frederick Buechner, *The Sacred Journey* (1982).
3. Frederick Buechner, *Now and Then* (1983).
4. Buechner, *supra* note 2, at 1, 4, 5, and 7.
5. Amos 2:6.
6. Isaiah 32:6, 41:17; Amos 4:1.
7. Amos 8:4–6.
8. Amos 6:1–6.
9. Isaiah 1:23; Amos 5:11–13.
10. Isaiah 5:23, 10:1–2, 24:5.
11. James W. Fowler, *Becoming Adult, Becoming Christian: Adult Development and Christian Faith* 95 (1984).
12. Walter Brueggeman, "Covenanting as Human Vocation," 33 *Interpretation* 115, 126 (1979).
13. James W. Fowler, *Stages of Faith—The Psychology of Human Development and the Quest for Meaning* 18 (1981).
14. Barbara B. Taylor, *The Preaching Life* 27 (1993).
15. Sacrament is anything which reflects God's presence and God's grace in the world.
16. Matthew Fox, *The Reinvention of Work: A New Vision of Livelihood for Our Time* 102–6, 296–308 (1994).
17. Jean M. Blomquist, "Discovering Our Deep Gladness: The Healing Power of Work," *Weavings—"Woven Together in Love"—J. Christian Spiritual Life*, Jan.-Feb., 1993, at 20 (many other excellent resources present some of this same thinking).
18. *Id*. at 25–26 (citing Frederick Buechner, *Wishful Thinking: A Theological ABC* 95 [1973]).

Neither Curse nor Idol: Towards a Spirituality of Work for Lawyers

Joseph G. Allegretti[1]

A few months ago, I had one of those weeks that is not life-sustaining but life-draining. I had been away at a conference and returned to find my desk cluttered with stacks of telephone messages, each more urgent than the next. When I was away I had missed several classes and was committed to making those up while preparing and teaching my regularly-scheduled classes. Months before I had agreed to give two talks and both were now due. I had prepared neither—the talks had seemed so far in the future when the invitations came, but somehow, mysteriously, the months had slipped away, like all my good intentions. I serve on several committees at the university where I teach. For over a year, everything had been quiet, but on my first day back in the office I received two frantic calls announcing emergency meetings. And to top things off, I got a call on Wednesday from a journal telling me that the article I had promised and was procrastinating over was due on Friday, no ifs-ands-or-buts.

That was not a good week. I staggered into work with the sunrise, slouched home way after dark, and was a surly grouch to anyone who crossed my path. I had no time for my children, who needed help with their homework, or my wife, who needed a break from my children. I had no time for anything but work.

My week was a blur. But soon afterwards I had the opportunity to spend a few days alone recharging my inner batteries and taking stock of where I was. With a little bit of detachment, I came to realize that during that frenzied week I had alternated crazily between two equally unsatisfactory visions of work: damning my work as a *curse* and transforming it into an *idol*. These polar extremes are the subject of this essay. In Part One, I discuss the temptation to regard work as a curse, and in Part Two the temptation to treat it as an idol.

Part One: Work as a Curse

I know I'm not alone in sometimes treating my work as a curse. We fall into this trap anytime we approach work as nothing more than a grim necessity, without any inherent meaning, utterly estranged from our spiritual life.[2] We spend our time just trying to get through the day and the week, divorcing the hours spent at work from our *real* life, which is reserved for evenings and weekends.

Lawyers are no more immune from such feelings than anyone else. More than a few lawyers have told me, in the quiet of my office or over a drink at a party, that they hate what they do. These lawyers are often quite successful, yet for some reason their work holds no intrinsic meaning for them. It does not provide sustenance for their souls, bread for the spiritual journey. Often their faces will brighten up—lighten up—the moment the discussion changes to what is really important in their lives, whether it be family, the arts, or golf.

Perhaps the most pessimistic account of being a lawyer that I ever heard came from a senior partner at a large firm who told me, "Look, law is like prostitution but it pays better." For this prominent lawyer, work was not only devoid of meaning, it had infected him with the deadly disease of self-loathing.

Most lawyers, though, do not hate their work as much as they are often overwhelmed by it. Anyone who is a lawyer can recount stories of days, weeks, or even months that rushed by in a frenetic blur of activity. At such times it is all-too-easy to look upon work as a curse where survival is the only victory.

Religion itself has contributed to this negative assessment of work. Work, back-breaking, mind-numbing work, is pictured in Genesis 3 as God's punishment for the primeval, original sin of humanity. More subtly, Christianity has sometimes encouraged the mistaken notion that God and the spiritual life are reserved for Sundays and special days, with the unfortunate effect of trivializing the value of our everyday lives. Too often spirituality in the West has been seen as something that you can do only if you *escape* from your ordinary life.

In the Middle Ages, for example, it was assumed that no one who remained in the secular world could live out the richness of the Christian faith. As philosopher Lee Hardy puts it, "Those who remained outside the cloister, who remained involved in the world, may be Christian, but they were less than fully Christian."[3] They were relegated to second-class citizenship in the kingdom of God.

The remnants of such a view haunt us still. To go on a retreat, sit in a church, read the Bible, meditate in private—that is spiritual. But the rest of life, the time spent at work, with the kids, fixing dinner, cleaning clothes, rushing to the veterinarian or the supermarket—that is secular, worldly, and decidedly not spiritual.

If we are to give work its proper due, however, we must reject this cramped notion of work as spiritually meaningless. We need to open ourselves to other images that link our work to our spiritual life. One helpful step is to think about our work not as curse, but more positively as both *calling* and *creation*.

Work as Calling

Throughout much of Christian history, the concept of calling (or vocation) was reserved for the few who renounced secular life to dedicate themselves completely to God. Looked at in this way, the concept has little to say to those who have not abandoned the world for God. A priest or a monk may have a calling, but certainly not me, a married man with two children and a job as a law professor!

The Reformation changed all this. The Reformers broke free of the medieval notion that only those who left the world for the church had a vocation from God. Instead, they insisted that there was no hard-and-fast distinction between sacred and secular work. Any job can be a calling if we approach it as an avenue of loving service to our God and our neighbor. Our calling is to serve God *in and through our work* no less than the rest of life.[4]

When lawyers approach their work in this way, they begin to see their clients in a different light. A client is not a mere commodity, but a human being: often a human being in pain and emotional turmoil, who has come to me for help. I serve my God by serving my neighbor. The concept of calling invites a relationship in which lawyers and clients come to know each other as children of God who share a common spiritual destiny.

The idea of calling also helps put the financial and business dimensions of lawyering in proper perspective. Money and success are still important—how could they not be? But they are not the most important thing. Our self-worth is not bound to the size of our paycheck or our office. If we approach our work as a calling from God, success becomes more a matter of helping others than of accumulating riches.

Work as Creation

Although it was the Reformers who first liberated the notion of calling from its medieval and monastic straightjacket, modern Roman Catholic theology also insists on the spiritual significance of work. Human work is seen as a participation in God's work.

In Genesis we read how God created the universe and fashioned human beings from clay, so we know that work is an essential part of God's very nature. Humans, too, are called to work, and by doing so they participate in the further unfolding of God's plan for creation. In the encyclical *Laborem Exercens*, Pope John Paul II speaks of work as a sharing in the activity of God; humans are, in a sense, co-creators with God.[5]

One implication of such a view is an ongoing commitment to excellence at work. To respond competently and diligently to the task at hand is part of a spirituality of work, for in this way we truly collaborate with God's creative activity. As theologian Elizabeth Dreyer reminds us, "Gradually we are learning that to be a good plumber, truck driver, nurse, or janitor is the way to be a good Christian."[6]

Such a perspective also puts the inevitable difficulties and problems of work in a different light. As Pope John Paul II says, "The Christian finds in human work a small part of the cross of Christ and accepts it in the same spirit of redemption in which Christ accepted his cross for us."[7] Work cannot be divorced from sweat and toil, but that does not mean it lacks spiritual meaning. Quite to the contrary! The toil itself has meaning. By our work we participate not only in God the Creator's ongoing work of creation, but in God the Redeemer's work of redemption.

Finding God at Work

I believe that it is useful to have some appreciation of these positive and negative images, for they often shape our approach to work without our even knowing it. Some of us find it easy to approach work as calling or creation. Others find it more difficult. As a check on myself, I occasionally reflect back over a few days or weeks and ask: What are the implicit images of work I have been carrying with me? Have I recognized the connections between my faith and my work, or have I approached work as devoid of spiritual meaning?

The difficulty with focusing on these images of work is that they are too general and abstract. Many of us experience all of them in a typical week; sometimes we treat work as a curse, other times as a calling or creation. We would like to integrate our work with the rest of our life and with our spiritual journey, but the images we carry with us cannot tell us *how* to bridge the gap.

Let me suggest a few steps we can take as lawyers to deepen the spiritual dimensions of our work. The first is simply to recognize that our God is the God of the whole week, not only Sundays and occasional moments of prayer. We must break down the artificial barriers that compartmentalize our life into neat little pigeonholes labeled "work," "family," and "religion." We must begin to think of ourselves as disciples of Christ not just when sitting in church, but when counseling a client, playing with our children, or visiting a sick friend.

Consider a typical day of a typical lawyer. You rise early, take a shower, and dress. If you have children, you get them ready for school or the babysitter. You gulp down a quick bowl of cereal and grab a cup of coffee. You rush to your office. You work all day, and you work hard, with maybe an hour off for lunch. More likely, you eat a hasty sandwich at your desk, have a "working lunch," or run a few quick errands. You usually work late into the evening. When you get home from work, dinner must be made. The dishes must be cleaned and the kitchen floor swept. Dirty clothes must be washed. If you have children, they need help with their homework. If you're married, you need to catch up with your spouse on the day's happenings. And then there are the everyday chores to be done: shopping for food, picking up a prescription at the pharmacy, trying to fix a balky vacuum cleaner, paying the bills and balancing the checkbook, finding a few minutes for exercise. Often you spend an hour after dinner reading the memos and files you never got around to at the office.

Finally, the children are in bed, the house is tidied up, and you collapse onto the sofa. Perhaps you try to read a book, or you flip through the pages of a magazine, but your eyes are heavy and you soon catch yourself dozing off. Maybe you listen to music or watch TV, but it isn't long before you give up the battle and turn in for the night.

Where do you fit your spiritual life into all this confusion and clutter? Where do you gain your spiritual nourishment? Where do you squeeze God into your already overscheduled and overburdened day?

As long as we live as if the spiritual life is one more task to get done, as long as we divorce the spiritual from the ordinary, then we have no choice but to cram God into our few free moments or abandon the whole idea of any kind of spiritual life except on Sundays and holy days. *There's just not enough time for God if God is one more responsibility in an already overcrowded life.*

If the Incarnation means anything, however, it means that God embraced and sanctified the whole of human life. By becoming a human being, like us, God in Jesus broke down the barriers between the sacred and the profane, so that what is done outside the Church is as important as what is done inside.[8]

If that is so, then our spiritual task is to wake up to the holiness of the office, the factory, the kitchen table, and the bedroom. As Reverend Davida Foy Crabtree puts it, the Christian message is that "no ground is more holy, no work more sacred, no life more worthy than any other. Every moment, every place and every interaction is sacred and holy, infused with the Spirit's presence."[9] This means that the lawyer is never far from God while at work. God is present "amid our daily chores and in all the legal institutions and systems: in the office, in the courtroom, the library, and the jail."[10]

A Spirituality of the Ordinary

If all of life is sacred, our challenge is to cultivate an awareness of the moments of grace that can occur at any time or place. Whenever two people are together, we know that God is the invisible third party, and so little miracles can happen at the most unexpected moments if only we develop the inner eye to see them. If God is in the details, as theologians are fond of saying, then we need to become sensitive to the manifold ways we encounter God—and are presented with opportunities to serve God—in the ordinary humdrum events of our ordinary, often humdrum lives. What we need is a *spirituality of the ordinary.*

Let me give an example. Many times I've had a student walk into my office and begin talking about a class assignment or an upcoming examination, only to gradually open up and reveal the deeper problem at the root of the visit: a family breakup, a vocational crisis, or nagging doubts about self-identity. Yet I'm embarrassed to admit that more than once I have caught myself surreptitiously peeking at my watch and wondering how I was ever going to get my "real" work done—preparation for a class, writing an article—if I spent so much time with this student.

Right now, at this moment, with this student, I have the opportunity to bring my faith and my work together, yet too often I find myself half-listening to my student and half-worrying about the other things I need to do. How often I've overlooked the opportunities for ministry in my work! How often I have forgotten what is called for: a ministry of the kind word, an attentive ear, a smile or a laugh, just being there for a friend, colleague, student, or client. A ministry of presence, not of great and glorious deeds.

What would such a spirituality mean for lawyers? I believe that we lawyers have many opportunities to minister to others in the ordinary course of our work. The very title *counselor-at-law* highlights our essential role as counselor and companion.

Ideally, lawyers and clients are bound by interpersonal ties of trust and mutual respect. They are not so much parties to a contract as partners to a covenant in which each partner wills the best for the other and stands with and for the other.[11] As a covenant partner, the lawyer is granted a host of opportunities to serve her clients. A client tells a story of a marriage or a business partnership gone bad. A client talks of an accident or an injury that she suffered or caused another to suffer. A client and a lawyer discuss a painful business decision that could put dozens of people out of work.

The stories are as varied as the people who seek our help. But they are tied together by a common thread: people in need come to lawyers, and lawyers are called—there's that word again!—to minister as best we can to those people. We are cognizant of our own shortcomings, to be sure, but confident as well that God can use us as instruments of grace and love.

Sometimes lawyers serve clients by the advice they give. Sometimes by assisting clients in navigating the dangerous shoals of the law. Sometimes by pursuing the justice denied their clients. Sometimes by prophetically raising issues or concerns that their clients would just as soon ignore. And sometimes just by being present and listening, by taking the client seriously and valuing the client as a person. Sometimes the ministry of presence is the best gift we can give to each other.

Likewise, there are opportunities for service to others as well, even if they are often mediated through our relations with our clients. In a business deal, for example, we can negotiate a contract that is fair to both sides. In litigation, we can help our client realize that reconciliation can take the place of acrimony and compassion can take the place of revenge.[12] God has given those of us who are lawyers a great blessing and a great responsibility to serve someone in some way.

There is another dimension to the spirituality of work that needs to be mentioned. An authentic spirituality resists the temptation to become privatized and insular. If the pressures of legal practice make it difficult for us to serve our clients well, or rob us of time for ourselves and our loved ones, then a reform of law firms and legal institutions is in order. If too many lawyers are living too hectic lives, the solution is not for individuals to slow down and catch their breath (although that would certainly help), but to transform law practice into something more humane. As one writer puts it: "[S]pirituality is about seeking and responding to God's presence. Good policies and humane institutions make it easier to see God. Therefore, far from being a distraction, the reform of institutions is a key ingredient to a spirituality of work."[13]

Any spirituality worth its name is interested not only in the solitary quest for meaning but also in the creation of a more just and more compassionate world.[14] As my Jesuit friends and colleagues remind me, Christians are called to be *contemplatives in action*. Each of us, in our own way, is anointed to preach good news to the poor, proclaim the release of captives, and bring liberty to the oppressed.[15]

Ultimately, a spirituality of the ordinary poses some simple questions: Where is God in my work? Where are the opportunities to minister and to serve? How can I live out the Christian message of love, compassion, and justice while at work?

Part Two: Work as an Idol

If one view of work devalues its significance and treats it as a curse, another perspective overvalues it, and threatens to transform work into something more than it is, something great, something godlike, an idol made not of stone or clay but of our dreams of worldly success and achievement. It is important not to lose sight of the paradoxical nature of work: work is an integral part of our spiritual journey and has great significance, but it is not of *ultimate* significance. Work should open us to God, not take the place of God.

Earlier I recounted a particularly hectic week I experienced. Thinking back, I realize that while one part of me was grimly intent on enduring the curse of work, another part of me, inconsistently but simultaneously, was guilty of investing too much of myself in my work. There I was, frantically struggling to get all my projects done, at the same time saying "yes" but never "no" to each new request. It wasn't enough to complete all my assignments—no, I had to do them all and do them all *perfectly*! I was using my work to prove myself, to validate my self-worth. I had confused *who I am* with *what I do*, so that my work had become a way of saying to the world and to God, "Look, I'm a good guy, I count for something."

I wasn't working to live, I was living to work. Work had become an end in itself.

I'm not alone in this. At a cocktail party we break the ice with strangers by asking, "What do you do? Where do you work?" The size of our paycheck or our office becomes a subtle sign of divine favor, proof that we're somebody good and important. We end up like the man I read about recently who, as he approached retirement, could only say, "All my life I've been an engineer. Now I'm nothing." Woe to the unemployed and under-employed in a society that enshrines work and productivity as the chief test of individual worth!

In his book *When Work Goes Sour*, theologian James Dittes makes the point well:

> [Our] most intense religious commitment is often to work. We give it absolute devotion, and we expect our work to save us, to make us feel whole and healthy and right, cured from the gnawing sense that there is something wrong with us. Sometimes it does this, for a while. But often the sacramental powers of work become crumbled idols, and we find ourselves religiously dedicated to a god unworthy of our ardor, trusting a god unable to deliver a saving.[16]

An idol need not be a piece of rag or a hunk of clay; it is any god unworthy of our ardor, any god unable to deliver salvation. This is what work can become if we let it.

The Overachieving Lawyer

I wonder whether idolatry isn't the occupational hazard for professionals like lawyers and doctors. Too many of us are over-achievers, workaholics, who place inflated value on our work in the hope that it will save us from our shadowy fears of emptiness and worthlessness.

For many lawyers, work becomes their entire life. Everything else suffers—families and friends fall by the wayside, hobbies are forgotten, health is jeopardized—in their ceaseless effort to work more, do more, accomplish more. I have seen lawyers spend so much time at the office that it becomes their surrogate home. I have listened to a senior partner at a prestigious law firm say that his only friends were his clients, because only with his clients did he feel that he was doing something *real*. The broken marriages, the drug and alcohol problems, the push-push-push mentality that can never slow down—all these are signs of the vain quest to grasp the Holy Grail of the workplace.

When we turn our work into an idol like this, we forget the fundamental teaching of St. Paul that we're already saved, not because of anything we can do, but because of what Jesus the Christ did. That is the simple point behind the mystery of the Redemption: while we were still sinners, Christ died for us. We are accepted. Just as we are.

As the great modern theologian Paul Tillich said, our only task—but this is no easy matter for most of us—is to accept the fact that we are accepted: "Do not try to do anything now; perhaps later you will do much. Do not seek for anything; do not perform anything; do not intend anything. *Simply accept the fact that you are accepted!*"[17]

This is the challenge for all of us who are prone towards over-achievement, towards investing work with more meaning than it deserves. We don't need our work to prove our self-worth. We're already worthy. We don't need it to prove our self-importance. We're already important, infinitely important. We don't need it to make life good or meaningful. Life already is.

If we are to smash the idols of work, we must first ease up on ourselves, and let go of the nagging suspicion that without our accomplishments and our corner office we are at bottom nothing. As Dittes suggests, we need to move from the belief that "I am worker" to the more realistic understanding that "I am someone who sometimes works."[18]

If we do not do this, we may become like the man whose gravestone was spotted in a Scottish cemetery: "Here lies John MacDonald, Born a man, Died a grocer."[19]

Born a man, born a woman—but died a grocer, a lawyer, a priest, or a painter, as if work and work alone gave meaning and purpose to life.

Giving Work Its Proper Meaning

The first step towards a healthier attitude is to admit our tendency towards work idolatry. This is a fact of life for most of us, to a greater or a lesser degree, because our work *does* matter. It does make a difference if we do it well or poorly. If our work was without meaning to us, then we would be treating it as nothing but a curse.

So let us admit that our work is important and that it is inextricably entangled with our self-identity. Problems arise only when it becomes so important that the rest of our life revolves around it like planets around a sun. When work is not just *meaningful*, but of *ultimate meaning* in our life.

I can begin to examine the effect of work on the rest of my life by asking myself a few questions: If things are going poorly at work, how does that affect my relationships with family and friends? How does it affect my health? Do I eat or drink too much? Does it rob me of my capacity for fun? And how does it affect my feelings of self-worth? Do the inevitable failures at work make me feel like a failure as a person?

I vividly recall my first weeks as a junior associate in a large law firm. Everything was new and intimidating. I was constantly trying to prove myself—everyday there was a new challenge, a new obstacle to overcome, a new chance to succeed or fail. I wanted so much to make a good impression on the partners who held my destiny in their hands. The slightest hint of praise or intimation of criticism could send me into hours of delight or despair. Even when I was at home on evenings and weekends, I was either working or worrying about work. Clearly my life was out of balance.

Two things helped me restore some sense of equilibrium. First, when we were at home my wife would plead, cajole, and sometimes physically push me out the door, so that we could go to a movie or a museum or take a walk in a park, anything to leave work behind for a few hours. Often I would resist but always I felt better for getting away and giving my nervous mind a rest.

Second, a few of my friends from law school were associates in other firms around town, and every two or three weeks we would meet for a combination lunch and b.s. session. Just having someone to talk to about my work, someone who understood in general what I was facing but who was not personally involved, did wonders for my perspective. I found myself becoming less self-absorbed and more confident as I discovered that my friends were dealing with the same pressures and worries I was facing.

In short, I began to put my work in a wider and more spacious frame of reference. My wife reminded me that I was more than just a worker, and my friends reminded me that work was just work, nothing more nor less.

And I learned something else. How important it is to have fun. All work and no play does indeed make you dull, and it also makes you cranky, upset, and full of doubts about yourself and your work. Ever since, I have tried—without great success, I admit—to bring a certain spirit of playfulness to my work, to take it a little less seriously, to laugh a bit more at the exaggerated sense of importance I invest in work. I believe it was G.K. Chesterton who said that anything worth doing is worth doing poorly—if it's important enough to do, then of course it's worth doing, even though I can only do it poorly and not perfectly.

I also try to make the physical surroundings of my office a visible reminder that work is not the only thing or the most important thing in my life. I have brought from home pictures of my wife and children, some *Star Trek* figures my sons gave me for Christmas, and a poster that proclaims "Everyone Should Be Italian At Least Once A Year." Near my desk I keep a copy of the prayer of St. Francis, a small cross, a postcard of Gandhi seated cross-legged at a spinning wheel, and a framed picture of a beautiful Russian church I once visited, its illuminated onion-skin domes shining bright in the night sky. These are but small efforts to tie together the parts of my life, to bring my whole self into the workplace with me.

I also find it helpful to get away once or twice a year for a few days at a local retreat house. There I think back and ahead about my life and my work: Have I been giving too much of myself (or too little) to my work? Have I been open to the opportunities for service in my job? What steps have I taken to achieve a balance between work and the rest of my life? How have I treated my family and friends? How have I related to God? How well have I taken care of myself, physically and mentally? What should I do differently in the future?

The point, again, is to embed my work in my entire life, to give it its due importance, but not to let it dominate my waking (or sleeping) hours. To take it seriously, but not too seriously.

****

Work is a paradox. We grant it both too little and too much meaning.

We treat it as irrelevant to our spiritual life, but worship it as a god. This paradoxical problem calls for a paradoxical solution: we must give work more and less meaning, invest more of ourselves into our work and less of ourselves. The challenge for me, and perhaps for you, is to hold together in creative tension the idea that work is holy, a place where I encounter and serve God, with the countervailing notion that work is not of cosmic significance, it's not the avenue of my salvation—Christ is.

What the great Christian novelist Flannery O'Connor said about life applies to work, too. O'Connor wrote, "You have to cherish the world at the same time you struggle to endure it."[20] Work is not a curse or an idol, but something else, something more and less. We must learn to cherish our work at the same time we struggle to endure it.

Endnotes

1. Roman Catholic. A.A. and Ethel Yossem Professor of Legal Ethics, Creighton University School of Law. J.D. 1977, Harvard Law School; M. Div. 1989, Yale Divinity School.

    This essay is a portion of a larger project on the religious dimensions of lawyering. Another portion of that work has been published by Paulist Press under the title of *The Lawyer's Calling: Christian Faith and Legal Practice* (1996). Although I write as a Christian, I hope that my reflections may prove helpful to persons of other faith-traditions.

2. I will not even attempt to give an all-inclusive definition of spirituality. For my purposes here, spirituality can be characterized broadly as *a person's orientation towards the divine*. As William Droel puts it, "Spirituality is the style, the awareness with which we orient ourselves to God." William L. Droel, *The Spirituality of Work: Lawyers* 12 (National Center for the Laity, 1989).

3. Lee Hardy, *The Fabric of This World: Inquiries into Calling, Career Choice, and the Design of Human Work* 24 (1990).

4. See Hardy, *supra* n. 3, at 44–76, for a good discussion of the Reformers' theology of vocation.

5. *On Human Work: A Resource Book for the Study of Pope John Paul II's Third Encyclical* 52 (United States Catholic Conference, 1982).

6. Elizabeth Dreyer, "Toward a Spirituality of Work," *New Theology Rev.*, May 1989, at 58.

7. *On Human Work: A Resource Book for the Study of Pope John Paul II's Third Encyclical*, *supra* n. 4, at 52.

8. More important, actually, according to the Hebrew prophets. See, e.g., Amos, chapter 5 and Isaiah, chapter 1.

9. Davida Foy Crabtree, "They Bring Their Work to Church," in *Of Human Hands: A Reader in the Spirituality of Work* 113 (Gregory F. Augustine Pierce ed., 1991).

10. Droel, *supra* n. 2, at 13.

11. See William F. May, *The Physician's Covenant: Images of the Healer in Medical Ethics* (1983). I examine the idea of the lawyer-client covenant in more detail in *The Lawyer's Calling*, *supra* n. 1.

12. I deal with the lawyer's responsibilities in litigation in more detail in *The Lawyer's Calling, supra* n. 1. There I argue that lawyers should see themselves less as the "hired guns" of clients and more as peacemakers and agents of healing.

13. Droel, *supra* n. 2, at 38.

14. I am painfully aware how little I have to say here about the pursuit of justice as an integral part of the spiritual life. My only defense is that the topic is too large to deal with adequately in these few pages. I do consider questions of justice in *The Lawyer's Calling, supra* n. 1. One potentially fruitful avenue to explore is the application of the insights of "liberation theology" to the legal system and legal profession.

15. Luke 4:18–19.

16. James E. Dittes, *When Work Goes Sour* 7 (1987).

17. Paul Tillich, *The Shaking of the Foundations* 162 (1948).

18. Dittes, *supra* n. 15, at 103.

19. James Luther Adams, *The Prophethood of All Believers* 152 (George K. Beach ed., 1986).

20. Ed Marciniak, "Toward a Catholic Work Ethic," in *Origins*, Feb. 25, 1988, at 632.

Engaging the Law

Thomas W. Porter, Jr.[1]

The relationship between my faith and my practice is of particular professional interest to me, as I am both a minister and a lawyer. To some people I may appear to be courting schizophrenia. My preference is not to live a schizophrenic life.

When I describe myself as both a minister and a lawyer, I often get strange looks and much wonderment. I also get more than my fair share of lawyers' jokes. The grocer in the little town in New Hampshire where my wife grew up is one example of the reactions I get. She always asks me whether my check was written in my capacity as a minister or a lawyer, so she will know whether the check is going to bounce. A young nephew recently asked, "Uncle Tom, why do they bury lawyers twenty feet underground?" The answer was, "Because down deep, lawyers are good at heart." Perhaps, my role as a lawyer should not take all the grief because the clergy are coming into their own share of criticism.

My attempts to understand and affirm the relationship between religion and law have occupied a significant part of my life during the last twenty-five years. These attempts either say something about the depth of the "split," my own particular slowness and obtuseness, or the importance and significance of the relationship between the two.

The summer before I went to law school, I undertook a study on worker-priest ministries for the United Methodist Church. After law school in 1974, I became associated with a new organization called the Council on Religion and Law. I presently chair the Editorial Board of the *Journal of Law & Religion* and serve as my Bishop's Chancellor. These organizations and activities have given me the opportunity to sit at the feet of, or at least be near, some of the great minds and souls exploring the relationship between law and religion. The friendships and wisdom I have received have been rich and profound.

Before I begin my reflections on where I currently find myself on my own faith journey, let me put what I am going to say in context, telling you a little bit more about my work as a lawyer and how I got to this point.

I grew up in Texas as a Methodist and became a Methodist minister. I was fortunate to grow up with the Bible read at home, grace at meals and a wonderful church community. As president of the Youth Council of the Fort Worth Council of Churches, I traveled around the City of Fort Worth and the State of Texas in the '50s with Eddie Edmonds, who was the vice president of the Council. Eddie is black, and in our travels together, I learned first-hand what racism in our state and church were all about. This was the first time I thought about becoming a lawyer.

While in college, I worked for a U.S. Senator from Texas named Ralph Yarborough. I was in Washington during the Summer of '64 when the Civil Rights Bill and other key legislation on the "War on Poverty" were passed. I became more interested in being a lawyer, impressed with what the law could accomplish.

After college and seminary, I became a minister in Paterson, New Jersey, working for three inner-city churches. Every Friday, I met with some of the brightest and most committed people I have known; a group of ministers and priests trying to "bring the Kingdom" to Paterson. We learned to celebrate small victories. Out of this grew a greater interest in the law. The lawyers we worked with seemed to get things accomplished that we as ministers could not do, like filing suits to desegregate the school system, helping to prosecute police officers for police brutality, and obtaining federal money for low-income housing.

After two years in Paterson, I decided to get a law degree so I could fight "City Hall" with more resources, the resources of the law. This was the '60s.

During law school, I worked as a law clerk in legal services. After law school, I tried unsuccessfully to get a job with the Boston Legal Assistance Project. My rationalization for not getting the job was that I did not fit the quota at the time.

I then started trying cases for a trial firm and I have been doing it ever since. I helped form a firm in 1983 which does only litigation. At present, I represent universities, product manufacturers, doctors, employers, insurance companies and other individuals and institutions. I have managed this firm since its inception, and it currently has twenty-five lawyers.

What does one say in the '90s about how one's faith affects one's practice? What do you say to your fellow law students who entered law school with much idealism and who still want to believe there is something important about what they do? What do you say when they tell you they have grown disillusioned and cynical and even depressed, and you know what they are talking about? How do you speak to the ongoing desire to reform the law and the practice, maintaining some hope that it is possible?

My response to these questions is to reflect on what the faith says to the practice of law and our legal system as a whole, speaking particularly to the questions of how faith helps us to see the importance of our work as lawyers, how faith speaks to the disillusionment and cynicism many feel today and how faith deals with the need of the law and the practice of the law for reform and redemption.

I am indebted to many people for getting me to the point where I can make some sense out of all this. I am only going to speak of one, however. Walter Wink's recent book, *Engaging the Powers*, has been particularly helpful in giving me an overall perspective in dealing with these issues of hope and meaning in the practice of law.

Walter was a professor at Union Theological Seminary when I was a student there in the late '60s. His book, *Engaging the Powers*, is a study of what the Bible refers to when it speaks of the "Principalities and the Powers," the Powers being institutions, such as the law and the legal system. In Wink's understanding these institutions are a critical part of God's creation as well as God's redemptive activity. "Humanity is not possible apart from its social institutions."[2] The Powers have an outer visible nature, but also an inner invisible, spiritual nature that must be understood in order "to engage" them. His main thesis, which he describes as a "drama in three simultaneous acts,"[3] is:

> *The Powers are good.*
> *The Powers are fallen.*
> *The Powers must be redeemed.*[4]

He goes on to say: "These three statements must be held together, for each, by itself, is not only untrue but downright mischievous. We cannot affirm governments or universities or businesses to be good unless at the same time we recognize that they are fallen. We cannot face their malignant intractability and oppressiveness unless we remember that they are simultaneously a part of God's good creation. And reflection on their creation and fall will appear only to legitimate these Powers and blast hope for change unless we assert at the same time that these Powers can and must be redeemed."[5]

Later he says, "To assert that God created the Powers does not imply that God endorses any particular Power at any given time. God did not create capitalism or socialism, but there must be some kind of economic system. The simultaneity of creation, fall and redemption means that God at one and the same time *upholds* a given political or economic system, since some such system is required to support human life; *condemns* that system insofar as it is destructive of full human actualization; and *presses for its transformation* into a more humane order. Conservatives stress the first, revolutionaries the second, reformers the third. The Christian is expected to hold together all three."[6]

The law is one of the Powers. To paraphrase Wink:

> *The law is good.*
> *The law is fallen.*
> *The law must be redeemed.*

And all three insights must be held together simultaneously. Wink's development of this thesis has been very constructive for me in putting the pieces together of my two vocations. The title is significant for Wink. He could not name it "confronting the Powers" or "combating the Powers" or "overcoming the Powers" "because they are not simply evil. They can be not only benign but quite positive."[7] Moreover, I would add that you could not name it "celebrating the Powers." Therefore, he names his book *Engaging the Powers* and I name this essay, *Engaging the Law*. I will first engage each of the three insights about the law and then deal with the three insights together.

The Law is Good

Wink begins his discussion with the hymn to the cosmic Christ in Colossians 1:16–17 which says, "For in him all things in heaven and on earth were created, things visible and invisible, whether thrones or dominions or rulers or powers—all things have been created through him and for him. He himself is before all things and in him all things hold together."[8]

God made the law. The law is a necessary structure of human life. "What the hymn sings is recognition that it is God's plan for us to live in interrelationship with each other, and to this end God has determined that there will be subsystems whose sole purpose is to serve the human needs of the One who exemplifies and encompasses humanity."[9] This means in part that the law has a divine vocation. Human community is not possible without law. Law defines and protects these interrelationships and establishes a necessary order for life to flourish. The law works to make these relationships just.

Justice, as I have come to understand it, means the fulfillment of the obligations and demands of relationships. The importance of God's good creation of law and the demands of justice are seen for me most dramatically when the Prophet Amos, speaking for God, says: "I hate, I despise your festivals, and I take no delight in your solemn assemblies. Even though you offer me your burnt offerings and grain offerings, I will not accept them; and the offerings of well-being of your fatted animals I will not look upon. Take away from me the noise of your songs; I will not listen to the melody of your harps. But let justice roll down like waters and righteousness like an everflowing stream."[10] For Amos, doing justice is more important to God than the worship of God. For Amos, doing justice is the worship of God that God yearns for.

So what does all this say to me? First, it tells me that the work of the lawyer is important to the extent this work serves in its own way the divine vocation of the law. As lawyers, there is much to which we can aspire and much to be proud of. Second, it helps me make sense out of what one of my professors in seminary, Daniel Day Williams, said to me when he heard that I was considering going to law school. When I discussed with him the possibility of going into legal services, he suggested that I do theology from the vantage point of a lawyer in private practice where most lawyers work, serving the institutions and clients that law firms represent. He thought that this would be challenging, creative and useful. His words were a challenge because working for Legal Services was for me, at the time, a much more Christian thing to do than working in a conventional law firm. Daniel Day Williams was not saying that one should not serve the poor or the oppressed. My sense now is that he was saying that the institutions that law firms represent greatly affect all God's good creation. The universities and hospitals that my firm represents have divine vocations as well. To the extent these institutions serve their divine vocations, they can have great influence for the good of all, including the poor and oppressed. We need lawyers who recognize the divine vocation of the institutions they serve and who attempt, in their own small ways, to keep the institution focused on its divine vocation. As lawyers trying to live our vocation of faith, we do not want to leave the field of our institutions to those who appreciate neither the demonic and the need for redemption nor understand the divine vocation of the institutions.

One personal note about my own practice. I have ended up primarily on the side of the defense in civil litigation. In many ways my natural leanings would be for the plaintiff. What I have discovered is that, as defense counsel, I like my role. I am in an unique position to assess the plaintiff's case as well as our defenses. I can work toward settlement of those cases where my client is liable and the damages are credible and to litigate those cases where either the client is not liable and/or the damages are not credible. At the same time, I am in a position to participate in decisions within the institutions that I represent that can, even if in very small ways, affect people in the future. Moreover, I have come to have a deep respect for most of my institutional clients who, for example, care about the safety of their products, the students they educate and the patients they serve. This is not to say that some day I might not want to be a plaintiff's attorney or a legal services attorney.

Not only are institutions created good but so are my clients. Unlike some, I find very few clients that I do not really like. I find more goodness than I find the demonic. As Tom Shaffer, the author of *On Being a Christian and a Lawyer*, has taught me, I learn from my clients and hope they will learn from me, "giving and receiving grace."

Finally, the perspective that the law is good opens up the possibility for a new understanding of natural law as having a place in our contemporary discussions of law. Studies of comparative law and interreligious dialogue can open us up as well to shared insights grounded in the created order. I will leave this discussion for another day.

Now, there is no question that it is "untrue and mischievous" to emphasize only the fact that the "law is good" because the law is fallen and the law must be redeemed. Emphasizing only that the law is good involves one in maintaining the status quo and using law to hold and seek power, being blind to the demonic.

Law is Fallen

Lawyer jokes are only the tip of the iceberg in terms of understanding the fallenness of the law. We know that there are laws that are harmful and oppressive. We know that the letter of the law kills. We know that law is supported by violence. We know that there are lawyers who worship money, power and winning at all costs, with little, if any, concern for the truth. I know that I have worshiped these gods as well.

Wink says that the Powers, including the law, are fallen. This does not mean for him that the law is evil in its essence or intrinsically evil. The fall is caused by idolatry—by law forsaking its divine vocation—by law becoming hostile to the purposes of God. What are some of the false gods that law worships: Money, Power, Violence and Domination of Others through racism, sexism, militarism and economic greed as well as the exploitation of God's creation. But Wink sees this as a perversion, not the essence of the law. Law is not evil by nature. Law is good as well as fallen. In Romans 7, Paul says that the law is "holy and just and good,"[11] even spiritual,[12] and yet fallen under the power of sin.[13]

Wink also understands that fallen institutions can mold good people to do things they would not otherwise do. The legal institution of segregation is a good example of this. My grandparents in the South could not see this. They accepted the law of segregation. What demonic form of the law do we accept today that our grandchildren will abhor? We need forgiveness today for complicity with that to which we are blind. Fallen institutions, such as law firms, can also be golden cages, enslaving people and destroying good people's sense of their divine vocation.

So what does this reality that the law is fallen say to me? First, it grounds us in a realistic assessment of the world as it is. From the perspective of faith, I have been able to see what Wink calls "the domination system." Moreover, a faithful person is neither surprised by the depths of evil nor as easily seduced by the demonic. This is a critical perspective for one who is a trial lawyer. Second, the doctrine of the fall, as Wink says, frees one from the idea of perfectibility, of utopian illusions. This leads to a healthy modesty and humility, and is a good antidote to both self-righteousness and burnout. I also know that reforms carry with them new possibilities for evil, as we continue to live in a fallen world. This is a particularly important message to the '60s generation. Third, in dealing with the fallen world, we must stand, as God does, with all those who are oppressed, particularly the weakest, because only through their eyes can we begin to see the fallenness of our institutions and recognize the need for redemption. Fourth, as expressed by Wink, the fallenness of the law is not seen as total depravity, with no health in it. This is a mischievous and untrue doctrine that lacks an understanding of the law as being good. Finally, this doctrine keeps one from satanizing one's enemies, from being paranoid, and even opens up the possibility of learning from one's enemies.

The Law Must Be Redeemed

Yes, the law is fallen, but not in its essence: only in its idolatry. Wink says that what is perverted in time can be redeemed in time. Moreover, Wink states that Jesus died for the Powers, for the Law, as well as for individuals.[14]

This concept of Jesus dying for the law has opened up for me real possibilities of social change. "It is these Powers that Christ reconciles to God through his death on the cross. That death is not, then, merely an unmasking and exposure of the Powers for what they are[15] but an effort to transform the Powers into what they are meant to be."[16] Jesus breaks the sabbath law in regard to healing on the sabbath in order to show that law is made for human beings not human beings for the law. Jesus opens up the spirit of the law, and how it builds relationships and community. We are freed from legalism. Being conformed to Christ, having the mind of Christ, the law is redeemed. Therefore, we can say that institutions can and must change. Institutions can and must rediscover their divine vocations. The law can and must be redeemed so that it works to create genuine human community. God's spirit is seen breaking down barriers created by unjust laws that divide people or create systems of domination. God's spirit gives us a sense of what is unjust, even if we do not see clearly what justice requires.

This creates a lover's quarrel with the law that would be a victim's plea if it were not that the law is good and can be redeemed. We know that the demonic will not win the day.

This creates the need for good advocates and good counselors and we should be proud of those moments when we achieve both. The role of advocacy, in light of the O. J. Simpson trial, for example, is recognized as fallen. But, advocacy on behalf of another is a divine vocation. God, throughout the Hebrew Bible, is seen advocating, among other causes, the cause of Israel. Jesus was the advocate for all creation. To stand up for someone, to receive the slings and arrows on behalf of another, to create a clear, cogent case for someone—this is a noble vocation. Good advocacy must be linked to good counseling—an aspect of our profession that gets less attention than it should. To hear the truth spoken with love is something our clients need. We need to hear it from our clients as well— where we can learn from our clients—where our client's goodness can convert our striving to win at all costs. Together we can work at the weightier matters of the law: justice, mercy and love.[17]

Finally, we must put on the full armor of God, nonviolent armor. Thank God for worship, where we remember who we are and what we are about. Thank God for prayer which unites us with the Spirit. Thank God for the Book which restores and judges.

As I write this, it sounds clearer than it really is. It is hard to see. We do see in a glass darkly. But, we do have moments of discernment. Most of my day is filled with mundane detail. The redemptive moments, the moments of lucidity, are not everyday events. Sometimes they come only after long periods of poor vision and even darkness.

A Drama in Three Simultaneous Acts

Wink's greatest insight is that we must never lose sight of the fact that we must simultaneously recognize that the law is good, that the law is fallen and that the law must be redeemed.

To paraphrase Wink, God upholds any given legal system because it is required to support life. God condemns any given legal system insofar as it does not serve its divine vocation. God presses any given legal system for its transformation into a more humane order. As a fallen people in a fallen world, we can live redemptively to restore God's good creation. This is what my faith says to my legal practice. This is why my practice can and must be a ministry.

Endnotes

1. United Methodist. Partner, Melick and Porter, Boston, Massachusetts. B.A. 1966, Yale University; M.Div. 1969, Union Theological Seminary; J.D. 1974, Boston University.
2. Walter Wink, *Engaging the Powers* 66 (1992).
3. *Id.* at 65.
4. *Id.* at 10.
5. *Id.*
6. *Id.* at 67.
7. *Id.* at 10.
8. Colossians 1:16–17 (New Revised Standard).
9. Wink, *supra* note 2, at 67.
10. Amos 5:21–24.
11. Romans 7:12.
12. Romans 7:14.
13. Romans 7:7–11.
14. Wink, *supra* note 2, at 82.
15. Colossians 2:15.
16. Wink, *supra* note 2, at 82.
17. Luke 11:42.

Aunt Nell's Disappointment

Robert W. Nixon[1]

You probably would have liked my Aunt Nell. She wasn't even a relative, really, just a neighbor who befriended teenagers in the 1950s in my home town, Alloway, New Jersey.

Poor but honest, toughened by a life of "takin' in laundry," as she liked to put it, Aunt Nell was sitting in her scarred oak rocking chair in her kitchen by the kerosene stove, gently wearing the print off the linoleum floor when I last visited her nearly a quarter century ago.

As I began to speak, Aunt Nell fumbled with her hearing aid, which promptly fell into one of its screeching fits. Adjustment made, she paused, her blue eyes piercing mine.

"I hear you're takin' law," she said. "Your mother told me."

She paused, and rocked some more, and then, with a skeptical frown, continued, "Robert, you were such an *honest* boy."

An education in the college of life somehow had left Aunt Nell with the inability to reconcile her concept of the legal profession with her concept of honesty. Unfortunately, Aunt Nell's conclusion wasn't an isolated one. More sophisticated observers over the centuries have made similar comments. That keen observer of Federalist times, Benjamin Franklin, commented: "A countryman between two lawyers is like a fish between two cats."[2] Carl Sandburg, the twentieth century poet, asked, "Why is there always a secret singing / When a lawyer cashes in? / Why does a hearse horse snicker / Hauling a lawyer away?"[3] In this decade, comedian Jay Leno doubtless drew cheers and laughter from his network television audience with this anecdote: "As we watched Judge Clarence Thomas's Supreme Court confirmation hearings, all of the commentators said the same thing: 'One of these people in the room is lying.' Do you believe that? You've got two lawyers and 14 senators in the room, and only *one* of them is lying?"[4]

But despite common stereotypes that generally place the ethics of the legal profession at or below that of used car salespersons, and despite the critical observations of poets and comedians, I have concluded, after more than twenty years of grappling with difficult legal issues and innumerable confrontations between my religious faith and my law practice, that today I could go to the small Baptist cemetery in my hometown, pause at Aunt Nell's tombstone, and whisper, "Aunt Nell, may you rest in peace with a smile. I'm convinced that, yes, an honest person *can* be a lawyer, and, Aunt

Nell, I've found that though it's an endless struggle, it *is* possible to be a good lawyer without abandoning my Christian principles."

How have I come to that conclusion? How have I reconciled my faith as a Seventh-day Adventist Christian with my profession as a lawyer? What milestones mark the professional road on which I have traveled as a believer for nearly a quarter century and on which I continue to travel today, a road that twists and turns from day to day and stretches toward distant curves and yet unforeseen intersections? Here are three that come to mind:

1. Without my faith I would be naked in the public square. When I was a college student in the early 1960s, I dreamed of going to law school, but the hurdles were many, and seemed quite high. My parents listened carefully as I explained my desire one night by telephone from college in Maryland. More diplomatic than Aunt Nell would be a decade later, they urged me to think carefully about my choice of careers and gently guided me into another, more traveled path for a young Adventist son. And even higher hurdles in those less accommodating days were law school administrators who looked to the rules and stated that a student who observed the seventh-day Sabbath[5] and who would not take classes or exams on Saturday should apply elsewhere. So I became a teacher and later an editor. But despite detours in my career into teaching and communication jobs, my dream of studying law never died. A decade later found me in law school, one that already had what I considered an enlightened policy of accommodating the Sabbatarian beliefs and practices of its students.

And as I reflect on the intervening years, I conclude that though my conservative religion had led many, like Aunt Nell and to a lesser extent my family, to be somewhat skeptical about a career in the law, I feel I have successfully reconciled my faith with my legal career. That conclusion does not really surprise me in the least because I had always assumed I could do it, for two reasons. The first is a biblical mandate that I take seriously: Just as God has reconciled others to Himself through Christ, we in turn are Christ's ambassadors to reach out in faith to others in our daily lives,[6] living out our faith in whatever our professions may be. The second is an admonition of Ellen G. White, one of the founders of the Seventh-day Adventist Church: "It requires more grace, more discipline of character, to work for God in the capacity of . . . lawyer . . . , carrying the precepts of Christianity into the ordinary business of life, than to labor as an acknowledged missionary. . . . It requires a strong spiritual nerve to bring religion into the workshop and the business office, sanctifying the details of everyday life, and ordering every transaction to the standard of God's word. But this is what the Lord requires."[7]

Reconciling faith with the everyday legal workplace takes persistent effort. My employer is my church, and perhaps the atmosphere where I work removes me to some degree from ethical temptations to compromise that exist in more secular law offices. But still I must regularly interact with other lawyers, outside counsel, and insurance lawyers, for example, who may have different religious or ethical values. My practice for a church, I must admit, does not completely insulate me from all temptations to ethical compromise. Early in my legal career I made a personal vow to always observe the highest ethical standard.[8] Trying to implement that standard into real life provides me both comfort and anguish.

For example, how should I react in discovery when outside trial counsel suggests a response that to me violates the biblical mandate to let my answers be truthful: "Simply let your 'Yes' be 'Yes,' and your 'No,' 'No'; anything beyond this comes from the evil one."[9] Do I insist on what I consider the "honest" answer, or do I rationalize, smile uncomfortably, and agree to something less, often much less? What if the proposed "lesser" response meets the requirement of every applicable procedural rule and every applicable section of the Code of Professional Responsibility, but still somehow fails to meet my perception of the biblical standard? Should I insist on the higher, biblical standard? Or is such thinking naive? Even professionally irresponsible? And what if my perception of the issue from an objective viewpoint turns out to be erroneous? Answer: I argue for the answer that under the circumstances meets the highest standard.

And how should I relate to the testimony of someone who accuses a church employee—pastor, teacher, or administrator—of sexual misconduct? Do I start with the assumption that men and women pastors are above sexual temptations and are to be believed regardless of what their accusers say? Do I assume that those who make such charges are mentally unstable and cannot be believed under any circumstance? Or do I assume just the reverse? Or do I make the effort to set the balances on as even a level as is humanly possible and then let the evidence settle the matter as it makes its way through ecclesiastical channels? Answer: I argue for starting with level balances.

Anguishing questions, these—and the answers sometimes are even more so. And do I have all the answers? Sometimes I think I had more answers—and they came easier—a quarter century ago. Perhaps legal issues were of a simpler nature then, with less conflicts with my ever-growing faith. But the intervening years have taught me that reconciliation of my faith and the law is not a static, one-time event. It's more like a kaleidoscope with constantly changing complex issues that challenge my constantly developing and maturing faith.[10] I also must conclude that faith is an integral, inseparable part of me, which I cannot discard when I venture into the public square. Without my faith I would be naked in the public square.[11]

2. My view of government and of the relationship of church and state are faith based. In an age when it's politically correct for some conservative and evangelical Christian activists to advocate taking wrecking bars to much of government, I—a conservative Christian and a child of a century and a half of politically conservative ancestors—feel increasingly uncomfortable with much of the rhetoric that now echoes through society and urges me to stride into the public square and to try to impose what often are described as Judeo-Christian beliefs on my state and my nation.

Why do I feel so uncomfortable? I've concluded I cannot reconcile much of the rhetoric with my faith-based concept of church-state relationships. The relentless attacking of government and what I consider attempts to impose all views, both political and religious, on civil society, all in the name of Jesus Christ or Christianity, just doesn't square with how I interpret the Scriptures.

For example, I believe government is ordained by God to commend those who do good and to punish wrongdoers.[12] Conceptually—and historically—governments, of course, can void this mandate by oppressing people of faith, depriving them of basic freedoms, but that, to my way of thinking, does not describe our current political system. In addition, my religion teaches that there are both good and bad laws and that I should obey all of them except those that ask me to disobey clearly defined biblical principles.[13] So the almost ceaseless attacks on government in the name of "Christianity" don't ring true to my way of thinking.

Second, I believe the Bible teaches me that government deserves its "due," commonly called taxes.[14] Perhaps this conclusion appears quaint, even muddled, in this age of tax rebellion. But after visiting scores of countries over the last quarter century and observing government and life abroad, I have concluded that my nation, my state, and my local government are *not* oppressing me with their taxes. For the standard of living that my family enjoys and for the government that protects my freedoms and provides the political stability our nation enjoys, I willingly pay my taxes without complaint, and with a spirit of genuine thankfulness and respect.

Third, I believe that even though God oversees the political affairs of humankind,[15] still His kingdom is not an earthly one. As Jesus said to Pilate, "My kingdom is not of this world. If it were, my servants would fight to prevent my arrest . . . ."[16] As a spiritual, not political, ruler, He does not force His way into anyone's life: "Ask and it will be given to you; seek and you will find; knock and the door will be opened to you. For every one who asks receives; he who seeks finds; and to him who knocks, the door will be opened."[17] My God wants volunteered obedience, not obedience compelled by government threats and force.

I conclude from these concepts that government should not force religious beliefs and practices on anyone. I believe my conclusion is reinforced by the story in which the tax protestors of 2000 years ago confronted Jesus with the question of whether they should pay taxes to the hated Romans. I believe His answer—"Give to Caesar what is Caesar's and to God what is God's"[18]—contains what we might today call a concept of separation of church and state that makes me comfortable with the nonestablishment concept of the First Amendment to our federal Constitution. Furthermore, I believe that in a pluralistic society, faith by force goes against the so-called Golden Rule: "So in everything do to others what you would have them do to you . . . ."[19] Home and church—not Caesar—should pass religious beliefs on to future generations. At the same time, however, every believer and every religious community has every right to participate in and speak out in the public square.

To the question of how believers, individually or corporately, can speak out without asking the government to impose religious beliefs on others, I must admit that I have no simple answer. As the old saying goes: "The devil is in the details." Overall, though, I feel our secular political process, including executive, legislative, and judicial branches on both state and federal levels, have done a reasonably good job of balancing free exercise and nonestablishment interests while deciding current issues in light of our constitutional provisions. Illustrative of how the branches work to preserve religious freedom is the Supreme Court's decision in *Employment Division v. Smith*,[20] which virtually wrote the free exercise clause out of the First Amendment. Congress, however, subsequently "righted the balance" by passing remedial legislation.[21]

Like most Seventh-day Adventists,[22] I strongly support the concept of free exercise of religion and am pleased that the Supreme Court has protected the free exercise of individual Seventh-day Adventists in several important immigration and unemployment compensation cases.[23] Congress has done likewise through accommodation provisions in the federal Civil Rights Act.[24] Since I consider myself, like my church, to be a church-state separationist with certain accommodationist leanings,[25] Supreme Court rulings in Establishment Clause cases generally do not offend me.

3. Only by the grace of God can I integrate my religion and my professional life. Humanly speaking, Aunt Nell was on to something when she confronted me with her concerns about a possible conflict between my ethics and a career in the law. It *is* difficult to integrate biblical principles into daily life, to reconcile faith and lawyering. In fact, from a strictly human viewpoint, it is *impossible* to perfectly live out those principles. As a mere mortal, I will make mistakes. I will fall short of the standard. Only through the grace of God, through dependance on Him, can the imperfect be made perfect.[26] Rather than digress into more abstract theological concepts, suffice it for me to say that I believe that the ascended Christ is my heavenly Advocate who pleads on my behalf: "Even now my witness is in heaven; my advocate is on high. My intercessor is my friend as my eyes pour out tears to God; on behalf of a man he pleads with God as a man pleads for his friend."[27] Only as I completely depend on Him will I be able to successfully implement His principles fully in my life.

These religious concepts—my faith—give me confidence as I go about my daily life as a lawyer. Every day I consciously strive to integrate my religion with the law as it comes to me in my practice. Every day I think and pray that whatever I do—both professionally and personally—will be perfectly reconciled with God's will. Every day that integration is imperfect. I don't assume for an instant that my efforts—my works—are of prime importance to my God, who said: "Woe to you, teachers of the law and Pharisees, you hypocrites! You give a tenth of your spices—mint, dill and cumin. But you have neglected the more important matters of the law—justice, mercy and faithfulness. You should have practiced the latter, without neglecting the former. You blind guides! You strain out a gnat and swallow a camel!"[28] I am mindful that the Old Testament prophet Isaiah attributed these words to God: "Maintain justice and do what is right, for my salvation is close at hand and my righteousness will soon be revealed."[29]

A key part of my thinking and praying about such subjects is referring by what I call the casebook approach to basic Bible texts on subjects that interest me. Rather than read redundant commentaries, I prefer, often with the aid of a concordance, to read and contemplate relevant Bible passages, such as I have cited in this essay. Most often I read in the Old Testament the books of Psalms and Proverbs and in the New Testament the books of Matthew and James.

For example, when I need spiritual encouragement, I meditate on a favorite Psalm: "God is our refuge and strength, an ever-present help in trouble. Therefore we will not fear, though the earth give way and the mountains fall into the heart of the sea."[30]

Do I have all the answers? No, absolutely no. But I do have a method that helps me search for reasonable answers that are reconciled with my faith, an effective method that would enable me today to reply to Aunt Nell with confidence, "Yes, Aunt Nell, it *is* possible to be an honest lawyer."

Endnotes

1. Seventh-day Adventist. B.A. 1961, Columbia Union College; M.S. 1964, Boston University; J.D. 1974, Washington College of Law, American University.
2. Rudolph Flesch, *The Book of Unusual Quotations* 147 (1957).
3. Carl Sandburg, *The Lawyers Know Too Much* (1920), reprinted in *Complete Poems of Carl Sandburg* 189 (1969).
4. Jess M. Brallier, *Lawyers and Other Reptiles* 12 (1992).
5. "Remember the Sabbath day by keeping it holy. Six days you shall labor and do all your work, but the seventh day is a Sabbath to the Lord your God." Exodus 20:8–10 (New International).
6. 2 Corinthians 5:16–21.
7. Ellen G. White, *Messages to Young People* 215–16 (1930).
8. "The greatest want of the world is the want of men—men who will not be bought or sold, men who in their inmost souls are true and honest, men

who do not fear to call sin by its right name, men whose conscience is as
true to duty as the needle to the pole, men who will stand for the right
though the heavens fall." See Ellen G. White, *Education* 57 (1952).

9. Matthew 5:37; see also Exodus 20:16 ("You shall not give false testimony
against your neighbor.").

10. "We have much to say about this, but it is hard to explain because you are
slow to learn. In fact, though by this time you ought to be teachers, you
need someone to teach you the elementary truths of God's word all over
again. You need milk, not solid food! Anyone who lives on milk, being still
an infant, is not acquainted with the teaching about righteousness. But
solid food is for the mature, who by constant use have trained themselves
to distinguish good from evil." Hebrews 5:11–14.

11. See Richard John Neuhaus, *The Naked Public Square: Religion and
Democracy in America* (1984).

12. "Everyone must submit himself to the governing authorities, for there is
no authority except that which God has established. The authorities that
exist have been established by God. Consequently, he who rebels against
the authority is rebelling against what God has instituted, and those who
do so will bring judgment on themselves. For rulers hold no terror for those
who do right, but for those who do wrong. Do you want to be free from fear
of the one in authority? Then do what is right and he will commend you.
For he is God's servant to do you good. But if you do wrong, be afraid, for
he does not bear the sword for nothing. He is God's servant, an agent of
wrath to bring punishment on the wrongdoer. Therefore, it is necessary to
submit to the authorities, not only because of possible punishment but also
because of conscience." Romans 13:1–5; see also 1 Peter 2:13–17.

13. "We have men placed over us for rulers, and laws to govern the people.
Were it not for these laws, the condition of the world would be worse than
it is now. Some of these laws are good, others are bad. The bad have been
increasing, and we are yet to be brought into strait places. But God will
sustain His people in being firm and living up to the principles of His word.
When the laws of men conflict with the word and law of God, we are to
obey the latter, whatever the consequences may be." Ellen G. White, 1
Testimonies for the Church 201–2 (1948). For example, Seventh-day Adventists historically have considered Sunday closing laws and laws uphold-
ing slavery to be in such conflict.

14. "This is also why you pay taxes, for the authorities are God's servants, who
give their full time to governing. Give everyone what you owe him: If you
owe taxes, pay taxes; if revenue, then revenue; if respect, then respect; if
honor, then honor." Romans 13:6–7.

15. "Praise be to the name of God for ever and ever; wisdom and power are
his. He changes times and seasons; he sets up kings and deposes them."
Daniel 2:20–21.

16. John 18:36.

17. Matthew 7:7–8.

18. Mark 12:17.

19. Matthew 7:12.

20. See *Employment Division v. Smith*, 494 U.S. 872, 876–90 (1990).

21. Religious Freedom Restoration Act, 42 U.S.C. §§ 2000bb-1(c) (Supp. V

1993). The Supreme Court voided this statue, however, after this essay was written. *City of Boerne v. Flores*, 65 U.S.L.W. 4612 (1997).

22. The General Conference of Seventh-day Adventists and its North American Division have filed numerous amicus curiae briefs, often in cooperation with other denominations, arguing for religious freedom for a wide variety of believers and their diverse religious practices. The North American Division publishes *Liberty* magazine, which is distributed to several hundred thousand opinion leaders and which promotes freedom of religion and separation of church and state.

23. *Girouard v. United States*, 328 U.S. 61, 70 (1946); *Sherbert v. Verner*, 374 U.S. 398, 403–10 (1963); *Hobbie v. Unemployment Appeals Comm'n*, 480 U.S. 136, 141–46 (1987).

24. For provisions recognizing some degree of accommodations for believers and religious educational institutions see 42 U.S.C. §§ 2000(e)(j), 2000(e-2)(e) (1988).

25. See North American Division Working Policy HC 05 03 Position Statement: "[W]e hold that religious liberty is best achieved, guaranteed and preserved, when church and government respect each other's proper areas of activity and concern. . . . Though the Bible does not specifically prohibit the acceptance of gifts from the government, such aid should be shunned when its acceptance would violate applicable law, would lead to excessive control by or entanglement with the government, would lead to dependence on government, or in any other way would compromise the integrity of the Church or reduce its ability to design programs and curricula to fulfill its gospel commission."

26. "Let us then approach the throne of grace with confidence, so that we may receive mercy and find grace to help us in our time of need." Hebrews 4:14–16.

27. Job 16:19–21.

28. Matthew 23:23–24.

29. Isaiah 56:1.

30. Psalm 46:1–2.

Lawyers and Sacred Gold

Michael Joseph Woodruff[1]

Religion concerns the spirit in man whereby he is able to recognize
what is truth and what is justice; whereas law is only the application, however imperfectly, of truth and justice in our everyday
affairs. If religion perishes in the land, truth and justice will also.
We have already strayed too far from the faith of our fathers. Let
us return to it, for it is the only thing that can save us.
—Sir Alfred Lord Denning, Master of the Rolls[2]

The Case of the Coughing Stenographer

It was an early fall morning in 1972, my first time at "Master Calendar."
The monthly case setting session was conducted by the presiding judge in
the Santa Barbara County Courthouse, a beautiful Spanish mediterra-
nean-style building. The presiding judge's courtroom was rapidly filling up
with people as I entered. The room was overly crowded with all the seats
taken and people lining the walls. Lawyers sat in the jury box. The court
stenographer was up close to the judge's bench. Two clerks, one a young
assistant, were sitting behind desks on one side, receiving lawyers as they
checked in for their cases. Near them, next to a water cooler, stood the
bailiff.

I found a space facing the center courtroom aisle in the middle of the
back wall next to several other lawyers and waited for my case to be called.
Everyone rose as the bailiff called the court to order and announced the
judge. The judge went through his preliminaries and began calling cases.

This judge was an intimidating character with a stern demeanor and a
reputation for being autocratic. I later observed in chambers a poster of
Marlon Brando as the godfather with the slogan, "Make me an offer I can't
refuse," on the inside of his closet door. He rarely accommodated out-of-
town counsel who had not bothered to learn the local rules and he was not
above rebuking lawyers for late submissions. On this particular morning,
the docket was long and the judge worked through it as the audience gave
him their rapt attention.

My unrestricted view from the back wall was perfect for learning how
lawyers worked in such a setting, where they would stand, and what they
would say. The local legend, a lawyer-octogenarian in a black pin-stripe
three piece suit, famous for his ancient ritualistic recitals of a case's status,
answered the call of his case in characteristic fashion. Before half a dozen
cases had been called, the stenographer began to cough occasionally as

though something were stuck in her throat. The frequency and intensity of her coughing gradually increased. I watched, puzzled that the judge and the lawyers close to her ignored her increasingly desperate state. I wondered what could be done. I spotted the water cooler and wondered why she didn't stop her machine and get a drink. Then I realized that the scene was a paralyzed triangulation between judge, stenographer, and audience, with the judge controlling the room. He wouldn't stop, she wouldn't move, and no one came to her aid.

Her face began to redden, her distress evident for everyone to see, as the coughing, now violent and desperate, continued. With one quick step, I was away from the back wall and moving down the center aisle. I passed through the bar, reached the water cooler and took a small paper cup from a stack of cups. Filling it with water, I walked fifteen feet and handed it to her. The judge stopped talking with counsel and a hush fell over the room. I became self-conscious, but determined to see her served regardless of whatever consequences awaited me. Her coughing not fully abated, I repeated my act.

I looked up at the judge, who was now waiting patiently for her recovery. After the stenographer nodded that the water was enough, the judge thanked me. As I retreated to the back wall, I realized from my pounding heart that I subconsciously believed there was some risk to my action. But I was new and there was a lot I didn't know.

I didn't really know the judge or the real person behind his brusque exterior. I didn't know then that the judge was a well-meaning man who worked hard at doing a good job, but wasn't beyond becoming preoccupied with problems and not seeing the need of someone near him. Years later I could see him in a wider context and appreciate him as an honorable and decent man who was intent on raising the standards of legal practice.

The incident passed and I appeared many times before the same judge. Some fourteen months later, I went to pick up a copy of a court transcript. When I entered the room at the courthouse, the stenographer greeted me. She had learned who I was and where I worked. She treated me like a friend. She thanked me and said my assistance that day was not a small matter to her. She died a few months later.

I consider this story embarrassingly simple. It was only a small act of providing a small paper cup filled with a little water. Not the stuff of real high drama. Was her life at stake? Probably not. I did think at the time, though, that she could have died and nobody in that crowded courtroom would have stopped to notice. The stenographer could have been born in Bethlehem or had shepherds for ancestors; the lawyers next to her didn't care. They were busy. They had other things to do. But the story illustrates a vital point of conflict for faith and law. *Faith demands attention to people's needs.* Sometimes the law responds swiftly and appropriately. At other times, it acts not at all. It is silent. The need is invisible, either ignored or denied, and people are sent away with a rationalization or a callous shrug of indifference.

This story serves me as a parable, about misplaced priorities, almost-missed opportunities, and the relationship between misperception and action or inaction. I do not expect that the story's meanings and their correlations to Scripture will well serve relativists or materialists or philosophical determinists. To them, I simply note that the intellectual journey through such material may be a cross-cultural challenge to answer the "riddle" of human motivation to respect and help another.

It should make a difference to others that a person has lived. As pilgrims on life's journey, we should contribute to the good, benefitting others, leaving the world a little better than we found it. Our choices, like lived-out ideas, have consequences. Each of our lives has the potential to be a one-of-a-kind story; what we experience, do, say, and think, gets into us somehow as part of us and becomes ours, not like a fingerprint, but a signature movie, a unique life on tape. We cannot edit what gets filmed; everything in which we participate goes into it: the wheat and the chaff, the good, bad, and the boring—all woven together in a mosaic of relation-ships and actions that to us may make as much sense as chaos theory. I think it is all, in an ultimate sense, editable and reportable. Like any story, not all of it is worth telling. But the telling should be more than it usually is, especially at the end of one's mortal life. As a society, we struggle to sum up a long life, even one lived well with lots of interesting experiences. If not captured by a biography or autobiography, one's life is unfortunately often relegated to a small obituary and a few lines on a granite slab. It doesn't seem fair, and it isn't if that's all there is.

The Relationship of Our Life Story to the Great Story

It has been suggested that each life lived is intended not only to be reportable, but accountable. The predicate for this is obviously more than an afterlife; something in itself suggested implicitly and inductively by the very dissatisfaction and unfulfillment that registers when life is gone at the height of its powers; the *angst* of knowing that the life lived was much more than what is reported in those last few lines; the frustration of those left behind to struggle to sum up what cannot be adequately totalled. So the question remains: Are reports kept on each life, what difference has that life made, and to whom does one account?

I have come to understand that our life is not only a story; life fits into a bigger story when it intersects with, and is measured by, the Great Story, a life template fit upon our own. The person in the Great Story is, for many, a kind of missing person, one seen leaving the scene of the accident, but who keeps showing up at unexpected times and places. The Great Story breaks off, apparently unfinished, because it continues and continues . . . off the page or off line . . . in life after life, mine and yours, in lawyer or client, in ways apparent and in ways not so apparent. So that even the reading of this essay becomes part of the story as well, linking author to reader ("I read *your* article." To which *I* reply, "Did it make any difference to you?" That is, did it contribute anything to *your* story?) To what extent do the shared meanings of our stories overlap? How is there a shared meaningful experience at all? How can there be an argument of words over the veracity of what was reported that is at all meaningful, unless there is real human contact in, for the moment, a common story? So, the little stories of our lives can be told from different perspectives when there are commonalities derived from the intersections (of course, the old word would be, without sexual connotation, "intercourse") with others. Could it be that there is another story that is summing up all of our lives, a Great Story into which all our small stories fit?

That audacious thought is precisely what has been suggested already by one who taught that a story was unfolding that fit precisely into the hoped for experience of prophets and kings. Their story was incomplete because they wanted to hear and know about the Great Story. "Blessed are the eyes that see what you see. For I tell you that many prophets and kings wanted to see what you see but did not see it, and to hear what you hear but did not hear it."[3]

Thus are identified certain pregnant possibilities: there is a kind of narrative quality about our lives that suggests a story with subplots and counterpoint themes; our story is one of those narratives that is not usually found in isolation from those of others, but, in context, is still very reportable *and*, if truth be told, very possibly accountable, as we seem to have such a preoccupation with holding *others* responsible for the minutest of details, while hoping for every consideration for ourselves. Additionally, we have been told that each life's story is measurable by and related to a Great Story, the one involving the Great Missing Person (GMP).[4]

The GMP's Solution to the Justice/Mercy Dilemma

According to the Book, the GMP's job was to defeat the law's requirement of holding individuals accountable for their defalcations—so that as Søren Kierkegaard noted, the light of justice does not just refract as it comes to illuminate what we are and have done, but reflect off the One who successfully intervenes to hide all that is unworthy of being seen. Because of the GMP, life, including the legal environment in which we work as lawyers, is therefore graced with the possibility of gifts that are undeserved; the problem is how to reconcile that mercy with the demand for justice.

The doctrine of substitutionary atonement has wrongly, in my view, been presented as a matter beyond the capacity of the finite mind to comprehend. We are told, "just accept it on faith." In an ethical analysis, giving due consideration to criminal responsibility, justice cannot be satisfied by the intervention of another, an innocent volunteer, to take the punishment for the guilty party. The punishment of the innocent for the guilty is immoral as a matter of ethical judgment.[5]

Without an ontological change,[6] the ethical demand for retributive satisfaction requires justice to be done, not mercy. But because justice will be satisfied when mercy's invitation is accepted on the condition of ontological change, the ethical demand is met. The benefits of the substitutionary atonement, a vicarious sacrifice, cannot be transferred to another to resolve the problem of guilt, unless there is participation in the life of the Substitute. The terms of mercy's reception require the occurrence of ontological change, so that when the atoning act as redemptive payment or repurchase satisfies the ethical demand for justice, the criminal "disappears" in favor of a "merger" with the GMP. The GMP's atoning sacrifice is thus the universal and infinite solution to guilt and shame, a means whereby forgiveness extends to not only acts but thoughts.[7]

In other words, the reason why conciliation and forgiveness can play a part in the lawyer's practice of law is not because those terms have been introduced in a religious and ethical lexicon to make law practice kinder and gentler, but because the GMP satisfied justice's demand and offers mercy to all who are willing to undergo a change in their nature or being, an ontological change.[8]

The Criminal Justice System Illustrates Mechanistic Justice

The criminal justice system represents a pervasive condition in society, and especially within the legal profession. When we are self-sufficient and complacent, we are in danger of spiritual blindness that misses our own need for God and the needs of our neighbor.[9] Narcissism not only blocks love for God and neighbor, it hollows out a culture, makes it superficial, introduces an arrogance of self-sufficiency that is false to reality. This puts the arrogant in confrontation with God. The ancient truth in the Jewish psalter will apply: "It is you who deliver lowly folk, but haughty eyes you humble."[10]

This understanding of morality, of ethical decision-making, is in conflict with a legal system that mandates sentencing guidelines, removes rehabilitation as a goal of the criminal justice system, and does not allow the judiciary to function with discretion beyond a mere clerk, a decision-maker who applies the law in the totality of the circumstances and with regard for equity as "law's conscience."[11] Society is less humane when justice without mercy is sought. Justice becomes mechanistic, serving retribution of a kind.[12]

The morality of faith goes further and sees the possibility of ontological change, of mercy participating with justice to affirm human responsibility, rehabilitation, and reconciliation with the victim. The goals of a humane society would exclude capital punishment except under extraordinary circumstances to preclude executing the innocent by mistake or those persons for whom repentance and ontological change will make them new persons, as well as to reinforce society's value that all human life is sacred.[13]

When law through its criminal justice system abandons any pretense of restoration of the wrongdoer to society through responsibility, rehabilitation and reconciliation, it is a conscious choice against many things: the moral significance and humanity of all persons, the necessity that mercy work with justice because of the possibility of ontological change, the understanding that the essential nature of the judiciary requires participating in moral decision-making by the exercise of discretion in appropriate circumstances, and our need for God's wisdom, especially for legal decisions. The irony of the situation is that society in its zealous pursuit of justice can forget that Scripture teaches that the God of justice is also a God of mercy. When society abandons His merciful ways, God becomes the enemy and its judge.

When a judge sentences a person convicted of crime, should not society's interest of safety be a predominant factor in sending that person to prison? Should not a judge consider carefully what alternatives are available to help maximize society's interest in the outcome of a case, including reconciling the offender to society and the victim? The legal profession sets itself a high task to treat each person, including those often invisible, but essential to the operation of a law firm or a court, as an important self in a moral space, responsible to act with significance, to exercise the power to do something good for the benefit of others. Lawyers can set the example, to show that there is a basis to act, to pursue the good of the other, and to make a difference in the world.[14] Charles Colson tells the story of an inmate without hope, whose life after years in prison was changed by a family who shared God's love with him, who visited him, who cared about him.[15] I wondered, on reading the story, whether he was represented by counsel and how his lawyer cared for him. Did his lawyer treat him as a neighbor when he was isolated, lonely, and in prison?

As I try to know the people around me in my practice (neighbors), the secretaries, clerks, law students, lawyers, receptionists, janitors, bailiffs, whether in person or on the telephone, and to listen and respond to them as persons, I constantly remind myself of their inestimable worth. Yet I know the inner tension that results from choices, leaving the computer, interrupting one's work. The effort to care has a price. The fact that I cannot measure the value of virtue, or what it means to others when they are treated as persons with respect, does not mean that the intangible is ultimately outweighed by the tangible, e.g., the recovery of monetary damages.[16]

Today, I like to think of the late stenographer as a former client, not one on retainer, but one for whom my brief service in a courtroom made a difference. Although "the case of the coughing stenographer" was measured in minutes, it reminds me that in our legal work, no one should be invisible, and that faith's duty to love our neighbor is also the law's duty to treat all persons with dignity and respect.

Faith addresses the ideal in law of seeking justice, by stretching our perception of what is really going on. Faith, by nature, is the intangible, "things hoped for, the evidence of things not seen."[17] Therefore, the questions raised do not necessarily admit to easy answers. The question we can never answer is, "Who has the most important claim in this situation for God's attention?" Scripture instructs us to look at those who need help, those who want help, those who are honest about their need and humble enough to admit that they can't help themselves. For example, in the wonderful parable Jesus told of the Good Samaritan, to identify our neighbors, Jesus chose a character who was offensive to make his point. He made a hero out of an ethnic outcast Samaritan at the expense of the "respected" people in his audience. The Samaritan was no respecter of persons as he met another's need. Similarly, the law's treatment of individuals with dignity and respect, during court time, should not be limited to the privileged.[18]

The law firm in which I work respects faith as an indispensable part of life. Many of our clients are leaders of religious organizations, colleges, and churches. Since the diversity of lawyers within the firm addresses their variety as clients, we are able to meet them with a common language, and with an understanding of their aspirations, goals and the ethos within which they function. By spending time together as lawyers on firm retreats and with regular interaction, we have glimpsed what a client-centered community of persons, holding each other accountable and sharing common goals for their practices, might be. We strive constantly to be in formation, always in process, adapting to change, and trying to improve. So we think less of what we are than what we want to be. We are defined more in our doing, by the projects undertaken, the cases being worked on, the needs being addressed, than by theoretical interests in law. We recognize that respect from clients and colleagues is earned daily and so we discuss how our clients' needs can best be served, how the delivery of our legal services might be improved, and whether a service should be provided *pro bono publico*. We try to deflate egos and not take ourselves too seriously, even if we all tend to work long hours and sacrifice other relationships and other worthwhile activities for the law. It is a life that strives for excellence, but always within limits.

If sharing the company of lawyers in the firm has been a benefit to me, and it has,[19] it has not displaced the challenge of being a lawyer today. The legal profession has an uneasy social relation to society.[20] We may subconsciously be motivated to be better lawyers because we know the public perception of lawyers is so bad. This is not consistent with Jesus' admonition about anxiety in his Sermon on the Mount.[21] We try to work *together* at being an example of what can be done, even if the contribution is of limited significance to a few people. We practice together as a firm, not as individuals, who are necessarily interested in ethically sound and practical solutions to the daily problems clients present. We maintain an interest in the academic and juridical debate about legal theory, because legal hermeneutics and constitutional interpretation are relevant to our religious liberty and constitutional law specialties.[22] The point is that Jesus' reminder not to be anxious about life and the nature of community does prompt a periodic collective review of the legitimacy or illegitimacy of the sources of stress and anxiety. We check and recheck priorities. We know we cannot do everything, but what we can and must do, we try to help each other to do with excellence.

One of the difficulties in representing clients with a conflict between law and their religion is that it is not always obvious why faith and law are in conflict. Religion is a complex phenomenon,[23] under criticism,[24] and its role in society is keenly debated.[25] When we pay attention to such claims, legitimate them as worthy of our attention as lawyers in the courts, we assume the burden that often is attached to unpopular causes, reconciling two differing worlds, and interpreting meaning in two directions. Some of the cases I have worked on are somewhat removed from the clients, e.g., participating as counsel for an *amicus curiae*. In others, the clients' burdens transferred directly to counsel. In either situation, the problems placed the lawyer in an "in-between" role—where law and religion were in conflict and where the lawyer's own religion was not necessarily implicated—but the advocacy role undertaken required a measure of burden-bearing that is the privilege and honor of being a lawyer in the service of a client. Some examples of such matters include:

(1) In separate cases, Native American Indians objected to government policies that either disturbed or prohibited their religious practice. The federal government allowed logging companies access to federal property, thereby disturbing Indians worshipping at ancient sacred burial sites.[26] A federal agency prohibited a Native American employee from giving an invocation at a federally sponsored meeting of tribal leaders.[27]

(2) Zoning regulations prohibited churches from feeding the homeless on the church premises.[28]

(3) Students were penalized for religious expression in public schools, notwithstanding the fact that it was clear that any other expression was acceptable.[29]

(4) One judge refused to hear our client's testimony during a no fault divorce proceeding. The client wanted to dispute his wife's allegation of irreconcilable differences that had caused an irremediable breakdown of the marriage.[30]

One of the authors in this Symposium, William Bentley Ball, known for his First Amendment work, including *Wisconsin v. Yoder*, once said, "These are sacred cases." As our clients' burdens become ours, I can think of the relationship that law shares with religion,[31] and even of the relationship of conflicting schools of legal philosophy to a trinitarian theology,[32] but when all is finally analyzed, I must ask whether the duty each requires has been discharged. I have learned that the issue of being available to meet someone's need precedes any issue of what that contribution might cost. Such was the case with Eleanor, a homeless person, whose story concludes this essay.

The Case of the Woman Who Lived in Her Car

My law firm represented one of the local banks in the mid-1980s. The bank had been the trustee for an estate for over thirty years. The estate portfolio was mostly stocks and real property valued in the millions of dollars. Due to a conflict of interest, the bank had to seek judicial approval to substitute another trustee. A complete asset inventory, including legal descriptions of all real property interests, had to be prepared, the first in many years. Day after day, as I worked on the project at my desk or attended meetings at the bank, I thought about the wealth behind this trust. It seemed a hollow reality, to have assets without a good end or a beneficial cause to serve. I wondered whether a new trustee would maximize trust income at the expense of the environment (one of the issues), and whether trust beneficiaries had lived happier lives because they had more money than they could spend. Finally, I wondered what I was doing spending my creative energies on something that was legally necessary but, in the larger scheme of things, seemed to serve no meaningful end.

After numerous hours on the project, I decided to spend a few minutes before work each morning studying the subject of God's concern for injustice and the poor, guided by the book, *Bring Forth Justice*.[33] I had to refer each morning to the many cited scripture references. The author asserted that "the materially destitute and socially marginal are the special object of God's concern and should be ours as well."[34] The exercise was convicting: I was living far removed from the destitute and socially marginal. I went weeks without meeting a truly poor person. I seemed to be serving the rich at this moment in my career for no defined end. After reading, thinking, and praying for the week, the juxtaposition of the morning study and the asset inventory convinced me that I was living in contradiction to the gospel of Christ, unless I was at least *available* to help the poor. My legal work was so far removed from human need that I could not imagine how justice for a poor person could be served by what I was doing. On Friday morning, after my reading, I prayed: "Lord, if you want me to help someone, I'm available." The operative word was *available*.

At four-thirty that afternoon, a woman named Eleanor called on referral from a doctor I had once met briefly. It took me a moment to even remember the doctor. Eleanor explained that she wanted help in securing a continuance of a trial scheduled to begin Monday morning, a mere three days away. Her illegally parked car had been towed away and had been stored by a private towing company. The daily storage charges now exceeded the value of the car. She needed the car back because she lived in it. The trial would decide, in effect, whether she got her home back, at least all the home she had.

I couldn't take a new case. I couldn't prepare for trial on Monday. My thoughts were racing with conflicts and excuses. But I also remembered that I said that morning that I would be *available* and I recognized in Eleanor's call a strange coincidence, a never-in-my-practice-before quality that connected this moment to my morning prayer and my week's reading. This was no coincidence. I had to do what I could. I interviewed her briefly, confirming the case information and why her request was for a continuance. I then asked if I could call her back after checking with the court clerk. She said she was calling from a pay telephone and she would have to call me again. We set the time so she would call before the switchboard closed for the weekend.

I immediately called the presiding judge's chambers and talked to his secretary, explained the circumstances and asked about the calendar for Monday. I asked if there was any possibility of having the matter continued while I looked into the matter. She said she would call me back. I was surprised when in five minutes she called back and said that the judge was willing to continue the matter. I thanked her.

When Eleanor called back, I told her that the court would continue the case. Before I could discuss with her my representation of her, she thanked me and hung up, never asking if I would represent her at the hearing.

The next day was Saturday and I awoke with Eleanor's continuance on my mind. I realized that I had to go to court on Monday morning to be Eleanor's safety net to see that she got her continuance.

On Monday morning, I got to the courtroom of the presiding judge for the Master Calendar call at 8:30 a.m. The room was crowded with familiar faces. I took a place against the back wall to be able to survey the whole courtroom and identify her if she stood up when her case was called. As the second item on the docket, her case was called and she stood at the front row. I saw Eleanor, a small elderly woman. But the judge referred her case to Department 3. He did not grant her continuance. She was confused and tried to talk to the judge. He told her to take the request up with the judge in Department 3. I started forward as she turned away from the judge and came up the center aisle. Meeting her half way, I introduced myself. She immediately gripped my arm, obviously relieved that I was there for her. We retrieved the court file and headed down to Department 3.

Nothing was said about a retainer, but I knew I had a client. We walked to Department 3, opened the door and looked in. The judge was talking to the bailiff in an otherwise empty courtroom. He hadn't put on his robe yet. When he saw me, he cheerfully greeted us and said he would be right back. By the time we walked up to the bar, and handed the file to the bailiff, the judge had come out, robed. He was formally announced by the bailiff as we stood respectfully. The judge sat down, took the file, looked through it, then asked where the other parties were. Learning that they had not appeared at the Master Calendar call, he said to Eleanor, "This is your lucky day. You win." He signed the order and said, "That will be all." I thanked the court and told Eleanor we were leaving. She held my arm as we quickly left the courtroom, went down the hall, descended a staircase, and exited on the first floor to the street.

"Do you know what just happened?" I asked her? "No," she said. "You just won your case. You did not get a continuance, but you won the case." She was speechless for a moment and as tears welled up in her eyes, she began repeating "God bless you! God bless you!" I felt the power of her words as a sense of peace came over me. We stood on the sidewalk and discussed the next steps to be taken and parted. I went back to my office, not knowing that my work for Eleanor would continue for several weeks. I checked my watch. It was 8:52 a.m. I had scarcely invested a half hour in Eleanor's project, including the calls on Friday. The only task so far seemed to be to just show up, to be "available."

It was 9:00 a.m. when I told the receptionist, "I went to court this morning and our client won." As part of a litigation firm where victories were important, she was pleased. I went on down the hall to my office. Apparently, she told others coming into work the news of my victory, but no one knew which case it was or that a trial had even been scheduled. Within an hour, I had a visit from a senior partner. He smiled and asked about my victory. I gave him the facts and left nothing out. His face showed his disapproval. He told me that doing such things could damage the reputation of the firm. He shook his head and left. The message to me was clear. We practiced law to make money, and we did it by representing a certain class of people. That was the bottom line for him.

My partner missed the satisfaction of serving a person in need and the experience of seeing hope in the client's eyes. Eleanor's victory brought relief to one who had nothing to offer in return and needed a lift from despair, a woman whose poor judgments and misfortunes resulted in tragic consequences to her life.

Eleanor's case taught me that *faith demands availability to meet people's needs*.[35] Faith sees significance in all people, not just the rich and the privileged. Faith makes helping others a matter of privilege and honor. Money did not come first: the barrister's gown with the pocket in the back of the hood was a constant reminder that compensation *followed* service. A primary motivation for work should be availability to help people without a preoccupation with the pursuit of money. Satisfaction in work is a gift of God.[36]

I know lawyers with kindness, competence, and generosity of spirit, who are sustained by a faith in which truth and justice are not matters of cosmic indifference. These lawyers have the humility to pray as they practice and the willingness to diligently practice before they preach. They serve their clients even if it involves a personal sacrifice or is emotionally difficult.

(Few find it easy to be present with a client in crisis.) They respond to success with thankfulness and do not take the credit. They only did their duty.[37] They respond to failure as an opportunity to learn what could or should have been done differently.

I know the numbers of these lawyers are small. But they are exciting to be around because the result of their work is not only an enigma to explain, but a miracle to be witnessed. They do not consider the question irrelevant or meaningless, "Which is greater: the gold, or the temple that makes the gold sacred?"[38] because they are custodians of the temple, carriers of a sacred tradition of serving clients as advocates and counselors, doing justice and loving mercy. With such as these we would not remain "a nation under lawyers,"[39] but become conscious of our duty to serve one another in the love of God.

Endnotes

1. Episcopalian. Partner, Gammon & Grange, P.C., McLean, Virginia. B.A. 1967, University of California, Santa Barbara; J.D. 1972, University of California, Los Angeles. The author gratefully acknowledges the helpful comments of Scott J. Ward, Esq. and Jonathan A. Ruybalid, Esq.

2. Alfred Lord Denning, "The Changing Law," 122 (1953), reprinted in *The Western Idea of Law* 393 (J. C. Smith and David N. Weisstub eds., 1983). Lord Denning's use of "religion" likely refers to the Church of England, but is used here to include those faith groups that comprehend and/or utilize certain vocabulary and concepts of the common law tradition, a synthesis of classical and biblical jurisprudence: God, justice, law, equity, reason, truth, good, guilt, duty, free agency, covenant, redemption, freedom, confession, mercy, and pardon, as well as their opposites. This is in accord with the root definition of *religio*, "to bind back," and the nature of religious conversion itself, a matter of intellection rather than the mere stirring of the emotions. See Malcolm A. Jeeves, "Psychology of Religion," in *New Dictionary of Christian Ethics and Pastoral Theology* 706–9 (David J. Atkinson, et al. eds., 1995).

   For the term "justice," used here, consistent with Lord Denning's usage, see John Finnis, *Natural Law and Natural Rights* 161–63 (1980) (the elements of other-directedness, duty, equality, and the *legis aeternae* in Thomas Aquinas's phrase, *participatio legis aeternae in rationali creatura*, id. at 398–403). See also Douglas R. Anderson, *Strands of System* (1995). For American philosopher C. S. Peirce, the universal laws of God require interpretation but are related to human experience. Like Aquinas and Peirce, Lord Denning posits a Creator as law-giver, affecting every aspect of human experience and providing a basis for understanding universal legal norms. He interpret's law's moral meaning in light of an understanding of divine interaction through information input and participation in the life of the world, a view that accords with Jewish and Christian understanding of the mighty acts of God and the mysterious, familiar, relational presence of the Word of God that addresses his people as his servant and by his Servant. See, e.g., Martin Buber, *The Prophetic Faith*

233–35 (1949) (discussing servanthood); Eberhard Jungel, *God As the Mystery of the World* 345–47, 373 (Darrell L. Guder trans., 1983) (discussing the distinction between law and gospel applied to the principle of God); John Polkinghorne, *Reason and Reality* 74–84 (1991) (discussing congruence between the physical universe and the rationality of God as creator); see also Karen Lebacqz, *Justice in an Unjust World: Foundations for a Christian Approach to Justice* 61–64 (1987) (discussing scripture as a starting place for understanding the law and justice); Karen Lebacqz, *Six Theories of Justice: Perspectives from Philosophical and Theological Ethics* (1986). For a valuable contrasting view, see Lloyd L. Weinreb, *Natural Law and Justice* 66 (1987) (asserting that the rational nature of law necessarily leads to atheism, and law as command leads to faith without reason). Weinreb's naturalistic legal philosophy seems a logical extension from Kantian presuppositions, namely, that reality is separated into *noumena* and *phenomena*, effectively representing the death of metaphysics and narrowing the epistemological methodologies available, and consistent with postmodernism. Without God, Weinreb's quandary is why law should have an aspirational dimension when, he assumes, we live in a "morally indifferent universe." *Id.* at 265.

3. Luke 10:23 (New International). Unless otherwise indicated, all subsequent citations to the Bible are to the New International version.

4. The characterization of GMP here is not of one who is lost, but whose physical presence is absent, explained by positing a multi-dimensionality beyond the space-time continuum. The theological warrant for such a reference is referred to as the Marcan hole at the end of St. Mark's gospel, as the most reliable early manuscripts do not include Mark 16:9–20. Frederick C. Grant, "Introduction to Mark," in VII *The Interpreter's Bible* 645 (George A. Buttrick, ed. 1951). The text abruptly ends after the announcement of the resurrection with the promise that "you will see him." *Id.*; Mark 16:7. This ending raises the question of when and how will the GMP show up, implying that the rest of the story is to be told by those in whose lives the GMP makes himself known.

5. There is no mention of mercy in Romans 13:1–5 when government authorities, as *servants of God ordained* to do justice, punish wrongdoers. *A Greek-English Lexicon of the New Testament and other Early Christian Literature* 238 (William F. Arnat and F. Wilbur Gingrich trans., 1957). They are acting as *ekdikos* or avengers, agents of divine wrath. The ethical equation demands justice without accommodating mercy.

6. The term "ontological change" is used here synonymously with the theological terms that sequence a new life, namely, "regeneration," and "sanctification." These terms refer to a divine action upon the human, a kind of continuing conversion so that change in "being" is about the presence of "faith," a "renewing of the mind," and an action upon the human personality to supply the wisdom and power to both apprehend and do the good. The sequence is completed theologically by the term "glorification" in which all residual impairment is removed. The transformation of personality in positive and virtuous character formation is an evidence of such change as is the commencement of new actions previously not considered possible, namely, the love of God and neighbor as self, and the forgiveness of adversaries. I am indebted to Tobin B. Woodruff for correlating my theory

of ontological change as resolving the justice/mercy dilemma in soteriology with Aquinas's views of Christ's atonement. See Eleonore Stump, "Atonement According to Aquinas," in *Philosophy and the Christian Faith* 61–91 (Thomas V. Morris ed., 1988).

7. An illustration of mercy's invitation on the condition of ontological change is found in the healing story involving the lame and the blind in Matthew 21:14. It is a violation for the lame and blind to enter the temple area. See 2 Samuel 5:8. The violation disappears when the healing occurs; there are no lame and blind persons present. Similarly, the expression "by his wounds we are healed," Isaiah 53:5, joins mercy's act with its effect, namely, an ontological change. The process begins with consent, a reception by the beneficiary of the benefits. John 1:12.

8. The servant metaphor is used to describe the humility of the divine action in being made man ("but made himself nothing, taking the very nature of a servant, being made in human likeness"), Philippians 2:6–7. God becomes man in order that man might become like God.

9. The American criminal justice system has responsibility for five million inmates. To the extent that it is inhumane, nonrestorative and nonrehabilitative, where work is excluded, therapy and medical care are unavailable, and the crowded conditions contribute to assaults, it is evil. Such a system denies the moral imperative to regard prisoners as bearers of the *imago dei*, as beneficiaries of divine grace. See Matthew 25:36; Luke 4:18; Hebrews 10:34; 13:3. Such a system may serve as a harbinger of civil disorder because without God, mercy is ultimately definitionless. Mercy cannot provide a boundary condition for justice, a rehabilitative intervention to ameliorate the inhumane. Human justice becomes a "terrible swift sword," serving vengeance and retribution. With God, there is meaning for being and doing: the rationality and suffering grace revealed by the *Logos* of God, the promise and vitality of spiritual life in the *agion pneumatos* (Holy Spirit), and the *shalom* (wholeness, blessedness, peace) for maintaining civil order without force or high cost.

10. Psalms 18:27–28 (*Tanakh—The Holy Scriptures: The New Jewish Publication Society Translation According to the Traditional Hebrew Text,* 1985) [hereinafter New J.P.S.]; see also, e.g., Matthew 23:12 ("[w]hoever exalts himself will be humbled. . . .").

11. See, e.g., Peter C. Hoffer, *The Law's Conscience: Equitable Constitutionalism in America* 17–20 (1990) (discussing development and discretion in court of equity).

12. Retribution as "pay back" punishment need not be inhumane or nonrehabilitative.

13. While this is not the place for an extended discussion of capital punishment, it is clearly a point of conflict between law and religion for many people, including myself, when it is seen as a remedy for all serious crime and when convictions are obtained on questionable circumstantial evidence, something not allowed in ancient Jewish law. One need not be an absolutist against its use to oppose the currently prevalent attitude that capital offenses should be increased in the penal code. The issue need not be oversimplified as society should have concern for deterrence, humane retribution, and reform. See, e.g., Jeffrie G. Murphy, *Retribution, Justice, and Therapy* (1979) (presenting essays on Kantian justifications for pun-

ishment in the context of a social contract); *Crime and the Responsible Community* (J. Stott and N. Miller eds., 1980) (discussing common justifications for punishment); Franklin E. Zimring and Gordon Hawkins, *Capital Punishment and the American Agenda* (1986) (discussing the distinction between public attitudes toward capital punishment and executions).

14. "Since one cannot do good to all, we ought to consider those chiefly who by reason of place, time, or any other circumstance, by a kind of chance, are more closely united to us." Augustine, *De Doctrina Christiana* I, 28. PL 34,30 (quoted in Saint Thomas Aquinas, *On Law, Morality and Politics* 191 (William P. Baumgarth and Richard J. Regan, S.J. eds., 1988)). Aquinas quotes, "He that . . . shall see his brother in need and shall close his heart from him, how does the charity of God abide in him?," Aquinas, *supra*, at 191 quoting 1 John 3:17, discusses the remedy of self-help and the obligation of close relations to assist their unfortunate kinsman before considering the lawyer's moral obligation to help. *Id.* at 192. "Therefore, an advocate is not always bound to defend the suits of the poor but only when the aforesaid circumstances concur, else he would have to put aside all other business and occupy himself entirely in defending the suits of poor people. The same applies to a physician with regard to attendance on the sick." *Id.*

15. *Crime and the Responsible Community*, *supra* note 13, at 177.

16. See Luke 12:13–21 (relating the parable of the rich fool: "[A] man's life does not consist in the abundance of his possessions."); Luke 16:19–31 (relating the parable of the rich man and Lazarus); 1 Corinthians 13 (defining love).

17. Hebrews 11:1 (King James).

18. Not to be confused with *disrespect*, the archaic use of *respect*, meaning to show favor or to give an advantage, is used in the older English versions of the Bible about God's impartiality, e.g., "God is no respecter of persons." Deuteronomy 10:17; see also Job 34:19; 2 Chronicles 19:7; Romans 2:11; Ephesians 6:9; Colossians 3:25. It is a standard to be applied at law. "You shall not render an unfair decision: do not favor the poor or show deference to the rich, judge your kinsman fairly." Leviticus 19:15 (New J.P.S.); Proverbs 24:23. It is also the standard to be applied in daily relationships. James 2:1–13.

19. The lawyers in my law firm uniformly share a respect for other lawyers who have thought and written about issues we face. To say this does not mean that each of the lawyers understands everything at the same level or wants to do so. Nevertheless, our collective strength as lawyers who take our faith seriously is deeply enriched by legal scholars and lawyers who have taught us about the relationship between law and religion. See, e.g., Milner S. Ball, *The Word and the Law* (1993); Harold J. Berman, *Faith and Order: The Reconciliation of Law and Religion* (1993) (discussing the theory that the legal order of a society is intrinsically connected with religious faith); Harold J. Berman, *Law and Revolution: The Formation of the Western Legal Tradition* (1983) (presenting a historical perspective on influence of theology on the development of the law); Harold J. Berman, *The Interaction of Law and Religion* (1974) (presenting the Lowell Lectures on Theology delivered at Boston University in 1971); Harold J. Berman, "Law and Logos," 44 *DePaul L. Rev.* 143 (1994) (integrating theories of law

in views of Christian jurisprudence); Jacques Ellul, *The Theological Foundation of Law* (1969) (examining natural law theory as common ground between Christians and non-Christians); Edward M. Gaffney, Jr., "Biblical Law and the First Year Curriculum of American Legal Education," 4 *J.L. & Religion* 63 (1986) (exploring the historical interaction of law and religion); David Granfield, *The Inner Experience of Law: A Jurisprudence of Subjectivity* (1988) (examining mental operations at work in law and ethics); Michael W. McConnell, "The Role of Democratic Politics in Transforming Moral Convictions into Law," 98 *Yale L.J.* 1501 (1989) (reviewing Michael J. Perry, *Morality, Politics, and Law* [1988]); Sir Walter Moberly, *The Ethics of Punishment* (1968) (exploring the interaction between Christian ethics and theology in relation to punishment); John T. Noonan, Jr., *Bribes* (1984) (exploring religious and legal injunctions against bribery); Michael S. Paulsen, "Accusing Justice: Some Variations on the Themes of Robert M. Cover's Justice Accused," 7 *J.L. & Religion* 33 (1989) (discussing fidelity to law and faithlessness to morality in applying abortion law); Sir Edward A. Parry, *The Gospel and the Law* (1928) (exploring the law in relation to the poor); Thomas L. Shaffer, *On Being a Christian and a Lawyer: Law for the Innocent* (1981) (exploring moral and ethical problems faced by Christian and Jewish lawyers); *A Keeper of the Word: Selected Writings of William Stringfellow* (Bill W. Kellerman ed., 1994) (presenting a collection of essays by the famed Harlem street lawyer); *The Weightier Matters of the Law: Essays on Law and Religion, A Tribute to Harold J. Berman* (John Witte, Jr. & Frank S. Alexander eds., 1988) (exploring the historical interaction of law and religion); *John C. H. Wu, Fountain of Justice: A Study in the Natural Law* (1955) (discussing the interaction between philosophy and theology in the development of law); see also *Christian Legal Society Quarterly* (1980–present), *J.L. & Religion* (1983–present). Lawyer organizations reflect or are inclusive of various faith traditions: e.g., Christian Legal Society (Nondenominational); Guild of St. Ives (Episcopalian); Thomas More Society (Roman Catholic).

20. See Mary Ann Glendon, *A Nation Under Lawyers: How the Crisis in the Legal Profession is Transforming American Society* 4–994) (discussing a widening gap between lawyers' and the general citizenry's perceptions about law); Sol M. Linowitz and Martin Mayer, *The Betrayed Profession: Lawyering at the End of the Twentieth Century* 5, 21–46, 207–26 (1994); Anthony T. Kronman, *The Lost Lawyer: Failing Ideals of the Legal Profession* 1–4 (1993); David Luban, *Lawyers and Justice: An Ethical Study* 48–49 (1988); see also James Luther Adams, "Conceptions of Natural Law, From Troelsch to Berman," in *The Weightier Matters of the Law, supra* note 19, at 188. Adams quotes from Professor Harold Berman's unpublished essay that law "no longer seems to be rooted in an ongoing tradition and guided by a universal vision." Adams then says:

> What has been lost is a sense of rootedness of law in the moral order of the universe and a sense of its transcendent qualities, the sense that it points to something beyond itself, to something dealt with by theology. In place of this rootedness, law is viewed as something "wholly instrumental, wholly invented, wholly pragmatic." Along with this attitude has come finally also a deep skepticism about law as a manifestation of justice. Id.

21. Matthew 6:25–34 ("Therefore I tell you, do not worry about your life . . . .").
22. See Antonin Scalia, "Originalism: The Lesser Evil," 57 *U. Cinn. L. Rev.* 849, 852–55 (1989); Morton J. Horwitz, "The Constitution of Change: Legal Fundamentality Without Fundamentalism," 107 *Harv. L. Rev.* 30, 34 (1993); Michael W. McConnell, "The Forgotten Constitutional Moment," 11 *Const. Commentary* 115, 119–20 (1994); Laurence H. Tribe, "Taking Text and Structure Seriously: Reflections on Free-Form Method in Constitutional Interpretation," 108 *Harv. L. Rev.* 1221, 1224, 1227–28, 1235–36, 1248 (1995); see also Sanford Levinson, *Constitutional Faith* 184–91 (1988) (arguing for discourse based interpretation); Robert H. Bork, *The Tempting of America: The Political Seduction of the Law* 241–50 (1990) (discussing moralism and moral relativism as outside forces impacting constitutional interpretation); cf. Jerry H. Stone, "Christian Praxis as Reflective Action," 103–21, in *Legal Hermeneutics: History, Theory, and Practice* (Gregory Leyh ed., 1992) (arguing for interpretation through application); Anthony C. Thiselton, *The Two Horizons: New Testament Hermeneutics and Philosophical Description with Special Reference to Heidegger, Bultmann, Gadamer and Wittgenstein* (1980) (presenting a masterful survey of philosophical issues in New Testament hermeneutics of special interest to specialists in legal hermeneutics).
23. See Thomas C. Oden, *John Wesley's Scriptural Christianity* 11 (1994) (describing the three houses of Christendom: the "Reformed House" with Lutherans, Reformed Churches, and Baptists, including those influenced by a revival tradition; the "Liturgical House" with Anglicans, Catholics, and Orthodox; the "Wesleyan House" with Methodists, Holiness, Pentecostal, and revivalist groups).
24. See Mark A. Noll, *The Scandal of the Evangelical Mind* 25–27, 109–45 (1994) (analyzing the anti-intellectualism of the recent expression of evangelicalism in America); Thomas C. Oden, *Requiem* (1995) (a critique of liberal Protestant seminaries).
25. See Sanford Levinson, "Religious Language and the Public Square," 105 *Harv. L. Rev.* 2061, 2061–63 (1992) (reviewing Michael J. Perry, *Love and Power: The Role of Religion and Morality in American Politics* [1991]).
26. *Lyng v. Northwest Indian Cemetery Protective Ass'n*, 485 U.S. 439, 451–52 (1988).
27. This case was resolved through mediation; the client was represented by a major Washington D.C. law firm.
28. *Western Presbyterian Church v. Board of Zoning Adjustment*, 862 F. Supp. 538, 547 (D.D.C. 1994) (granting permanent injunction), *appeal dismissed*, No. 94-7104, 94-7189, 1995 WL 118016 (D.C. Cir. Feb. 3, 1995).
29. *Perumal v. Saddleback Valley Unified Sch. Dist.*, 198 Cal. App. 3d 64, *cert. denied*, 488 U.S. 933 (1988).
30. See *Sutherland v. Sutherland*, 112 S.Ct. 2002, *cert. denied* (1992) (deciding case in which petition raised Contracts Clause and Procedural Due Process claims). There have been three historic shifts in American law's treatment of marriage. In *Trustees of Dartmouth College v. Woodward*, 17 U.S. (4 Wheat.) 518 (1819), marriage was treated as a contract within the Contracts Clause. In *Maynard v. Hill*, 125 U.S. 190, 210 (1888), marriage was treated as an exception outside the Contracts Clause, but the Court had to ignore Chief Justice Marshall in *Dartmouth College* on when exceptions

were justified. Finally, with California's Family Law Act (1969) the no-fault revolution began, sweeping into their orbit even prior marriages entered into and defined under earlier rules and concepts. Where marriage had been regarded as an institution that was more than contract, with hybrid characteristics of a relationship (status) and obligation (contract), it was set aside only upon a showing of adequate justification. Today, the deconstruction of marriage's former meaning provided by religion and law is complete with the no-fault system allowing unilateral termination of the relationship for any or no reason at all and is applied even to marriages entered into before the law's enactment. The adverse social consequences for children and women have been documented. See Mary Ann Glendon, *Rights Talk: The Impoverishment of Political Discourse* 107 (1991); Bruce Hafen, "Individualism and Autonomy in Family Law: The Waning of Belonging," 1991 *B.Y.U. L. Rev.* 1, 27–30.

31. Berman, *Faith and Order, supra* note 19; Berman, *Law and Revolution, supra* note 19, at 226–30; Berman, *The Interaction of Law and Religion, supra* note 19.
32. Berman, "Law and Logos," *supra* note 19, at 143.
33. Waldron Scott, *Bring Forth Justice* (1980).
34. *Id.* at 159 n. 34.
35. John 15:12; James 1:27; 2:8–9, 14–26; 1 Peter 2:12, 15; John 3:17. Christian faith cares for the poor, Galatians 2:10, demonstrating true repentance by deeds, Acts 26:20. The Christian faith is not irrelevant to or disengaged from the needs of society. Any neglect of the duty of Christ's followers to be rich in good deeds, 1 Timothy 6:18, and to care impartially for others in need, especially the poor, was said to have serious consequences. See Matthew 25:31–46.
36. See Ecclesiastes 2:24; 3:13, 22.
37. "So you also, when you have done everything you were told to do, should say, 'We are unworthy servants; we have only done our duty.'" Luke 17:10.
38. Matthew 23:17.
39. See Glendon, *supra* note 20.

Maybe a Lawyer Can Be a Servant;
If Not . . .

Thomas L. Shaffer[1]

> Then a jealous dispute broke out: who among them should rank
> highest? But he said, 'In the world, kings lord it over their subjects;
> and those in authority are called their country's 'Benefactors.' Not
> so with you; on the contrary, the highest among you must bear
> himself like the youngest, the chief of you like a servant. For who
> is greater—the one who sits at table or the servant who waits on
> him? Surely the one who sits at table. Yet here am I among you like
> a servant.[2]

The religious heritage of Jews and Christians (and Muslims, too, I think)
is an awesome, demanding, put-it-absolutely-first set of habits, propositions, and pressures. It is not something to be reconciled with something
else, not something that informs some other thing that is in need of being
informed. It is, rather, dissonance with faith that must be reconciled with
faith. Whatever is not consistent with faith must be conformed, not informed.

This is so, even among those in the American Christian mainline—if not
as a way of life, at least as a theological proposition and an occasional
discipline. I have seen it that way, even during periods of lapse. I was raised
a low-church American Protestant, in a tradition (Baptist) that centers on
adult *conversion* to this God-comes-first point of view: In the church of my
boyhood, everybody is a convert; the church is a "free" church, freely chosen,
not (in theory) a matter of culture.[3] Sometimes the convert to the faith is
knocked to the ground on the Road to Damascus. Sometimes he has been
observant in the denomination from birth and takes its customs and
commonplaces for granted. But in the latter case, he is expected to seek
the experience of conversion so that he can be a real Christian. Sometimes
the moment of conversion is less a moment than a movement, in which a
day comes gently when, in C. S. Lewis's phrase, she is "surprised by joy."[4]

I was "converted" in the routine way, in early teen-age, the age when, if
I had been a Lutheran or an Episcopalian, I would have been invited to
prepare for confirmation—or, if I had been a Jew, for admission into the
adult community of worshipers. My Sunday School teacher and my mother
told me what was expected; my father nodded his head; the pastor paid a
visit to our house and invited me to accept Jesus as my personal savior,

which, of course, I did. My sins were washed away, by faith, an event that was symbolically observed in total-immersion baptism in the tank behind the pulpit, in the church, on a warm summer evening.

For all of that customary drama, my adherence to the church became what it had been all along. There had never been a time when I did not think of Jesus as my savior—not that I can recall. But, after the ceremony in the tank, others in our small town who made up their minds about me from what they saw me do, and may therefore have doubted my righteousness, were invited to put away their doubts. Whatever I had been, I had become a Christian. One of the things that meant was that I was vulnerable to anybody telling me I should behave like a Christian. Several people mentioned that to me.

However it comes, when it comes, in the faith of my youth, acceptance of the Lord is the first day in a life which the Lord is then seen to rule. Everything gives way before that lordship. My daughter Mary, when she was confirmed as a Roman Catholic, was told that she had become a "mature Christian." My friend David Bauer, after his bar mitzvah last winter, was welcomed by his community as an adult Jew, one of the chosen and consecrated, priestly People of God. The traditional prayer for a parent on that occasion is, "Blessed be He Who has relieved me of the responsibility for this boy."

The point I want to make about absolute priority would be true of Mary and David, as it would be true of an adult Christian who changes denominations: I am a Roman Catholic now and have been for the last forty-five years. I switched Christian denominations out of teen-age rebellion against the denomination of my family. When I did, I was told by those who accompanied me to a redundant and timid baptism in the Catholic tradition that the faith of the church comes first—ahead of "the world," ahead of my Baptist family, ahead of the pernicious tendencies I had inherited from the Protestant Reformation, all of which I solemnly renounced at the Mary altar in Immaculate Conception Cathedral in Denver. I was told that I had been given my one chance to triumph over innocent error; if I should happen to slip back toward the Baptists after that, I would have to answer for it.

(The conflict in *denominational* priorities has, in local Christian custom, as well as in minds like mine, been pretty much resolved. I often think that Pope John XXIII and the Second Vatican Council gave me back my Baptist youth. When Protestant Christians become Roman Catholics now, they do not renounce their former Christianity; they are not re-baptized; they are treated sort of like people who went to college at Texas Tech and then decided to study law at Yale.)[5]

Thus the memory of the church[6] offers a clear priority to a Christian in the law, one that we Christians share with one another and, in a different but vital and important way, with Jews. A priority that law school and being a lawyer does not trump—at least not finally or theologically. If I got confused along the way about that—and I did—I want you to know that I have been brought back to an understanding that faith is not something added on, not something that "informs" what I am otherwise about, or something that needs to be reconciled with the more important business of being in the legal profession in America.

My instinct and experience parallels inherited theological sources. When Israel is camped on the borders of Canaan, the Lord takes the occasion to say to them, through Moses: "You are a people consecrated to the Lord your God."[7] He invites them to contemplate the people who are already in the Promised Land, and He says, "You shall not intermarry with them. . . . You shall tear down their altars, smash their pillars, cut down their sacred posts, and consign their images to the fire.[8] You shall not worship their gods."[9]

The Apostle Paul, speaking to the primitive church (as I grew up, I understood him to be speaking to me), said, "I pray that your inward eyes may be illumined, so that you may know what is the hope to which he calls you, what the wealth and glory of the share he offers you among his people in their heritage, and how vast the resources of his power open to us who trust in him. They are measured by his strength and the might which he exerted in Christ when he raised him from the dead . . . far above all government and authority, all power and dominion, and any title of sovereignty that can be named . . . ."[10] "Far above all power and dominion." Far above—especially for lawyers—especially among believers who come to law school and go out into the practice with a commitment to "God and the law," as if the two were somehow to be coordinated and, when expedient, fashioned into a civil religion.[11]

Consider the way we American lawyers learn about the relationship between the church and the law: This grand constitutional and legal order we propose to serve is unfolded before us and built up in our minds and hearts; it comes to us out of multi-volume sets of course books, and, like the gods of Canaan, it comes to us *as religious*: Thomas Jefferson said America was God's New Israel; David Hoffman, the grandfather of legal ethics in America, spoke of the law as a temple and of us lawyers as priests who served in the temple; Law Day speakers commonly talk about our duties in this "calling" as the highest duties we have. Most of us aging males in the trade can look back with some regret at the many times when we believed that stuff and neglected family and psychic health as well as the moral implications of our being among a consecrated people.

We are formed by legal education for service in the temple of the law, and then along come people like Professors Floyd and Baker, who reasonably, plausibly raise the question: "How do you reconcile your faith with *that*?" It should be a painful question for a believer whose professional formation says that faith cannot be allowed to complicate, confuse, or confute the imposing legal order we were taught to admire and serve above all other orders. But the priority I identify here would say that faith among

Christians is nothing until it can be allowed to mess up American democratic, constitutional, legal, professional commitment.[12]

If the present question were put right, I think, it would go like this (I speak now in the language of some believers, not others): How does a Christian go about being a lawyer? In William Stringfellow's phrase, the issue is about being "a biblical person who works as a lawyer."[13] Stripped of the pretensions of professionalism, the question would be much the same for a biblical person who worked as a plumber or a clerk for the Bureau of Motor Vehicles. But, for a lawyer, it is a particularly difficult question, if you take it seriously, as a few of my students have done over the years, because "the law" is a grander thing than pipes or papers. Because the law is grander, and therefore more like the gods of Canaan, some of my students have taught me to remember this: "Maybe a Christian *cannot* be a lawyer."

* * *

More important than how this question is put, is *where* it is put. In the texts I suggested as fundamental on the theology of the matter, the implicit questions were put *among the faithful*—on the borders of Canaan, and in those odd little household sects St. Paul wrote to. These discussions were what Walter Brueggemann calls "conversations behind the wall," among the faithful—only among the faithful—in the language of the faithful—although often also in preparation for further conversation *on* the wall, in the world.[14] The notion would be that a discussion such as the one in this volume is prior, in time and in importance, to preparation for practicing law. What is really important will then have gone before. When questions of informing or reconciling seem to come up in the future, this something important must continue to come first, both as to the question that comes up and as to the place and time in which it is discussed and resolved.

Putting the question and the site of the question together, and talking behind the wall, then, what is asked, over and over, is this: Should one of *us* work as a lawyer? *What do you think*? I have imagined and described elsewhere some settings that might make this notion of time and geography more concrete. One can think, for example, of a primitive Christian or Jewish community within imperial Rome, as the place where a member of the community, among other members, and among them only, asks such a vocational question. (I suppose there were Christian and Jewish lawyers in imperial Rome, and I suppose they were among their sisters and brothers in the faith when they figured out how to work as lawyers,[15] or how to avoid that sort of work.)

Or a local, rural, small Anabaptist community such as the one Garrison Keillor talks about, from his youth in Lake Wobegon, Minnesota, when he recalls being a child among the Sanctified Brethren: What I have imagined is one of those people asking the others whether she ought to go to law school.

Or in the church as Walker Percy described it, "at a time near the end of the world," in an AIDS hospice at the foot of a fire tower in the forests of South Louisiana. Dr. Thomas More, in those stories, became a distinct sort of physician and psychiatrist, and I suppose that, if someone in that group had become a lawyer, she would have been a distinct sort of lawyer.[16]

That, I hope, gives you an idea of how I approach the issues of reconciliation and informing that were put to me. I want, for the remainder of this essay, to ponder two of the problems my idea poses:

(1) What, for one who is no longer in the primitive church, nor in a "sectarian" worshiping community, nor at the foot of the fire tower in Louisiana, is the site and the time in which questions are asked about working as a lawyer?

(2) How, given that the processes of this distinct community are somehow and somewhere invoked, does a lawyer's community translate these distinct determinations into the practice of law?

*   *   *

The Community. The short-hand Christians use when they talk about the community of the faithful is "the church."[17] Christian scripture appropriates Jewish tradition and claims for the church a priestly place among the nations and within the nation. It then raises the importance of its sense of itself as a priestly people when it says that the church is the body of Christ, from which metaphor (but it is more than a metaphor) it claims, in one way or another, that the substantive witness of the church, in the world, is infallible—or, at least, that, whatever mistakes and depredations the church commits in the world, God will stay with it and bring it safely home.

Now, I am talking about this "church" as the place where questions of priority and behavior are resolved in discussion, imagining the sort of thing St. James spoke of, in the Acts of the Apostles, when the early Jewish followers of Jesus got together and threshed out answers for a series of questions on what to do about Gentile converts: Whether, for example, they were to follow the moral and legal system Jewish Christians followed. When they were through threshing, St. James announced their decisions with this prelude: "The Holy Spirit and we have agreed . . . ."[18]

What I need to locate, with regard to being a biblical person who works as a lawyer, is a forum that is able to conclude its business with that credential: The Holy Spirit and we have agreed. I have not often found evidence of that credential in my own institutional Roman Catholic Church, where the church as commonly spoken of identifies a hierarchical structure of officials, still following a governmental system it borrowed from the Roman bureaucracy in the fourth century. That church certainly has a way to resolve questions, but it rarely considers questions that resemble those Stringfellow wrote and talked about—and, in any case, it is not a community; it is not what I am talking about when I talk about the church as a place where these questions are resolved.[19] On reflection, I notice that I have not resorted to my (bureaucratic) church, at any level, for guidance in how to work as a lawyer. But I have resorted to the church conceived of, not as a hierarchical structure of government, but as the people of God. (This is, by the way, a distinction preserved firmly in Roman Catholic tradition, which also recognizes, as I do, a certain amount of overlap between the bureaucracy and the people of God.)[20]

> [T]he church is not the institution of salvation which can remain stable on this earth and which discharges, one by one, into God's incomprehensibility only those whom it has embraced with its saving care. Rather it is the pilgrim people of God who, as such, await the coming of Jesus and stand under the law of his Spirit which redeems and triumphs only through death. . . . Aren't we . . . [t]oo anxious . . . [i]n the face of the dangerous and the not yet secure? As if we had to defend a church that itself were already the definitive kingdom and not just the tent (that needs ever again to be dismantled and put up again provisionally) of the pilgrim people of God, which, with inexorable courage, is even now in the period of time heading toward that point where there will be no church.

I suppose I could narrow the focus a bit and put a question about reconciling and informing to my local pastor, an unmarried professional male clergyman duly appointed to his full-time clerical duties by my diocesan bishop, who lives fifty miles from my house and whom I have never turned out to meet. My pastor would listen to my questions seriously, I am sure, and would probably say something like, "Well, do your best."

What my pastor would not do, but what the biblical model seems to assume for the people of God, is to convene the local congregation to consider my question. The congregation would be important, even essential, since my biblical theology says "the people of God" is a people; it is not the executive director of a people; it is not a company commander or a parish council or a vestry. I would need here more than the judgment of an administrator or a committee.

If it were convened for the purpose, would the local congregation meet that need? It might; I don't doubt that it could. But if my pastor convened the local congregation to talk about reconciling Christian life with working as a lawyer, and about informing a lawyer's life from the faith, the project would be unfamiliar. The Roman Catholic congregation in which my wife and I are enrolled gathers for worship on weekends, and once in a while for a picnic or a fish fry. It does not gather for moral deliberation. My sisters and brothers would be surprised at being called together to talk about Christian law practice. As I say, though, it might work. Maybe we lawyers should try it.

Conventional, mainline congregational discussion is implausible. But, still, such vocational questions, if they are to be resolved biblically, are to be resolved with what John Howard Yoder calls "the communal quality of belief."[21] But I don't think my congregation is going to be the community Yoder proposes for the job. Nor would any Catholic parish be, nor would any congregation in a mainline Protestant or Orthodox denomination, and neither, I think, would a Jewish congregation work for a Jew. I suppose there are congregations of fundamentalists, Pentecostals, Orthodox Jews, and Anabaptists, and, occasionally, people in mainline denominations who are isolated by choice or circumstance, in which the worshiping community and the deliberating community are *routinely* the same—and in which these questions could be put, discussed, and resolved under the authority of the Holy Spirit. I have no experience of them.

But, still, I claim that I have a way, a way I have used, to submit these lawyer's questions to the communal quality of belief—which is a blessing, because it is essential to faithful obedience for me to resort to such a community. The prescriptions for it, and the requirement of it, are clear in Christian scripture, and, I think, in rabbinical[22] tradition. Both Jews and Christians represent and think of themselves—on moral questions put by individuals, as well as in terms of religious witness in the wider society—as communities; in unavoidable ways they understand themselves as standing before God *together*, and therefore, in unavoidable ways, as accounting collectively not only for what they do together, but also for what each member of them undertakes to do. It is not biblically sufficient for a believer to go off by himself, alone with God, and figure out how his faith is to be reconciled with what he works at, or how his faith is to inform what he does when he works.

For this purpose, for me, the church has been a small group. Jesus said two or three were enough.[23] Once or twice the small group that has been the church for me has been loosely organized, within the law school where I taught, sometimes as a Christian "fellowship." More often it has been a circumstantial group of believers on a university faculty—in somebody's office, in the hall, on a walk outdoors, or at lunch. Always it has come to include my faithful wife Nancy (faithful to the faith, and my faithful friend). Sometimes it has included one or more of my children. Often it has included students and sisters and brothers I dealt with by letter.[24] On all of these occasions I have been able to see, as Karl Barth says, that God will find us where He has put us.[25] And on most of these occasions I could perceive at least the faint presence of the offices and procedures for discourse that St. Paul prescribed for communal moral discussion in the primitive church— "agents of direction . . . agents of memory . . . agents of self-consciousness . . . agents of order and due process," respectful attention to everyone who speaks, and a consensus that the discussion, conducted with this process, is able to claim the promises of God (Yoder's list).[26]

The church I belong to, when I seek guidance as one who works as a lawyer, is otherwise a fragmented church. The fragmentation is no doubt the product of the radical separation, in our culture, of faith from public life, a separation that also results in the separation of worship from the communal moral discourse faith requires. I tend to think that, in an ideal world, the community in which Nancy and I worship would also be a community for moral discourse. God did not put us in such an ideal world, but, still, He will find us where He has put us.

* * *

The Practice of Law. The eloquent Protestant theologian Walter Brueggemann poses a provocative architectural distinction from the story of the siege of Jerusalem, in II Kings chapters 18 and 19: The Assyrian army has laid the siege; agents of the righteous king of Judah, Hezekiah, stand on the city wall and discuss grave matters of public policy with the chief officer of the Assyrian army. The negotiators for Judah ask the Assyrian officer to speak in Aramaic, which is in the circumstances the language of official discourse—the language of the law, if you like. (The King James Version calls it the Syrian language.) Aramaic, not Hebrew, is the language to be used "on the wall." But when Hezekiah, behind the wall, ponders with his agents what action to take—there also to pray and to consult the prophet Isaiah—he speaks in Hebrew ("the Jews' language").

The (if you like) lawyers of Judah are bilingual, not only in their words but also in their "perceptions of reality." The language behind the wall expresses (Brueggemann's term) a "sectarian hermeneutic"; that is, it is not only for talking, but is also the language of moral deliberation. It is not that God acts and lives with His people only behind the wall, of course, but that, for the people of Jerusalem, behind the wall is where they remember who they are. And, because they there remember who they are, they do not forget who they are when they get on the wall.[27]

The dialogue on the wall is neither unimportant nor merely sequential. For one thing, as Brueggemann puts it, the fact that ambassadors of King Hezekiah there speak to the Assyrians in Aramaic keeps consideration of public policy (of jurisprudence, if you like) from becoming either a "totalitarian monologue" or the harangue of demagogues. But it is behind the wall where the King, the Prophet, and the priestly people—the lawyers, too, if you like—figure out what to do.[28]

* * *

What guidance might such a conversation behind the wall produce for a biblical person who works as a lawyer? The epigraph I borrow from Luke's Gospel suggests New Testament answers. John Howard Yoder argues that Jesus's command of servanthood can be taken in three parts:

— First, Jesus notices "the brute existence of dominion": Kings lord it over their subjects.
— Second he notices that rulers justify their power by claims of beneficence (as the Assyrians did during the siege): They are called benefactors.[29]

— Third, Jesus announces an alternative (if you like) professional ethic: Here I am among you, a servant; follow me.

Yoder's reflection suggests from this text alternative possibilities for a biblical person who functions as a formulator of public policy and as an advocate (as a lawyer does). Both of these alternatives rest in the second part of St. Luke's text; both of them appear to be available for practice by a biblical person who works as a lawyer:

— The first alternative is to claim power—a steady temptation, if not a realistic prospect, for a lawyer in a democratic society.[30] The question it asks and answers is this (Yoder): "If we had the power to set up the situation so as to be as fair and as foolproof as possible, how would we set it up?" In modern American circumstances, the language used in pursuing this first alternative is the language of liberal democracy; a familiar and even characteristic arena for it among academic lawyers is the law of church and state.[31]

— The other alternative makes rhetorical, manipulative, tendentious use of the ruler's justification for power—always at least mildly cynical, particularly in modern representative democracies. "If the ruler claims to be my benefactor, and he always does, then that claim provides me as his subject with the language I can use to call him to be more humane in his ways of governing me and my neighbors." And my clients. Unlike the first alternative, here the biblical person who works as a lawyer is using the ruler's language for purposes worked out (in Brueggemann's image) behind the wall. The language of the ruler —the language of the law, I think—is here used "as a fulcrum for constructive criticism" *but not as the primary language of moral deliberation*. The deep answers are located, as Yoder puts it, in "the faith community speaking internally."

The heart of the theological argument I borrow from Yoder is the insistence that the priority in moral deliberation remain behind the wall, in the church. (Brueggemann is, for me, too sanguine about moral deliberation on the wall.)[32] The deep influence runs for the most part in only one direction.[33] The reasons are evident in American church history, even if they are not evident in more detached theological reflection. The danger Christians should by now have learned to avoid is what has happened to the mainline church in America: In the quest for a "public theology," a primary language for moral deliberation that is worked out "on the wall," most Christians in America have surrendered their distinctive witness as a priestly people. They and their most influential theologians have lost sight of the fact that (as Father Michael Baxter puts it), "Christians are citizens of another *patria*, one that identifies them as strangers and aliens in this and all other nation-states through which they pass on their pilgrim journey."[34]

Which does not necessarily mean (although it might mean) that a biblical person should not even try to work as a lawyer—or, if she does, that her work as a lawyer will be so stridently restricted as to be ineffective for the ordinary business clients bring to her. From the perspective of "the faith community speaking to the nations" (Yoder), and more specifically from the perspective of a biblical person going out from such a community to work as a lawyer, I discern from Yoder's reflection on the text from Luke's Gospel three practical guides for thinking about what a lawyer is to do:

First, *servanthood*: Whatever a Christian does in any job is primarily oriented to following Jesus, who said, "Here I am among you like a servant." In Yoder's explication, in "the vocational decisions of persons committed to Kingdom ethics as they decide how to be active in the wider society . . . preference will not be for dominion roles but for servant roles." Reflection on biblical servanthood thus argues, in Yoder's theology (and in mine), against the claim of lordship that characterizes other and more prominent American Protestant and Roman Catholic political theology and that is, in my observation, a steady temptation for Christian lawyers in a modern liberal democracy such as that of the United States.

Second, *particular attention to the oppressed*. I understand that category of persons ("oppressed") as it is understood in the story of II Kings, where Jerusalem is threatened with destruction by armed force; in liberation theology, where perceptions of deep injustice benefitting the ruling class in modern democracies leads Christian thinkers to seek God among the poor; and, for that matter, as almost any county-seat American lawyer would understand it. (We lawyers know who the oppressed are, if only because we know whom we oppress.) Roman Catholic leaders thus advise, in moral and political and economic deliberation, a "preferential option for the poor." Yoder goes beyond an "option" derived from considerations of justice; he identifies the alternative with the New Testament biblical model: "[T]he paradigmatic person by whose situation my ethic must be tested would not be the oppressor but the oppressed, not the most powerful or even the most righteous person, not my representative or my ruler, but the one with whom Christ in his servanthood is first of all identified."

Third, and critically kept last, *attention to effectiveness*, to the extent that effectiveness is consistent with clear-sighted attention to servanthood and to care for the oppressed.[35] Effectiveness not disciplined by being considered last might become a matter of "taking the Caesar model and modifying it by adding certain kinds of Christian modesty and morality." By contrast, "the model of the empirical availability of ways to be socially effective with integrity" (Yoder) is disciplined by considerations of servanthood and care for the oppressed.[36]

Endnotes

1. Roman Catholic (formerly Baptist). Robert and Marion Short Professor of Law, Notre Dame Law School and Supervising Attorney, Notre Dame

Legal Clinic. B.A. 1958, University of Albuquerque; J.D. 1961, University of Notre Dame.

2. Luke 22:24–27 (New English Bible).

3. William Henry Brackney, *The Baptists* 71–86 (1988); James Wm. McClendon, Jr., *Systematic Theology: Doctrine* 361–72 (1994).

4. C. S. Lewis, *Surprised by Joy* (1955).

5. I describe what happened in 1951. The relevant legal guidance for pastors, then and now, is in *Canon 869 of the Code of Canon Law*: "Those baptised in a non-Catholic ecclesial community are not to be baptised [again] unless there is a serious reason for doubting the validity of their baptism . . . ." *The Code of Canon Law in English Translation* 160 (Canon Law Society of Great Britain and Ireland 1983). The assistant pastor at the cathedral must have had doubts about the Baptists (as most Roman Catholics in those days did), but, whatever its doctrinal defects, baptism in the church of my boyhood cannot be faulted for want of thoroughness. The comparison reminds me of a story I heard, years ago, from my friend Dean Willard Pedrick: A man was asked if he believed in baptism. He said, "Believe in it? Man, I've *seen* it."

6. I borrow from Dietrich Bonhoeffer the phrase "memory of the church" as a substitute for "theological knowledge." Clyde E. Fant, *Bonhoeffer: Worldly Preaching* 27 (1975).

7. Deuteronomy 7:6 (Jewish Publication Society).

8. Deuteronomy 7:3–5 (Jewish Publication Society).

9. Deuteronomy 7:16 (Jewish Publication Society).

10. Ephesians 1:17–21 (New English Bible).

11. This raises a question of ecclesiology, of what the church ("ecclesia") is to be when it is faithful. My position on such a question is radical when compared to those of my sisters and brothers who find lingering vitality in "the church-state nexus," that is, in the Christendom that came to be when the Emperor Constantine was baptized (313 C.E.) and that was continued in the alliances Protestant reformers made with governments. See Robert E. Rodes, Jr., "The Last Days of Erastianism: Forms in the American Church-State Nexus," 62 *Harv. Theological Rev.* 301 (1969). This is not a denominational disagreement; just in terms of the few theologians I discuss here, I share it with Baxter, a Roman Catholic; with Yoder, a Mennonite; and, for the most part, with Brueggemann, a Presbyterian. I discuss it in law-school terms in "Erastian and Sectarian Arguments in Religiously Affiliated American Law Schools," 45 *Stan. L. Rev.* 1859 (1993), and "Stephen Carter and Religion in America," 62 *U. Cin. L. Rev.* 1601 (1994).

12. Michael J. Baxter thus criticizes the "political theology" of the mainline church, theologians for which "never acknowledge that mediating love of neighbor might require *disloyalty* to the country." Michael J. Baxter, "Review Essay: The Non-Catholic Character of the 'Public Church,' " 11 *Mod. Theology* 243, 254 (1995).

13. "A Lawyer's Work," *Christian Legal Soc. Q.*, Summer 1982, at 17.

14. See *infra* note 27 and accompanying text.

15. My friend Mark H. Aultman observes: "The wall, of course, provides more protection to those who are behind it than to those who are on it." Letter from Mark H. Aultman to Thomas L. Shaffer (July 28, 1995). The point

fits II Kings chs. 18 and 19, where the attacking Assyrians spoke in the language of the besieged inhabitants of the city, in an effort to threaten the populace into submission. The representatives of the defending king, standing on the wall, had to resist that effort and they no doubt had also to resist the effort of the populace to understand what the Assyrians were saying. "The transition in language from going behind the wall to on the wall (and vice versa) also involves a diminution in meaning," Aultman says, which is what the representatives of the king wanted. "One can be very accomplished in two languages (as many French Canadians are), but for the most part one's audience will not be." Aultman describes, in the metaphorical or symbolical use I am making of Brueggemann's essay, the situation of a lawyer. See *infra* note 27 and accompanying text.

16. Thomas L. Shaffer, "The Church and the Law," in Andrew W. McThenia, Jr., *Radical Christian and Exemplary Lawyer* 103 (1995) (discussing *Love in the Ruins* [1971] and *The Thanatos Syndrome* [1987]).

17. I don't have a useful word for the parallel among Jews for the word "church." Still, the essentials for understanding an association of Jews as the people of God are, I think, parallel: communal quality of belief; local group as the place for moral discourse; respect for teachers. In fact, those qualities of faithful community are among the lessons Christians have learned from Jews.

18. Acts 15:28 (Good News Bible).

19. Which is not to deny respect for teachers—for what Catholics call the "magisterium" of the church ("magister" means "teacher"). This respect for teachers has nothing to do with papal infallibility; in my view it is best understood as resembling the rabbinical tradition in Judaism. See 2 Richard P. McBrien, *Catholicism* 821, 834–35 (1980).

20. See *Catechism of the Catholic Church* 197–98 nos. 687–88 (1994); Karl Rahner, *The Great Church Year* 209–10 (Albert Raffelt ed., Harvey D. Egan, S.J., trans. 1994).

21. All references here to Professor Yoder's work are to *The Priestly Kingdom* (1984), most of them to pages 151–71, a chapter entitled "The Christian Case for Democracy." The "communal quality of belief" is explained at pages 15–45, a chapter entitled "The Hermeneutics of Peoplehood." John H. Yoder, *The Priestly Kingdom: Social Ethics as Gospel* (1984).

22. See, e.g., the preface to Roger Brooks, *The Spirit of the Ten Commandments—Shattering the Myth of Rabbinic Legalism* (1990).

23. Matthew 18:20.

24. See *infra* note 36.

25. Karl Barth, *Ethics* 193 (Dietrich Braun ed., Geoffrey W. Bromiley trans. 1981) (1928).

26. See *supra* note 21. It is important to notice that answers given in such deliberations (i) are not inevitable and (ii) when concrete and useful are nonetheless only provisional. Aultman raises these considerations when he writes:

> [D]iscussions do not necessarily "resolve" things; they can both clarify and confuse. That a hierarchy can no longer give an authoritative answer does not mean that current discussion will either. Sometimes only time will tell. The advantage of most churches is that they can engage in moral discourse over time.

See Aultman, *supra* note 15. I suppose there is no better demonstration of Aultman's point than some of the specifics in the resolution reached by the primitive church in Jerusalem: "[E]at no blood; eat no animal that has been strangled." Acts 15:29 (Good News Bible). I am not aware that Christians since then or in other places have worried much about those "resolutions."

27. All references here to Professor Brueggemann's work are to *Interpretation and Obedience*, a chapter entitled "The Legitimacy of a Sectarian Hermeneutic: 2 Kings 18–19." Walter Brueggemann, *Interpretation and Obedience* 41–69 (1991).

28. Baxter thus speaks of "an intrinsically Christian understanding of politics, presented through historical texts which have no permanent, transcendental place apart from the practices and forms of life which produce them." Baxter, *supra* note 12, at 256. He argues there and elsewhere that these "practices and forms" include worship—sacraments, liturgy, preaching, and prayer. See Michael J. Baxter, "Overall, the First Amendment Has Been Very Good for Christianity—NOT!: A Response to Dyson's Rebuke," 43 *DePaul L. Rev.* 425 (1994); see also Richard P. Baepler, "Religious Challenges to Legalism," *Occasional Paper Number One, Section on Law and Religion, Association of American Law Schools* (1980).

29. The King of Assyria sent this message to the people of the city: "Make peace with me. Come out to me, and then you shall each eat the fruit of his own vine and his own fig tree, and drink the water of his own cistern . . . grain and new wine . . . corn and vineyards . . . olives, fine oil, and honey—life for you all, instead of death." 2 Kings 18:31–32 (New English Bible).

30. Baxter suggests that formulation and advocacy from the church are ad hoc, pragmatic, circumstantial; the church does not take on responsibility for the civil order—does not adopt its narrative. See Baxter, *supra* note 12.

31. See *supra* note 11 and accompanying text.

32. Brueggemann thus seems to me to depend on the civil conversation on the wall as a source of discipline for the conversation behind the wall—this mainly because the conversation behind the wall has been corrupted. No doubt he is right that "the technicalities of policy questions" are for the language of Syria, provided, as he also says, "a transformed imagination" is for behind the wall. Brueggemann, *supra* note 27, at 64. I mean here to speak of the way influence works, not of the way language works. Aultman, *supra* note 15 writes, "While a separate theology cannot come from 'on the wall,' neither can a primary language for moral deliberation for action 'on the wall' come from 'behind the wall.' These *are* two different languages." The advocate has to be able to translate back and forth. Somewhat the same point is made in the documents of the Second Vatican Council:

> With the help of the Holy Spirit, it is the task of the entire People of God . . . to hear, distinguish, and interpret the many voices of our age, and to judge them in the light of the divine Word. In this way, revealed truth can always be more deeply penetrated, better understood, and set forth to greater advantage. . . . Indeed, the Church admits that she has greatly profited and still profits from the antagonism of those who oppose or persecute her.
>
> *Gaudium et Spes: Pastoral Constitution of the Church in the Modern World* ¶ 44, reprinted in *Catholic Social Thought: The Documentary Heritage* 166, 194

(David J. O'Brien and Thomas A. Shannon eds., 1992); see also Baepler, *supra* note 28 (making the point from his Lutheran heritage).

33. See the sources *supra* note 32, especially that of Baepler.

34. See Baxter, *supra* note 12 and accompanying text.

35. Aultman: "I really think this is the most important point. By effectiveness, however, I would understand not simply achieving what you hope or intend, particularly in a broad sense of social policy, but attention to the actual effects of what you do and say. Eventually, I think, this sets up (an awareness of) a dichotomy between much of what is intended or hoped for by what is done and said, and the effects of what is done and said as it is mediated through social systems, organizations, and bureaucracies." Aultman, *supra* note 15. Aultman, a practicing lawyer, would no doubt agree that these "actual effects" occur, usually and primarily, in work (i) with and for clients (ii) that falls within Yoder's other two criteria. An instructive parallel comes from rural, in-the-field, medical care, provided in Haiti by a physician who is also a thoughtful student of liberation theology: Paul Farmer, "Medicine and Social Justice," *America*, July 15, 1995, at 13.

36. I am grateful for the assistance of Mark H. Aultman, Michael J. Baxter, C.S.C, Nicholas Chase, Robert F. Cochran, Jr., Robert E. Rodes, Jr., Nancy J. Shaffer, and John Howard Yoder. Such a group of faithful friends exemplifies a blessing, on me as a student of religious legal ethics. They are the church in moral deliberation.